Praise for The Reformation: A I

At a time when texts on the Reformation abound, one might ask whether there is room for yet another entrant into this crowded historiographical arena. My response after reading Appold's book was an enthusiastic yes. In clear and lively prose, Appold weaves the threads of a complex theological, economic, cultural, political and institutional story into a coherent narrative. Luther is clearly a central figure in the telling of his tale, but he is firmly located within the deep context of the medieval heritage, and other voices of the sixteenth century—perhaps most notably, the Anabaptists— get an ample and fair hearing as well. This deft, nuanced survey will serve general readers and classroom teachers alike as a reliable introduction to the Reformation era. I recommend it highly.

John D. Roth
Goshen College

This well-written, clearly told account of the Reformation in central and northern continental Europe is both traditional and innovative. A masterful synthesis of the latest scholarship, it combines top-down studies of the theology and polemics of leading reformers with bottom-up analyses of the reception given to their ideas by urban dwellers and oft forgotten rural folk. It provides new perspectives by tracing the pre-Reformation papal, conciliar, and royal efforts to control the Church that found resolution in several models of the Church that emerged from the Reformation. It also traces the age-old quest to lead a purer form of Christianity modeled on the apostolic church that found its expression in the medieval monastic and mendicant orders and in various Anabaptist communities of the Reformation era. It concludes with a brief survey of reform efforts in the Catholic Church and with an epilogue assessing the significant changes wrought by the Reformation struggles. Those interested in a scholarly, up-to-date, and fresh study that privileges the perspectives of the Protestant reformers need look no further.

Nelson Minnich
Catholic University

BLACKWELL BRIEF HISTORIES OF RELIGION SERIES

This series offers brief, accessible, and lively accounts of key topics within theology and religion. Each volume presents both academic and general readers with a selected history of topics which have had a profound effect on religious and cultural life. The word "history" is, therefore, understood in its broadest cultural and social sense. The volumes are based on serious scholarship but they are written engagingly and in terms readily understood by general readers.

Other topics in the series:

Published

Heaven	Alister E. McGrath
Heresy	G. R. Evans
Death	Douglas J. Davies
Saints	Lawrence S. Cunningham
Christianity	Carter Lindberg
Dante	Peter S. Hawkins
Spirituality	Philip Sheldrake
Cults and New Religions	Douglas E. Cowan and David G. Bromley
Love	Carter Lindberg
Christian Mission	Dana L. Robert
Christian Ethics	Michael Banner
Jesus	W. Barnes Tatum
Shinto	John Breen and Mark Teeuwen
Paul	Robert Paul Seesengood
Apocalypse	Martha Himmelfarb
Islam 2nd Edition	Tamara Sonn

Forthcoming

Utopias	Howard P. Segal
Sufism	Nile Green

The Reformation
A Brief History

Kenneth G. Appold

A John Wiley & Sons, Ltd., Publication

This edition first published 2011
© 2011 Kenneth G. Appold

Blackwell Publishing was acquired by John Wiley & Sons in February 2007. Blackwell's publishing program has been merged with Wiley's global Scientific, Technical, and Medical business to form Wiley-Blackwell.

Registered Office
John Wiley & Sons Ltd, The Atrium, Southern Gate, Chichester, West Sussex, PO19 8SQ, United Kingdom

Editorial Offices
350 Main Street, Malden, MA 02148-5020, USA
9600 Garsington Road, Oxford, OX4 2DQ, UK
The Atrium, Southern Gate, Chichester, West Sussex, PO19 8SQ, UK

For details of our global editorial offices, for customer services, and for information about how to apply for permission to reuse the copyright material in this book please see our website at www.wiley.com/wiley-blackwell.

The right of Kenneth G. Appold to be identified as the author of this work has been asserted in accordance with the UK Copyright, Designs and Patents Act 1988.

Library of Congress Cataloging-in-Publication Data

Appold, Kenneth G., 1965–
  The Reformation : a brief history / Kenneth G. Appold.
    p. cm. – (Blackwell brief histories of religion ; 35)
  Includes bibliographical references and index.
  ISBN 978-1-4051-1749-4 (hardback) – ISBN 978-1-4051-1750-0 (paperback)
1. Reformation. I. Title.
  BR305.3.A67 2011
  270.6–dc22
                                                        2010050368

A catalogue record for this book is available from the British Library.

This book is published in the following electronic formats: ePDFs 9781444397673; ePub 9781444397680

Set in 10/12.5pt Meridien by SPi Publisher Services, Pondicherry, India

1 2011

To George Lindbeck

Contents

Preface

Writing a "brief history of the Reformation" poses several challenges. The greatest of these comes with the word "brief"—a deterrent to most any historian. The following book does, however, aim at brevity. It accomplishes that by making a number of sacrifices, and some readers will notice these. Certain subjects are missing; editorial decisions precluded treating the Reformation in Britain, for example. Other regions have received less attention than they deserve—particularly those to the south and east of the Holy Roman Empire. And while the book's methods are eclectic, drawing on several disciplines and approaches, some readers may lament the relatively scant attention to academic theology. That, too, comes as a result of a conscious decision. (Disappointed readers are welcome to read this author's other works.)

Virtually any of the book's topics could be treated at much greater length. But most of them already have been. Herein lies not only a challenge, but also an attraction to writing a survey work. One needs to absorb vast amounts of material—but one also has the chance to take a step back and to craft an overarching narrative. For students of the Reformation, now may be an ideal moment to do that. We have seen old "grand narratives" displaced and partly discredited; we have witnessed a generation's worth of attention to "micro-histories"; and we have absorbed lessons from an unexpected variety of sources and angles, changing forever the way we approach the period. The time may be ripe, therefore, to shake the kaleidoscope and create a new synthesis.

Many traditional histories have portrayed the Reformation as an event that "divided" Western Christianity. The following account challenges that view. It argues that medieval Christianity was still searching for unity when the Reformation began. Several ideological models of church unity—among them papal, royalist and conciliar—were competing for dominance for much of the Middle Ages, and that competition was not settled in 1517, when Martin Luther published his famous "Ninety-Five Theses." Luther somewhat unintentionally exposed those fault lines and brought to the surface forces that eventually led to a long-term settlement. By the time these events had run their course, not one, but several "victors" had emerged, and several kinds of church were established. That process, which took different paths in different places, is called the Reformation.

The Reformation occurred within a larger dynamic driven by the Christianization of Europe. After the fall of Rome, Western Europe became the scene of a vast mission initiative that would last more than a thousand years. It had both an "institutional" dimension (the organization and administration of church and state), and an "ethical" one (the moral and spiritual transformation of individual lives and communities). These were often in tension with each other. At times, the desire of Christians to live holier lives and to pattern their communities after biblical examples conflicted with the more profane needs of institutions seeking to establish power and authority amidst the chaos of post-Roman Europe. Such tensions provided much of the energy that gave the Reformation its unique character—a mix of religious, theoretical, social, political, and economic forces that, taken together and harnessed to a number of extraordinarily charismatic people, proved remarkably combustible. The added invention of the printing press turned these forces into a continental conflagration. As a result, a new landscape emerged.

Sixteenth-century Europe was rural. Nearly nine-tenths of its people lived in the country. That fairly basic fact has rarely figured in traditional histories of the Reformation. Recent research into the lives of the period's "common people," however, has made it possible to begin creating more representative narratives—and that is something this "brief history" has aimed to do. That brings a shift in overall perspective. Events such as the German Peasants' War acquire a more central position, as do religious groups such as the Anabaptists who, often expelled from cities, took refuge and built Christian communities in the country. Because most of the rural people were poor, issues relating to poverty (both as an unwelcome condition and as a religious value) and to property (both the defense and critique of its ownership) take on a greater importance than they have in most previous Reformation histories. Readers may be surprised at some of the results—and are invited to consider their implications for the present.

I am indebted to very many people, ranging from students to colleagues, family and friends, who have provided direct and indirect inspiration for this book. In keeping with its spirit of brevity, I would like to single out three Reformation historians whose influence has been particularly important: Carter Lindberg for his pioneering work on organized charity and for providing an inspirational model with his own superb textbook; Scott Hendrix, my predecessor at Princeton, for alerting me to the importance of Christianization for understanding the Reformation; and Peter Blickle, whom I have not met personally, but whose work on the 'Revolution of the Common Man' revolutionized my own thought on the subject.

Finally, I would like to extend my special thanks to the editors and staff at Wiley-Blackwell for their exceptional support and patience throughout this process.

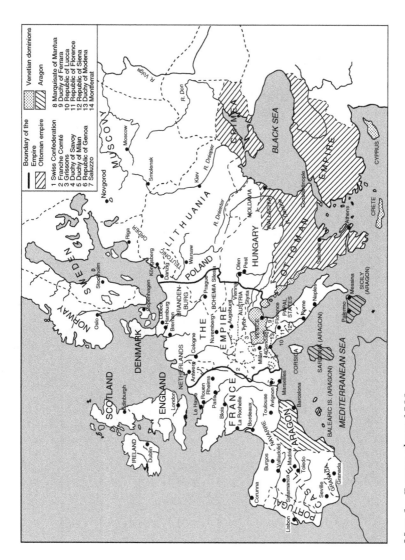

Map 1 Europe about 1500

Chapter 1

The Different Paths of Medieval Christianization

Christianity among the Rural Poor

Medieval Europe was rural. The vast majority of Europeans who lived in the Latin West of the continent were scattered about the countryside in villages, small towns and settlements. In most regions, less than 10 per cent of the population had come to live in cities by the year 1500. This is an important fact to keep in mind when studying the developments that led up to the Reformation. Medieval Europe's rural demographics, its feudal social structure, and its minimal rates of literacy all influenced that history to an enormous degree.

There was probably no such thing as a "typical" medieval village, since their populations could vary from a few dozen to several hundred or even a thousand. Most rural communities, however, shared a number of important characteristics that remained remarkably constant over the centuries. For one thing, village economies were almost entirely agrarian. Villagers farmed the fields that surrounded their homes. Their lives were organized by the chores of the seasons: plowing, planting, cultivating, and harvesting. Winters were times to be endured, especially in places where they were long and hard, and villagers only survived them if they had stored enough grain and produce to make it through. The fortunate had livestock to help with the chores and to produce additional food. Not surprisingly, life-expectancies

The Reformation: A Brief History, First Edition. Kenneth G. Appold.
© 2011 Kenneth G. Appold. Published 2011 by Blackwell Publishing Ltd.

were low by modern standards: few villagers could hope to live much past 40. Poor harvests, malnutrition, and vulnerability to disease kept that number low, as did additional factors such as childbirth, attacks by outsiders, or war.

Many village economies in the Middle Ages were self-sufficient and therefore isolated. Their inhabitants were subsistence farmers who produced just enough to feed themselves: grain for bread, fruit and vegetables, eggs, and occasional meat from livestock or hunting and fishing. More complex village societies included artisans, such as blacksmiths or carpenters, who played supporting roles in the economy. Beyond the village itself, trade was limited. Peasants would have produced little surplus, and communication between communities was sparse. These villagers relied on themselves. As a result, strangers were greeted with suspicion. Outsiders were not part of the village production cycle and represented additional mouths to feed, or, worse, a threat of violence or exploitation.

Some outsiders, however, had to be accepted. The most common of these were landlords. Many villagers were tenant farmers who paid rent to a landlord who often lived somewhere else and only appeared, in person or by emissary, to collect his due. In exchange, the lord offered promises of protection. The arrangement was a basic feature of feudal society, the dominant social order of medieval Europe. In such a society, peasant farmers enjoyed varying degrees of freedom. Some actually owned their own land and had no lord above them. Most, however, were subject to rental agreements and to someone who owned the land. As time went on, those agreements became more and more restrictive. Many peasants had the status of serfs; they were often tied to their landlord's land and not allowed to move. Such serfs had virtually no freedom to travel—or even to marry without the lord's approval. They paid a significant portion of their produce to the lord in rent and provided labor for the rent they could not pay. By the time of the Reformation, many contemporaries regarded serfdom as a form of slavery.

Within the village, one building towered over all the rest. It was the church. The church is fascinating for a number of reasons. For one thing, churches had no obvious utilitarian function within an agrarian economy. They did not house farmers or animals, nor did they store grain. They mostly stood empty. Second, they were the domain of another village outsider: the priest. Priests, too, had no obvious economic function. In many cases, they acted as landlords, which meant that they had to be paid rents by those who planted on church property, and thus consumed part of the village's goods without producing anything tangible in return. Given the parameters of these societies, living on a knife's edge between subsistence and extinction, one has to wonder how it came to be that churches and clergy could exist at all in their midst. Why would these people want a church?

The answer to this question lies in a complex historical process known as Christianization. After Germanic hordes swept through Western Europe in the fifth century, destroyed the urban-centered civilization of late antiquity, and settled amidst the rubble that remained, a long process of rebuilding began. Buried among the ashes of a plundered Rome, isolated embers of thought survived. From here, and from other former cultural centers, sparks of learning spread and began to illumine, very gradually, the newly dominant barbarian peoples. The primary means of transmission was religion. Religion lends meaning to existence; it also contributes to everyday existence by identifying and communicating with the powers that determine life's trajectories. The Germans were interested in religion; some in fact were Christian, converted long before they began their westward run. Christianity, the religion of the late Roman Empire, the religion that had absorbed so much of Greek, Roman, and Jewish thought and learning, now spread to the German tribes, who had previously seen that culture mostly from afar. In so doing, Christianity became the driving force in the recultivation of Europe.

Framing the narrative in this way opens the door to a common misunderstanding. The Christianization of Europe was not simply a process that brought learning and high culture to a primitive people. For one thing, the vast majority of Europeans were illiterate and Christianity did not change that fact. Ninety-five per cent of Western Europeans remained illiterate at the time of the Reformation, which in some cases was more than a thousand years after initial Christianization. It would be a mistake, therefore, to reduce Christianity to its intellectual components, its theology, and doctrines. Most medieval Christians had little comprehension of such things, and abstract theological discourse, aside from being exceedingly rare through much of the Middle Ages, had little direct impact on their lives. Christianity was more than learning. Christianity was a religion. It included—and inspired—intellectual activities of profound quality, but it did much more, especially for common people. It embraced their lives by bringing them into contact with a power beyond their existence in the here-and-now, and by describing that power as benevolent. While that assuaged concerns about an afterlife, it also affected their present lives. People turned to Christianity for blessings on their activities and relations, or for protection in a perilous cosmos filled with forces they could not control. Those aspects were particularly important to agrarian people, whose lives depended upon successful harvests, on finding a partner for procreation, and on protection from crop-ruining weather or plundering armies. Christianity also brought a specific ethos to medieval societies: a way of being "holy" and of following the life-example of Jesus Christ. At the very least, such values affected the way people related to each other—or, barring that, it affected the way they felt they *ought* to relate to each other.

Christianity was not simply a religion for individuals; it was an *organized* religion. From its beginnings, Christianity has had a corporate, communal dimension. Christians refer to themselves collectively as one "Body of Christ." Much of medieval history revolved around various attempts to translate that notion of a singular body of believers into an institutional and political reality. That task was made all the more urgent by the collapse of the Roman Empire, which left Western Europe without a central or unifying political authority. By offering the concept of a "universal church," Christianity provided an important resource in that effort. Furthermore, because the most prominent church leader of the Western Empire, the bishop of Rome, continued to reside in the former capital, a vision for a new Roman Europe, consolidated under the auspices of the church's leadership, began to emerge. While that vision never came to full fruition, it did contribute to a long-term interweaving of religious and political institutions. There would be no "separation of church and state" in the Middle Ages. As Christianity expanded, its church organization sought to keep pace. As it did so, it stepped into a political vacuum, assuming many of the functions of secular government. It also began to organize itself hierarchically in order to bring communities under joint regional oversight. In both cases, urban bishops were the key figures, supervising churches in their dioceses and functioning as governors in their cities. While the bishop of Rome early on claimed a unique position atop the entire hierarchy, those claims had little practical meaning before the eleventh century. Instead, Western Christianity began organizing its institutions at an intermediate level, with leadership located in a variety of centers, such as Tours, Reims, Mainz, Rome, or Canterbury.

Even from these more local vantage points, medieval Christianity remained more chaotic than united. Contemporary authors often underestimate this, either because they project a version of today's Roman Catholic church and its papal leadership onto the past, or because they take the past's papal apologists too readily at face value. Unity—however it was imagined by medieval leaders—proved elusive. That becomes increasingly evident as one considers the case of village life.

As Christianity spread through Europe, more and more villages acquired churches. Often, these were built by local lords, who also assumed rights to nominate priests (rights of patronage) and to claim a portion of the church's income, which consisted largely of tithes (10 per cent of one's earnings or produce) paid by the peasant villagers. The peasants themselves appear to have had an ambivalent attitude toward the church in their village. If complaints registered by priests are to be believed, most peasants had very little interest in organized worship—which, of course, is what the priest thought important. They did attend mass, but ignored most of the proceedings. In their view, "church" was a place for social interaction, and this did not require clergy. And so they talked during the readings and sermons, filed in and out during the liturgy, and behaved as though the priest were not present. If anything was likely to capture their attention, it was the elevation of the host at communion. The wafer—taught to be the body of Christ—was thought to radiate benevolent and protective powers. This was worth a moment's attention, and many parishioners who were busy socializing outside made sure they were in the church in time to witness the event. Once it was over they went back to what they were doing.

Accounts such as these are many, but one should remember that they are usually written from the priests' perspective. Had one surveyed peasant parishioners, one may have heard a different story, since complaints about priests' frequent absences, negligence of duties, or onerous demands of rent and taxes were common. The fact that relations between priests and peasants were often strained does not mean that peasants were not interested in religion—or that they were only superficially Christianized, as some have argued. It simply means that many common people sought forms of religious expression that bypassed clerical control. Pilgrimages, to cite a prominent example of medieval piety, did not require clergy once they were established. Veneration of local saints, or of relics, took place outside the regular mass and was often private. Objects such as holy water, crosses, or the eucharistic host were taken out of their "proper" liturgical context and used to ward off evil spirits, bless crops, or control the weather. Clergy—and later Reformers—often criticized such practices as superstitious, but the underlying conflict is one over power and control: who has access to spiritual powers? Clergy sought to control that access on their terms, but many laypeople simply ignored those efforts and made use of Christian rites and symbols on their own. Who represented the "true" Christianity? That, in part, was at issue.

All of these factors make it difficult to speak of "the church" as a unified hierarchical institution during the Middle Ages. Even if such a hierarchy was united at the top—and as we shall see, that was seldom the case—it still needed to find a way to organize the widely scattered faithful into a coherent flock. Such institutional unity was predicated upon clerical authority and control. At the very latest, that control tended to break down at the local level, where Christians typically created their own religious programs and frequently marginalized their priests. Medieval Europe was a mission field, and Christianization was a kind of mission. As in any mission setting, the recipients of a new faith tend to appropriate it on their own terms. The results are not always what the missionaries envisioned. That was certainly the case among the rural poor who comprised the vast majority of medieval Christians.

Nonetheless, the very fact that nearly every village came to have a church building and most people looked to that church to provide basic spiritual services such as baptism, marriage and funerals, arranged their lives according to the festivals and fasts of a Christian liturgical year, and engaged in devotional practices that in some way drew on Christian thoughts and images, points to a large-scale cultural phenomenon with more than minimal coherence. For all their obvious differences, people as far apart as Italy and Iceland still attended Easter services on the same day every year and had compatible notions of what the day was about. Even when the institutional church was in disarray, such commonalities continued. That was Christianization—and the following pages offer a brief account of how it came about.

Two Sides of Medieval Christianization

Christianization refers to the process by which groups of people become Christian. Normally, this involves some form of voluntary assent to Christian truth-claims, symbols and values. Barring outright coercion, people become Christian because they are persuaded, at some level, by the new religion. Many people who become Christian—and this is true of those who inhabited early-medieval Europe—already were religious and now find themselves replacing or adapting parts of their old belief-system. Something old and familiar is replaced by something new and alien that is brought in from the outside. Accordingly, during Christianization a people's religious life becomes formed and regulated according to Christian norms and contents. Both aspects—personal persuasion and external regulation—are part of the process.

Inevitably, Christianization is a complex phenomenon. It merits a much fuller theoretical discussion than is possible here. For the present historical survey, however, a broad distinction between two sides of medieval Europe's Christianization may prove helpful. They correspond roughly to the two aspects of the process sketched in the section "Two Sides of Medieval Christianization." The regulative challenges were met by *institutionalization*. This included, but was by no means restricted to, the creation of a hierarchically organized institutional church. That process was not only a matter for the clergy. As we shall see, non-clerical authority figures such as kings and emperors also felt responsible for the custody and supervision of the Christian religion. In medieval Europe, Christianity's institutionalization went hand in hand with the challenge of building and rebuilding a society. That makes it hard to distinguish between political and ecclesial agendas. If kings felt responsible for the church, it is also true that priests and bishops felt responsible for society.

The second factor has to do with the persuasiveness of Christianity. If Christianity had not seemed worthy of adoption, if it had not seemed attractive and compelling on a personal level, it would not have spread. Coercion would not have sufficed (though, as always, there were some who thought it might). As it happened, one factor seemed particularly important for this development: *the moral and spiritual integrity of those who brought the message*. In many cases, these people were monks. It was they, more than any other representative of the church, who exemplified in their own lives what it meant to follow Christ, both on an individual and on a communal level. They presented a pattern of what a life of holiness, a Christ-like life, could look like—and their example proved inspiring. Without monks, and without their monastic ethos, there would have been no Christianization. The institutional church would have had far less credibility. This, then, is the other side of the process.

Christianity flourished when both factors—institutionalization and a compelling spiritual example—were united. Regrettably, that was not always the case. Tied as it was to the rebuilding of European society, Christian institutionalization made use of power structures that, by their very nature, were "worldly" and often indistinguishable from those of secular or even non-Christian political life. Subjugated peoples were no more likely to respect an urban bishop acting as local governor than they were a local governor who had no relationship to the church. That was all the more true if such urban bishops draped themselves with the usual secular accoutrements of wealth and power that, in their eyes, were necessary to communicate "status" (and made life more pleasant to boot). If, moreover, those same bishops preached sermons about renouncing the world and serving Christ in humility, the combination could not help but seem hypocritical. Who would believe such a man?

Such situations arose often as Europe was rebuilt after the fall of Rome. Through his conversion in 312, and subsequent rise to power as Emperor of Rome, Constantine the Great had established state sponsorship of the Christian religion. This not only allowed Christianity to move out of its minority niche, it also designated properties as belonging to the church, thereby setting an important, if controversial precedent. While that sponsorship ended in the West after the Empire's decline, it was revived, at first on a more local level, by the Frankish kings. Beginning with Clovis (c. 466–511), whose conversion account mirrors that of Constantine in many ways, royal support of the Catholic faith and its institutions returned.

The interconnectedness of ecclesial and temporal powers took several forms. In cities that had long served as episcopal residences, the bishop in many cases remained the most significant person of authority after the empire's disintegration. As the Franks established new administrative structures in their kingdoms, those bishops served in both a secular and religious role, at the same time governor and pastoral supervisor. The ambiguity resulting from such arrangements was exacerbated by the wealth and property that the bishops accrued.

The very notion that the church could own property remained problematic. Legally, there was the question—not fully clear from precedents in Roman law—of *who*, exactly, the owner in such cases was. Some deeds designated Jesus Christ; others mentioned individual saints. Even if one conceived of a corporate identity defined as "the church," there still remained questions of who acted on behalf of that church. In practice, bishops felt that they did. That assumption was often contested by lords and kings, however, and such conflicts permeate the entire era.

The situation was even less clear in rural regions. Here, most churches were built and maintained by local lords. Those lords understandably felt that they owned that church. They nominated and paid the clergy; they retained a portion of the parish income. In principle, all of this required approval by a bishop, but that had little impact on the day-to-day workings of these so-called "proprietary churches" under a lord's control. The priest was, for all practical purposes, a subject of his landlord. At the same time, the priest drew a portion of the parish's income himself. That placed him in a social position above that of the peasants whose rents and taxes helped support him.

Politically, even the wealthiest Frankish bishops had to face the reality that their king guaranteed the viability of their claims and protected them from outside aggression. They were dependents of the king. That dependency was all the more obvious when the church did not own properties outright, but received property rights from a lord or king. The transfer of such rights was typically accompanied by a ritual known as "investiture." This was not the same as consecration, by which the bishop received his spiritual authority from other bishops, but it was significant nonetheless. In investiture, the king solemnly handed the bishop symbols of authority—a ring and staff—and said the words *accipe ecclesiam*, or "accept this church." That effectively made the bishop a vassal to the king. He now owed fealty to his worldly superior, and in turn exercised land-owning privileges over all those who, by living on "his" land, became his worldly subjects. In this way, clergy were integrated into the feudal system. If Christianity had a long history of placing itself over and against "the world," that notion now became harder to maintain. The church was a full participant in the world, a player with a vested interest in, rather than a critic of, feudal realities.

Defenders of this development argued that the church needed material resources to carry out its mission in the world. A major part of that work had always been care for the poor. In some cases, income derived from properties did in fact go toward supporting the poor and the sick. In many cases, it stayed with the bishops or other clerical elite. Such developments generated criticism, much of which arose from within the church. The emergence of powerful monastic movements bore witness to that critical moment. The most celebrated pope of the early Middle

Ages, Gregory I, "the Great" (c. 540–604), was famous in large part because, as a former monk, he took his monastic values into office. One of the few early bishops of Rome whose pastoral charisms filled the idea of a "pope" with real meaning, Gregory preferred his monk's habit to expensive garments and called himself "servant of servants" as a sign of the humility that he felt belonged to the office.

The fact that Gregory's example still resonated nearly a thousand years later with Reformers such as Luther who otherwise had little sympathy for the papacy says something about the quality that monastic values lent to church offices. It also reminds us that Gregory was an exception. Given the connection of high church offices with wealth and property, they tended to attract a very different sort of man. Becoming a bishop was a smart career move for scions of the local aristocracy—and that applied in Rome as much as anywhere. This meant that, despite prominent and influential counter-examples such as Gregory, bishops as a whole were seldom potent instruments of Christianization.

A far more significant counterbalance to the worldliness of early medieval clergy came not from Rome, but from the Celtic outskirts of the British Isles. Irish and Scottish monks had developed a distinctive Christian culture far away from the tumultuous continent. Its polity was organized not around episcopal dioceses, but around monastic abbeys, which functioned as centers of spiritual life and learning. They also served as sources of missionary activity. Aside from rigorous "askesis" (self-denial and discipline practiced to heighten spiritual focus), these Celtic monks cultivated a practice known as *peregrinatio*, or wandering. Renouncing the comforts and security of a fixed home, they left their communities to go out into an often hostile world and evangelize. In that fashion, the Irish monk Columba (521–597), one of the best-known of these early figures, left his homeland to establish a monastery on the island of Iona, thereby helping to introduce Christianity to Scotland. His countryman Columbanus (543–615) went even further, gathering a small group of fellow-missionaries and leaving his monastery in Bangor, Ireland, for France. Divided into several kingdoms, much of France was nominally Christian when Columbanus arrived around 585, but the state of its churches was deplorable. Corruption among the clergy had helped undermine Christianity's credibility and eroded the religion's foothold in the Frankish kingdoms. Columbanus counteracted this by circumventing the established church and by securing the support of a king—the King of Burgundy—rather than that of a bishop. Based in a monastery provided by the monarch, Columbanus and his fellow monks began a wide-ranging ministry to the surrounding areas. The rigor and authenticity of their example and the depths of their spirituality proved compelling. Attracting countless visitors from far and wide, the Celtic monks launched a revival of Christianity in Burgundy and beyond. This set a number of important precedents.

For one thing, the Celtic monastic missions continued. Columbanus himself moved across the Alps to Italy late in life and established an influential monastery in Bobbio, between Milan and Genoa. He also left a monastic rule that stood alongside Benedict's for two centuries. His friend and disciple, Ursicinus (d. 625), founded a mission in Switzerland. Other Irish missionary-monks included Kilian (640–689), who left Ireland for Franconia and evangelized part of modern-day Germany before he was beheaded by a German noblewoman's henchmen; and Virgilius (c. 700–784) who traveled from Ireland to Salzburg, where he eventually became bishop. Celtic influence also extended to England, from whence a second movement swept eastward to the continent. Willibrord (c. 658–739) and Suitbert (d. 713) went from Northumbria to evangelize Frisia and today's Netherlands. They were joined by the better-known Boniface (c. 672–754), who departed from England for France and, together with the Carolingian kings and their armies, launched a large-scale Christianization of Saxon Germany. Boniface, who became the first Archbishop of Mainz, was later martyred while seeking to convert hostile Frisians.

In addition to their mission work itself, the northern monks brought a new kind of polity to continental churches. The Roman model of church organization was diocesan. It consisted of geographic areas (dioceses) whose churches were supervised centrally by a bishop. As already mentioned, the Celtic churches favored a non-diocesan structure in which abbeys served as spiritual centers.

This was the model Columbanus and his followers brought to France. Given the weakness of the Frankish bishops, the monks' ability to bypass episcopal jurisdiction—and interference—was important to their success. Needless to say, bishops were not enthusiastic about the presence of an alternate polity in their territories because it created churches that were both exempt from their supervision and beyond their financial reach. Bishops worked hard to reverse that process and to integrate the abbeys into their dioceses, and the issue remained contentious for centuries to come.

Celtic piety also left a lasting imprint on the face of medieval Christianity. Its powerful ascetic ethos, promoting poverty, chastity, and humility, was spelled out in *The Rule of Columbanus* and set the tone for monastic discipline. Monks embodied a readily identifiable lifestyle of "holiness." On top of that, many monks became martyrs, laying down their lives in the mission field. All of this heightened the respect they earned in a land on the cusp of Christianization. To a society whose pagan memories remained fresh, monks fit a familiar religious category: they were "holy men." They may have been different from the holy men of pre-Christian times, but they were much easier to identify in these terms than were bishops, who resembled government officials more than anything obviously holy. The numerous accounts of miracles and other legends that attached to the Celtic missionary monks testify to the impression they made in their day.

It was the Celtic practice of private confession and penance, however, that affected medieval devotional life most directly. While some form of ritualized confession and penance had been practiced in the ancient church, it eroded almost entirely under the rapid coarsening of moral standards in post-imperial, Germanic Europe. Early medieval authors such as Gregory of Tours (538–594) paint a dire picture of a society dominated by violence and brutality, economies based on plunder and corruption, and justice executed through vengeance and vendettas. Aside from "a few sincere ascetics and a small minority of respectable clergy," church leaders were no less degenerate than society as a whole, and therefore ill-positioned to impose Christian discipline. The Celtic missionaries, on the other hand, had developed a detailed system of penance to support their robust notions of moral discipline. Less interested in building institutional bureaucracy than they were in reforming a society from individual to individual, the northern monks placed their emphasis on private, rather than public, confession and penance. Confession was secret. It was made to a suitable person who was generally, but not necessarily a priest. Confessors, who occasionally included ascetic women, were spiritual guides, or "soul friends" according to Irish tradition.

Acts of penance that the confessor assigned after confession were also private, though not always secret, particularly if they also involved some form of satisfaction to an injured party. The monks developed manuals for penance and circulated them once they arrived on the continent. These handbooks stipulate penalties for a wide variety of transgressions, ranging from murder and theft to sexual offenses, perjury, and heresy. They typically distinguish between clergy and laypeople, assigning different degrees of guilt—and punishment—to each. Penalties usually involve fasting, which typically means a diet of bread and water only. So, for example, the *Penitential of Columban*, written around 600, assigns one year of penance for theft, two for masturbation, and anywhere from three to 10 or more years for murder. Sodomy committed by a priest resulted in 10 years' penance, while lay sodomy incurred only seven. Penalties for fornication depended in part on the degree of social disruption caused by the offense: if a man slept with an unmarried widow, he did one year; violating a girl brought two years plus compensation to her parents; impregnating another man's wife incurred three years, during which the offender not only fasted, but abstained from relations with his own wife and made restitution to the cuckold; the penalty for sex between unmarried persons was marriage.

As several of these examples illustrate, penance was often coupled with satisfaction, that is, with restitution or compensation to the injured party. This was particularly important for a mission context, which aimed not only at disciplining individual conduct, but also at reshaping society as a whole. While penance healed the soul, satisfaction mended relationships. It also paved the way for the penitent's eventual reconciliation with the church. Successful penance ended with re-admission to communion, which, particularly in a parish setting, has social implications since religious and secular communities are largely identical. The mission context of these handbooks is also evident in their efforts to incorporate values of local pre-Christian cultures. An obvious case involves Germanic notions of *wergeld*, or "blood money," according to which every person's life had a "price." Penalties for killing someone could be reduced and even eliminated if the killer paid the victim's family the appropriate price. Such practices were retained by many of the penitential guides, which lessened the time of penance when blood money was paid. While these concessions to local sensibilities probably broadened the guidebooks' impact, they also created dangerous ambiguities for penitential practice by suggesting that relief of penance could somehow be "bought."

Fascinating as these catalogues of penitential penalties are, it is important to remember that they served merely as practical guidelines, not as codes of law. They were meant to assist confessors in their tasks. As a result, there is a good deal of variety among the handbooks, and while the basic pattern is similar, specific penalties are far from consistent. Far more important than the lists themselves was the underlying relationship that confession established between penitents and a confessor. This was the key ingredient of the process. The role of a "soul friend," or spiritual mentor, became central to this approach to religious reform. In the early stages of the Celtic missions, that person was likely to be an ascetic monk, a man—or in some cases a woman—whose personal example had the power to inspire. Ultimately, the aim of such mentoring lay in changing the attitudes and values of a society so that un-Christian behavior would be less likely to arise. "True penance," begins the *Penitential of Columban*, "is to refrain from committing deeds for which penance is to be done."

As the new form of penance spread, it sparked bitter controversies between the Celtic monks and Frankish church leaders. Bishops, fearing a subversion of their own influence, opposed the new practices vehemently and used all of their institutional power to suppress them. A long and acrimonious conflict between episcopal and monastic visions for church life ensued. After several centuries, though, even bishops came to recognize the value of private confession and sought to give it greater institutional grounding. Confession was defined as a church sacrament, declared valid only if performed by an ordained priest, and, in 1215, made mandatory for all Christians. The penalties, too, were institutionalized, progressing from the informally compiled Celtic handbooks into universal standards of canon law.

Private confession's journey into the institutional church highlights important aspects of early-medieval Christianization. Emerging from the rubble of post-Roman Europe, Christian leaders worked to build institutions that could organize and regulate the society they sought to convert. To do so, they wedded themselves to the feudal political structures that arose at the same time, thereby acquiring property, wealth, and social influence. That came with a price, however: a worldliness that compromised many of the basic values of their faith. The fact that Christianity grew nonetheless was thanks to the efforts of wandering monks from the North who embodied a different and more recognizably "Christian" ethos. As their arguments over the status of abbeys and private confession show, the two forces found themselves in frequent conflict. On a purely abstract level, such conflicts—between the institutional and the innovative, between form and content—are probably eternal. In the history of Western Christianity, however, they were partially resolved during the eleventh century, when monastic innovators became a driving force in the church's institutional life.

The Rise of the Papacy: Centralization and Reform

Libertas ecclesiae!—"freedom of the church!"—was the battle cry of an eleventh-century reform movement that changed the face of Western Christianity. It was this movement, dedicated to "liberating" the institutional church from secular influences, that also created an effective papacy.

The notion of a "pope" at the top of the church's hierarchy was nothing new. Ancient Christianity had five patriarchs—the bishops of Jerusalem, Antioch, Constantinople, Alexandria, and Rome—whose authority surpassed that of all the other bishops. The see of Rome, drawing on a history that included two apostles, Peter and Paul, as well as on its cultural status, periodically claimed preeminence among the five and tried to assert a universal authority, but those attempts were rebuffed. The Council of Chalcedon (451), one of the definitive gatherings of the early church, formally rejected Rome's claims of primacy and accorded "equal privileges" to Constantinople. Bishop Leo of Rome declined to accept the council's decree, and the conflict caused a lasting estrangement between the churches of the Greek East and the Latin West. Within the West, Rome had less direct competition. Had the city produced better bishops, Rome's preeminence in this part of Europe may have been more meaningful before 1050. As it was, the notion of a universal bishop residing in Rome was significant mainly as an idea.

Even that idea had its challengers, however. Authority over the church lay in more than one pair of hands before the eleventh century. The most obvious obstacle to universal church leadership (in the West) was political disunity. Political rule was concentrated locally. Kings and dukes controlled a patchwork of individual territories, and they saw themselves as custodians of the churches within those lands. There was a strong set of precedents for such a view. Because their personal conversions effectively "converted" their subjects, too, both Emperor Constantine and later Clovis, king of the Franks, understood themselves as leaders of God's people—and therefore of the church. It was they who convened church councils, for example, and set the tone for important decisions of doctrine and polity. Clovis did this deliberately, convoking the First of Council of Orléans in 511, which established the king as head of the Frankish church and gave him the right to name bishops within his kingdom. Other regions across Western Europe followed similar patterns and saw the emergence of largely independent Christian cultures not only in Gaul, but on the British Isles, in Visigoth Spain, in parts of Italy, and eventually across Germany and Scandinavia. Even at the most local level, rural lords built and oversaw their "own" proprietary churches.

Royal leadership of the church was particularly notable during the Carolingian Age of the eighth and ninth centuries. Two incidents are emblematic of the relations between Frankish monarchs and the papacy during this period. In 751, Pepin the Younger (or "the Short," 714–768) was crowned King of the Franks, inaugurating the "Carolingian" dynasty (named after Pepin's father, Charles Martel). Elected by the Frankish nobility, Pepin was anointed by a bishop, underscoring the sacral character of the king's rule. In addition, Pope Stephen II, needing Pepin's military support to protect Rome from attacking Lombards, made the long journey to Paris to consecrate him again—the first time a pope consecrated a king. The pope also named Pepin and his sons *Patricius Romanorum* ("Patrician of the Romans"), placing the city under Carolingian protection. In return, Pepin mobilized his armies to defeat the Lombards and then "donated" the liberated territories to the pope. Though the precise terms of "Pepin's Donation" remain obscure, the agreement laid the foundation for papal rule over the Italian territories that were known as the "Papal States." At the time, it also demonstrated the pope's political and military dependence on the Carolingian king.

Pepin's son Charlemagne (c. 742–814) signaled the pope's secondary stature even more forcefully. Famous for his vast expansion of the Frankish kingdom, Charlemagne, who read assiduously church fathers such as Augustine, also implemented wide-ranging reforms of the churches in his growing domain. Liturgy, prayers, and church administration were overhauled under his custody. It was he, not the pope, who enforced liturgical consistency in the realm. On Christmas Day, 800, Charlemagne became more than a Frankish king: he was crowned Emperor of the Romans—reviving the idea of a Western Empire and setting the cornerstone for the office of Holy Roman Emperor. Charlemagne saw himself as crowned by God. The agent acting on God's behalf was the pope, who placed the crown on the new emperor's head and afterwards knelt before his ruler in a gesture of submission. Later popes would interpret the event differently, emphasizing their right to crown emperors rather than their submissiveness, but at the time, the message was clear. As a letter by Charlemagne to Pope Leo III declares, the emperor would defend, guide, and reform the church—and the pope would be his assistant.

Medieval kings understood themselves as religious figures and therefore as natural heads of their churches. Both modern-day notions of secular government and the separation of church and state, as well as the anti-royalist polemic of the eleventh-century reformers tend to obscure that. In their own minds, however, medieval kings thought it was perfectly appropriate for the church to be governed by a monarch rather than by a priest. After all, that is how things were in biblical times under Kings David and Solomon. Drawing on such scriptural precedents, medievals developed notions of sacral kingship. Kings did not simply take the crown, they were anointed in an act of consecration. One of the most eloquent formulations of this principle came in a series of treatises known as the *Norman Anonymous*, or *Anonymous of York*. Written during the heat of the royal vs. papal polemics around 1100, it articulates a longstanding position of royal church governance:

> By divine authority and the institution of the holy fathers, kings in God's church are ordained and consecrated at the sacred altar with holy unction and benediction, that they may have authority to rule a Christian people..., i.e. God's Holy Church. [...] When kings are consecrated, they receive the power to rule this body: to rule it, to confirm it in judgment and justice, and to organize it according to the system of Christian law. (O'Donovan and O'Donovan, 1999: 252)

Like most medievals, the *Norman Anonymous* envisions a hierarchically organized church. That hierarchy includes bishops and priests. At the top of the order, however, stands the king—to whom all bishops and priests are subject.

The royalist authors reject a competing intellectual position, one that was similarly ancient. In a widely read letter to the East Roman Emperor in 494, Bishop Gelasius of Rome made a distinction between ways in which the world is ruled: by the authority of consecrated priests, and by the power of kings. Of these, the former is preeminent because it deals with matters of salvation. Consequently, kings need to subordinate themselves "in religious matters" to the authority of priests. The letter gave rise to a "two swords" theory of government that was highly influential throughout the Middle Ages. The theory draws on Augustine's distinction between spiritual and worldly things, assigning priority to the spiritual as the greater good. In *City of God*, Augustine develops this distinction further by describing a heavenly "City of

God" and an earthly "City of Man." While Augustine does not connect those two literary "cities" with concrete types of government, some of his medieval interpreters did. In their eyes, the heavenly city represented the church; it was to be ruled by men versed in spiritual matters. The earthly city was the realm of kings. This dualism is what tracts like that of the anonymous author of York reject. They take issue with the notion that human existence can be separated into "spiritual" and "bodily" components, each with its own ruler, "as though souls could be ruled without bodies and bodies without souls!"

Philosophically, the debate is fascinating in its own right. It did not, however, take place in a vacuum. Given the worldliness of so many medieval bishops, it seems remarkable that they would employ Gelasius's Augustinianism to make a case for their distinctiveness. They were not very distinctive. But that is precisely why the "two-swords theory" was so attractive: there was an urgent *need* to define a recognizably spiritual priestly class. In that sense, it was a matter of self-protection, of maintaining some theoretical hold on what it meant to be a priest in such a gray-shaded City of Men. Cynics could argue that it was also a matter of self-deception. There is some truth to that. But in the hands of a reformer, theory can be a powerful tool. Deep change sometimes requires a City of God, if only as a goal.

Not surprisingly, the eleventh-century road to reform was laid by monks. It began 100 years earlier in a Benedictine abbey in Cluny, France, from whence a powerful wave of spiritual and liturgical reform swept across much of Western Europe. Initially driven by a desire to restore ascetic discipline and strict adherence to the Rule of Benedict within monasteries, the Cluniac Reform movement soon inspired countless Christians in non-monastic settings, as well. In order to further their reform agenda, the Cluniacs took what turned out to be an enormously significant step: they insisted on exemption from supervision by their local bishops and made themselves accountable directly to the pope. This, of course, revived an age-old conflict, present since the arrival of Irish monks in France more than 300 years earlier. Because bishops so often were enmeshed in the machinery of worldly rulers and interests, the monks viewed them as an impediment to reform. In this case, they went over the bishops' heads and sought support from the pope.

The problem with this scheme lay in the poor quality of the Roman popes. If papal support were to have any meaning, the popes needed to be able to command respect. And because popes had no armies, that respect could not be won by force. Instead, a moral integrity needed to attach itself to the office. This happened in two ways. The first was luck. The reformers profited from a coincidence: Henry III, German king and Holy Roman Emperor, was a deeply religious man who happened to support the Cluniac agenda. He was also the most powerful man in Europe. When the papal throne became vacant in 1048, Henry used his influence to nominate a suitable successor. His choice, Bruno of Eguisheim (1002–1054), soon to become Pope Leo IX, was a stroke of genius. Leo was a truly great pope.

Leo IX quickly convened synods in Rome, passing sharp decrees against clerical abuses. More importantly, he followed up these efforts by traveling outside of Rome and calling together councils in France and Germany that promulgated similar decrees. This was an effective way of establishing the pope's authority over the larger church. The fact that it found widespread support had as much to do with the strength of Leo's character as it did with the popularity of the reforms themselves. Leo died in 1054, but his legacy was profound. Wisely, he had called other reformers to Rome and made them cardinals, giving that office considerably more substance than it had hitherto shown. From the ranks of those cardinals, the drive to reform now accelerated.

The second part of the reform effort targeted the process of papal succession. One of the greatest weaknesses in the office came from its vulnerability to political influence. Without a clear procedure for appointing successors, papal vacancies were met with unseemly wrangling and maneuvering by a whole range of parties with a stake in the outcome. These included prominent Roman families, bishops, and kings and emperors. To avoid this, and to minimize such influence, the reformers drafted a new set of rules for papal election. They made it an inner-church process. Considering that none of the reformers would have been in Rome without Henry's appointment of Leo IX, there is a certain irony to this. But royal "interference" was not always so beneficial. In fact, since both Henry and Leo died before their agenda was secure, the reformers came under considerable pressure from opponents eager to name a more malleable successor to the papal throne. The future of the movement therefore depended on a speedy conclusion to electoral reform. This came in 1059, when Pope Nicholas II promulgated a decree on papal election. The decree established a "college of cardinals," consisting of specially appointed Roman clergy, as the primary electoral body. From here on, cardinals elected the pope. Even if the process still contained an opportunity for "the people" to voice their assent, it was now firmly in the hands of the elite clergy who were most familiar with the office. As the decree states: "The most eminent churchmen shall be the leaders in carrying out the election of a pope, the others followers" (Tierney, 1988: 42).

To reformers interested in "liberating" the church from control by secular rulers, this was their project's cornerstone. The papacy had become "free," and, equipped with a newfound moral authority, could now begin a process of reforming the church with the reins of centralized leadership. Using papal election reform as a model, the reformers sought to apply the same standards to the appointments of all other clergy. The principle, spelled out in further legislation of 1059, was clear: no more influence by laypeople: "That no cleric or priest shall receive a church from laymen in any fashion, whether freely or at a price" (Tierney, 1988: 44). That, simply put, amounted to a political revolution. Given the enormous diversity of church polities in the Latin West, and the deep entanglement of clergy in the web of dependencies that made up feudal society, calling for an end to lay investiture was an extraordinarily bold and assertive step. Implicitly, it was an indictment of the feudal system itself, suggesting that the church, in order to be spiritually pure, had to be free of feudal loyalties. Priests would not be beholden to laypeople; they would be subject only to one Lord: Jesus Christ. In practice, of course, they would also be subject to the Lord's earthly representative, the pope; but even that was a radical departure from the feudal world.

One sees in these reform efforts the imprint of a monastic ethos. When eleventh-century reformers such as Leo IX, or Hildebrand of Sovana (c. 1020–1085), his most influential assistant and later successor as Pope Gregory VII, spoke of liberating the church from lay influence, they did not just want to make it vaguely more spiritual, they sought to make it specifically more monastic. Most members of the circle had been influenced by Cluny, including Hildebrand, who was a Benedictine monk and had spent time in Cluny. When he took the name Gregory VII, he claimed the spiritual mantle of the most celebrated monk-pope of all: Gregory the Great. Convinced as they were by the value of life in the monastery, these men built their reform efforts (often called "Gregorian reforms") on a desire to make all the clergy more monk-like and more recognizably "holy" in comportment. A basic distinction between "clergy" and "laymen" was one part of that program. Another targeted two of the medieval clergy's most blatant moral abuses: simony and concubinage. Simony is the sale of spiritual services and, more specifically, church offices. Leo's circle was not the first to outlaw such practices, but they hoped that putting an end to lay investiture would diminish the opportunities for financial corruption that made simony so attractive.

Concubinage meant living with a "concubine," or common-law wife. While continence—abstaining from sexual intercourse—was not formally required of clergy until the twelfth century, it seemed an appropriate part of ascetic discipline and was strongly encouraged by some church leaders much earlier. It proved difficult to enforce, however, and hypocrisy became common as clergy claimed celibacy while carrying on relationships with women whom they did not marry (that is, "concubines"). Others married openly. This, too, was criticized and earned the pejorative term "Nicolaitism." Aside from the social disruption concubinage caused—such as the uncertain status of the women and the production of illegitimate offspring—sexual relationships of any kind contradicted the ascetic ethos of the Gregorian reformers. If priests were to become more monk-like, they could not have sex.

The reform movement's success was mixed. Curbing concubinage and simony proved difficult. Even after clerical celibacy was made a legal requirement at the Second Lateran Council in 1139, most priests ignored it. Throughout the centuries leading up to the Reformation, even bishops and popes kept concubines, and most rural villagers would have been surprised to find a priest without a common-law wife. Simony, too, continued, along with a wide range of related financial corruption, and ranked at the top of the agenda at every council for the remaining Middle Ages.

More successful were efforts to create a potent papacy. Along with the pope's increased status came a considerable rise in political influence—not only over bishops and clergy, but over kings and princes, as well. In fact, by the time of Gregory VII's pontificate, one could argue that the reformers' original motto of "free the church" had mutated into something more like "rule the world." Popes began stylizing themselves as monarchs. They let themselves be crowned; their installation was referred to as "enthronement"; they assembled a court of advisors and bureaucrats, known as the "curia"; and they commissioned legates to travel abroad as their representatives and enforcers. Popes did indeed serve as temporal rulers over the Papal States of central Italy, but their political ambitions had grown much larger.

A list of 27 propositions ascribed to Gregory VII appeared in 1075, and reveals how far papal thinking had moved in this direction. Known as the *Dictatus Papae*, the document makes a case of unprecedented strength for papal supremacy. Arguing "that the Roman Church was founded by God alone" and "that the Roman Pontiff alone is rightly to be called universal," *Dictatus Papae* builds a case for centralizing authority in Rome, and for subjugating worldly rulers to the pope. The pope alone may "enact new laws according to the needs of the time," "he alone may use the imperial insignia," "the Pope is the only one whose feet are to be kissed by all princes," and he "may depose Emperors." A pope had the power to name bishops and other clergy "of any church he may wish"— thereby expanding his episcopal jurisdiction beyond his own diocese and over the universal church (Tierney, 1988: 49–50).

Significantly, the document maintains that only popes be allowed to convoke synods and councils. The pope also claimed ultimate authority over truth: "He himself may be judged by no one," "no sentence of his may be retracted by anyone," and "no chapter or book may be regarded as canonical without his authority." Against this background comes a remarkable dogmatic assertion: "That the Roman Church has never erred, nor ever, by the witness of Scripture, shall err to all eternity." Rome's effort to centralize ecclesial authority comes in the next-to-last statement: "That he should not be considered as Catholic who is not in conformity with the Roman Church." Its political ambitions come in the last: "That the pope may absolve subjects of unjust men from their fealty." Kings may have been prepared to ignore most of *Dictatus Papae's* claims, but this last one contained a powerful threat. If one's feudal subjects really believed that the pope could absolve them from their oaths of fealty then one papal pronouncement would undercut an entire political order. A king could no longer rule. While papal apologists might argue that *Dictatus Papae* was interested in advancing justice (after all, only *unjust* rulers would be deposed), most secular rulers read the document with a stronger sense of realism. In their eyes, it was about claiming power—at their expense.

Statements such as *Dictatus Papae* reveal another side to the eleventh-century developments. More clearly than ever before, "the church" is here defined as a papal institution (that is, "the Roman Church"). Rome decides who its members are; Rome decides where its boundaries lie. Significantly, that attempted monopoly is meant to exclude competing notions of sacral kingship. Kings and princes are dismissed as "laypeople," as far removed from clergy as were peasants. This conception of "the church" introduced a basic dualism: it existed over and against "the world." The dualism itself is not new—Christianity had long operated with variations of this same theme—but it was now being filled with very specific contents. "The church" meant the papally-led institution. Non-clergy belonged to this "church" only insofar as they participated in the institution's sacraments—and access to those sacraments was governed by clergy. As time would tell, that new definition of the church had political implications. It also had challengers.

The strongest opponent of Gregory's ambitions was King Henry IV of Germany. Lay investiture was the issue that focused their conflict. In Henry's eyes, if Gregory succeeded in prohibiting lay investiture then the pope would indeed have taken an enormous step toward subverting royal power. He therefore opposed those efforts and continued his practice of investing bishops. Their struggle lasted years and precipitated a Europe-wide battle of propaganda. An initial standoff, during which Gregory excommunicated the king, was resolved at the castle of Canossa, in northern Italy, in 1077; Henry assumed the attitude of a penitent and was reinstated. While propagandists portrayed this as a victory for the pope, the conflict in fact continued. Prohibitions against lay investiture increased at local levels, but lay rulers also retained many of their traditional prerogatives. Henry even recovered enough strength to invade Rome in 1080, and appoint an anti-pope to Gregory. Gregory had to flee the city and later died in exile.

Despite such turbulence, however, the papacy had achieved a remarkable rise to power. Prior to Gregory VII, no pope had confronted a king in this fashion. Even if the outcome remained something of a stalemate, the papacy had established itself as a serious player on the field of European politics. A century later, during the reign of the brilliant Pope Innocent III, monarchs truly were inclined to kiss the pontiff's feet.

Under the aegis of robust central leadership, Western Christianity attained an entirely new level of institutionalization. The popes of the twelfth and thirteenth centuries solidified their control over the institutional church by several means. Creating a canonical process for electing popes gave the papacy a more secure legal footing. While outside influence continued and even produced an astonishing number of anti-popes during the twelfth century, having a legal standard in place gave the papal party an important resource to survive those conflicts. Intertwined with the politics of papal elections were territorial claims over the Papal States, the lands in central Italy over which the pope had temporal jurisdiction. During the course of the twelfth century, papal dominion over these states, contested by other rulers and resented by many Romans, stabilized, providing a measure of security for the Roman see. An assertive system of church taxes extended the papacy's financial reach over most of Western Europe. This, too, contributed to centralization of power both symbolically and in the unmistakeable "hard" form of cold currency.

Canon law was perhaps the most significant tool used to establish a centralized church administration. Animated by the Gregorian reformers, as well as by the rediscovery of Roman civil law, church lawyers and other scholars began compiling collections of papal decrees, both past and present, and arranging them systematically in law books for the church. A milestone in that development came with the twelfth-century Bolognese jurist Gratian's *Decretum*. Gratian's collection lay the foundation for the *Corpus Iuris Canonici*, a body of texts that, continually expanded, would remain in use until it was replaced by a simplified codex in 1917—nearly 800 years after Gratian's initial recension. Canon law enabled the papacy to govern in an unprecedented way. There was now one set of laws for all the Western churches. Importantly, those laws came from Rome. The pope was the final judge in matters of church law. He was also the direct source of many laws, since the collections preserved papal decrees. This ensured that a pope's pronouncements could be both disseminated broadly and applied for years to come. Aside from increasing the pope's power considerably, the establishment of centralized canon law carried the promise of strengthening church discipline. It gave substance to the idea of a universal church.

While most popes stayed near Rome, they used two instruments to execute power in other regions. The first was the papal legate. These men represented the pope, traveling to places where he wished to make his presence felt and outranking all the local church authorities upon arrival. For this reason they were seldom popular, but often effective. The second tool proved even more problematic. It was the council. As *Dictatus Papae* indicates, part of the papal reform effort made sure that only popes could henceforth convoke councils—not kings, as had been the case in previous centuries. Between 1123 and 1215, there were four such councils in the Lateran Palace, where the pope resided in Rome. Three more took place in France over the next century. They were important politically as well as for legislative purposes. The most significant of the medieval councils, the Fourth Lateran Council of 1215, called by Innocent III, enacted wide-ranging reforms of church life, including the requirement that all Christians attend the eucharist at least once a year, preceded by confession. Since councils gathered representatives from many geographic areas, their influence could radiate widely when those people returned home—presumably taking the council's pronouncements with them.

Closer to the heart of church life lay the pope's authority over sacraments. Most medieval Christians had no personal contact with popes, but many experienced this side of the pope's office at least indirectly. There were three ways a pope's disciplinary will could impact a person's sacramental life: *excommunication* prohibited an individual from receiving communion and in severe cases (*e. major*) banned that person from church attendance; *interdict* was generally applied to places rather than individuals and prohibited entire regions or countries from receiving the sacraments; *suspension* applied to clergy and forbad their administering the sacraments and providing pastoral services. In addition to regulating access to the sacraments, popes had another tool at their disposal: they could render feudal rulers powerless by unbinding their subjects from oaths of fealty. If that proved insufficient, they could follow up with a formal deposition. During their struggles with the Empire and other European powers, popes made liberal use of all of these measures. In some cases, they combined them. Between 1207 and 1215, Pope Innocent III displayed his full arsenal: He placed an interdict over the entire kingdom of England, excommunicated King John, and freed the king's subjects from their fealty. After lifting these measures and restoring John to power, Innocent suspended the archbishop of Canterbury for his role in advancing the Magna Carta.

The Papacy's Decline

Innocent's pontificate marked the high point of papal power. From here began a long decline from which the office never fully recovered. Less than a century after Innocent's death in 1215, the popes gave up their residence in Rome and moved to Avignon, France. Eventually, efforts to restore the Roman papacy led to the election of two simultaneous popes, one in Rome, the other in Avignon. Both were elected canonically by the same college of cardinals, and each attracted his own group of supporters across the continent. Christendom was divided. Initially an instrument of unity, the papacy had now become a cause of division.

Even at its apex, the papacy never headed a "universal church." In 1054, shortly after the death of Leo IX, mutual excommunications split Rome and Constantinople, sealing a centuries-long process of cultural estrangement. The Christian East had always rejected the pope's claims to primacy. Now, with the "Great Western Schism" (1378–1417) that pitted Rome against Avignon, the West was divided within itself, pope vs. pope, obedience vs. obedience. For a short time there were even three competing popes—the third elected in Pisa. After the Council of Constance finally resolved the crisis in 1417 by causing the removal of all three popes and electing a new one, the papacy's image was badly damaged. Its supporters worked frenetically to restore papal authority over the following century, but the pope's position remained insecure atop an institution that had developed a taste for alternatives. The sixteenth-century Reformation made good on those alternatives—and put an end to the dream of universal pontifical rule. Even in the West, there would now always be Christians who belonged to churches without a pope.

The papacy's decline went hand in hand with its increased worldliness. Paradoxically, efforts to "free" the church from secular governance made the church's own governance appear more secular. As kings were shouldered aside, popes themselves began behaving more like kings. The monastic spirit that had fueled eleventh-century reform was largely lost along the way. Tellingly, whereas Gregory VII had been a monk, major thirteenth-century popes such as Innocent III, Innocent IV, and Boniface VIII were lawyers and aristocrats.

If the initial cries for a "free church" contained an implicit critique of feudal society, by the end of the thirteenth century the papacy had mutated into a major participant in that society. The church's property claims were an increasingly important part of its institutional life. Ending lay investiture could have had the effect of divesting clergy from their entanglement in secular property structures. The opposite happened. Their involvement grew. Rather than representing an alternative to feudal lords, bishops and popes now competed with kings and princes for bigger slices of the same pie. Popes, in particular, were always eager to claim territories for the church and insist that kings only "borrowed" those lands as fiefs. Such efforts did not go unchallenged. When, for example, Pope Hadrian IV wrote a letter to his rival, Emperor Frederick II, in 1157, and suggested ambiguously that the Emperor's rule may be a feudal "benefit" bestowed by the pope—essentially making the emperor the pope's vassal—it caused an international scandal that moved even bishops to protest.

As popes positioned themselves as competitors in the feudal system, they made a number of serious miscalculations. For one thing, they failed to recognize in time the emergence of an entirely new type of political rival: the nation-state. They had no compelling answer to the absolutist agendas advanced by monarchs of those states. They also misjudged the kings themselves. This became evident when Boniface VIII sought to prevent King Phillip the Fair of France from taxing the French clergy in the years before and after 1300. When Boniface challenged Phillip's sovereignty and threatened the king with excommunication, Phillip responded by freezing exports of French gold to Rome. Boniface was stunned. The pope depended heavily on French revenues, and now had no choice but to give in—exposing the vulnerability of the popes' worldliness. Phillip was able to tax "his" French clergy. Several years later, Boniface tried again to assert his authority over the king. Issuing the bull *Unam sanctam* (1302), which presented the medieval era's farthest-reaching assertion of a pope's lordship over earthly powers, Boniface planted a flag deep into the sovereignty-claims of the French monarch. For good measure, the pope closed the bull with a statement that went far beyond even *Dictatus Papae* in its efforts to define a Roman church: "Therefore we declare, state, define and pronounce that it is altogether necessary for salvation for every human creature to be subject to the Roman Pontiff." (Tierney, 1988: 189].

Boniface underestimated the king. Phillip and his entourage were a new type of political animal: cynical and ruthless, they were unimpressed by excommunication. They also had little patience for notions of a "Roman" church. With a few swift strokes, the French king turned the tables on the pope. Phillip accused Boniface of heresy and of criminal conduct. He then sent an army of mercenaries to capture the pope. Boniface managed to escape but died a few weeks later. This was a turning point in papal history, equal in significance to Gregory VII's conflict with Henry IV two centuries earlier. For the foreseeable future, popes would be French and reside not in Rome, but in Avignon, close to the French king. Romanist critics came to call this the "Babylonian Captivity" of the church. Whatever its name, it was worlds away from the *libertas ecclesiae* envisioned by Leo IX and Gregory VII.

The claims asserted by documents such as *Dictatus Papae* or, more extremely, by *Unam Sanctam*, proved unworkable. Instead of creating a church "free" of worldly influence, they led to an even more worldly church. By the fourteenth century, the papacy had politicized itself beyond recognition. Efforts to define the church exclusively as a "Roman," or even as a "papal" institution, had run aground. The reasons for this are complex, but they have to do, at least in part, with a loss of vision. Arguably, papal apologists had spent so much time trying to define their church that they had, along the way, lost their focus on Christianity.

The Mendicant Critique of Wealth and Property

To many Christians, the worldliness of popes and their clergy stood in crass contradiction to the example of Jesus Christ. Would Jesus have built himself a palace and donned a tiara? The clergy's investment in feudal society further cost them credibility. Even people who knew no alternative recognized that feudal relations were strongly exploitative. Initially, the servants of the church offered a kind of refuge from that world. There are accounts of persons pressured by local lords to give up their inherited lands in exchange for "protection," but resisting those mafia-like tactics and instead bequeathing the property to a local abbey. The abbey represented something more charitable; in their eyes it was governed by Christian values rather than a desire for profit. By and by, those impressions changed. Even abbeys became so attached to their property that their Christian image slid behind a more venal and ruthless façade. By the time of the Reformation, abbots were among the most loathed of the peasants' enemies. Again, many people looked at the church and asked: is this what Jesus would do?

Increasing numbers of Christians thought not. They sought a life that was in closer harmony with Christ's example and teachings. The four centuries between 1100 and the Reformation saw repeated attempts by both clergy and laypeople to establish alternatives to a property-owning church. Not surprisingly, church leaders sought to suppress them. Still, many prevailed for a time and formed a vital Christian counterculture, testing not only the patience of popes and bishops, but also their conscience.

During this same period, medieval economic life changed fundamentally. The eleventh century brought relief, at long last, from the waves of outside invaders—Vikings from the North, Hungarians from the East, and Muslims from the South—who had terrorized the continent and pillaged its communities in the centuries before. As some historians have remarked, Europeans were now safe to plunder each other. They took advantage of this opportunity by creating economies based on money and market exchange. In what has been called a "Commercial Revolution," profit supplanted survival as a primary economic goal. Two important demographic factors were connected to this change in economic direction: an overall increase in population density, and the growth of cities. Cities are particularly interesting because they were home to a new social class that did not fit into the traditional categories of feudal society. Craftsmen and merchants were neither lords nor peasants. To the aristocracy's chagrin, money made them self-confident, and they not only defied subjugation, they insisted on a share of governance. In time, they got it. In time, too, they amassed more wealth than the nobles, and it was the rising bourgeoisie and its bankers who made dependents of princes and bishops.

The new profit economy did not replace feudalism's agrarian economy any more than the city replaced the countryside; it emerged alongside and modified it. Feudal relations continued, but they were now augmented by the mechanisms of trade. Whereas previous ages might have seen surplus produce distributed in an act of largesse, it now would likely be sold, and the money saved. Church institutions engaged in both forms of economy—largely without self-reflection or criticism of the principles involved.

This began at the level of religious behavior. The central feudal relationship, that of lord to vassal, was sealed by a religious rite that made free use of Christian idioms. In such rites of "homage," the vassal knelt before the lord, placed his clasped hands inside those of his future master, and swore an oath of fealty, most often using visual aids such as Scripture or relics to emphasize his sincerity. Even more overtly Christian were the rites of investiture that followed. Witnesses to such performances must have felt the allusive similarities to Holy Communion: here, too, recipients knelt before a superior and received benefits from a "lord." There was a grammatical similarity between the two ceremonies as well: in both cases, the recipient was expected to keep up his own end of the bargain—to go forth and serve the lord. Against such a background, the mass itself could be read as a spiritualized enactment of feudal subjugation. Such ambiguities in religious practice help explain why so many critics of the institutional church, from the twelfth-century Humiliati to the sixteenth-century Anabaptists, rejected the swearing of oaths and sought radical revisions of the mass and eucharistic practice.

The church used feudal economic structures directly, as well. The most obvious example is that of the *benefice*. Closely synonymous with "fief," a benefice is property given by a lord to a vassal in exchange for service. The church made use of that arrangement to pay its clergy. Bishops or ecclesial patrons granted benefices to priests so that the latter might have a source of income. That income typically came from peasants who rented the property. On the surface, the practice made financial sense for the institution. At the same time, though, it contained a number of problems. The least of these, from the perceptions of those involved, was the vassal-like relationship of the priest to his ecclesial superior; people who served the medieval church were used to such hierarchies. Somewhat more troubling was the lord-like relationship of the priest to "his" peasants, particularly since these people were also his parishioners. It complicated his pastoral role, identified him with the ruling class, and cemented his outsider's status. Even more problematic were the abuses that such arrangements invited.

Many benefices were obtained (often purchased) by wealthy people who had no intention at all of serving the corresponding parish but were simply interested in its income. In fact, many were not clergy. They "sublet" the property to a vicar and paid him a small part of the proceeds. That subverted oversight and church discipline, and encouraged absenteeism, a common scourge of medieval church life.

One could name many more examples of medieval church economy. For our purposes, it is sufficient to note that, during the period in question, churches acquired a great deal of property and wealth. In addition to their involvement in feudal practices, they received goods and money through trade, from "souvenirs" of the Crusades, from fees exacted in exchange for spiritual services, and from an extensive system of taxes. Individual parish priests may not have been well off, but many of their superiors certainly were.

Critics took issue with those developments and the new mentality that they engendered. In a move that recalls the influx of a Celtic monastic ethos during the early stages of Christianization, these critics espoused a deeply ascetic spirituality. Its hallmark (though by no means its only feature) was a rejection of property. Its proponents took vows of poverty.

Attempts to introduce a more ascetic attitude toward clerical property were already part of the Gregorian reform effort. At a synod in 1059, Hildebrand (later Pope Gregory VII) and his colleague Peter Damian issued harsh rebukes against cathedral canons who lived "like laypeople." In their view, canons (groups of priests who were attached to specific cathedrals or other churches) should live an "apostolic common life," cloistered within the church's premises, eating and praying together, and separate from the town's laypeople. Many canons had instead taken up residence in their own houses, living like lords and aristocrats. Not only were they unavailable for much of the church's desired common life, but—and this was a centerpiece of the reformers' criticism—they were amassing private possessions. Owning private property was considered un-apostolic. Renouncing it therefore became a key part of reforming the canons' lifestyle. Though they encountered considerable resistance, the Gregorian reformers did succeed in launching a partial overhaul of the system by establishing the "Rule of Augustine," a rigorous, ascetic regulation of the common life, for canons. Though only a minority adopted the Augustinian rule, it established a significant alternative to the prevailing clerical culture of the time and reveals a lot about the kind of Christianity that Gregory and his supporters sought to create.

As the tepid response to these reform measures indicates, most representatives of the institutional church were not enthusiastic about criticizing the principles of property ownership. One sees this in the development of theological and legal theory as well. Early authors held up the biblical ideal of common ownership, based on passages such as Acts 2: 44–45, which describe how members of the apostolic community "had all things in common; and sold their possessions and goods and distributed the proceeds to all, according to need." As medieval economies came to develop entirely different values, and most Christians behaved in a manner diametrically opposed to the apostolic example, theologians began to adjust their theories. By the twelfth century, prominent legal scholars such as Rufinus the Canonist (1150–c. 1191) maintained that, while having possessions was not in and of itself a part of natural law, the corruption of human behavior required that such provisions be added. People needed to be able to define what is "mine" in order to protect such things from the avaricious hands of their neighbors who lacked respect for common ownership. A century later, Thomas Aquinas (1225–1274) was already arguing that private property was, indeed, safeguarded by natural law. This fit nicely the acquisitive mood of the era's elites and became their preferred theological position.

As the Gregorian spirit of reform waned, popes and bishops not only lost interest in changing the church's relation to property, they began to persecute reformers who did. Arnold of Brescia (c. 1100–1155) was one such reformer. As head of a community of canons, Arnold took a particularly rigorous stance against ecclesial materialism. In his view, any clergyman who owned property would not be saved. If that statement was straightforward, so was the papacy's response: Arnold was thrown out of office, expelled from Italy, and later hanged. Prominent theologians such as Bernard of Clairvaux (1090–1153), abbot and a leader of the immensely wealthy Cistercian order, saw in Arnold an "enemy of the Lord."

Some of the most meaningful alternatives to a property-owning church came from laypeople. Christian men and women, often living in urban settings and troubled by the effect of commercial culture on religious values, organized spiritual communities dedicated to a purer, more apostolic life. One such group called itself "Humiliati," or "Humble Ones." Emerging in northern Italy during the 1100s, the Humiliati adopted simple clothing, rejected oaths, and shared their possessions while living in a community. Seeking to spread their faith, they also preached in public. That combination of alternative communal living and public preaching (by laypeople) incurred the suspicion of successive popes. Pope Lucius III condemned the Humiliati as heretical in 1184. That changed under the more sympathetic papacy of Innocent III, who recognized the Humiliati as an official order and even gave their lay members permission to preach. Within a century, the Humiliati had attracted so many members that they needed nearly 400 convents in northern and central Italy to house them.

Somewhat less fortunate was a similar group of Christian laypeople who originated at roughly the same time in Lyons, France. Organized by a wealthy merchant named Waldes (?–c. 1218), who had sold his possessions, the Waldensians espoused many of the same apostolic values as the Humiliati. Their rejection of property was more rigorous, however, and the French Waldensians had no convents. Instead, they traveled about, wearing coarse garments and often going barefoot, to preach to a broader public. Their message was based on following the example of Christ and the apostles, whose stories they told with the help of Gospels translated into the vernacular. Their rapid spread throughout and beyond France to Italy and Germany incited the same hostility that greeted the Humiliati. While some of the Waldensians were reinstated by Innocent III, most were persecuted. Many of those who survived withdrew into underground communities away from episcopal control. As a result, their existence remained precarious and continually threatened, but their church lives on to the present day.

The same cannot be said of the Cathars, still another group dedicated to a life of Christian purity. Little is known about the movement, in part because most of the source-material was written by its enemies, and also because it was eradicated so completely. Congregating in southern France during the late 1100s, the Cathars, sometimes called "Albigensians," also sought to restore the ascetic spirit and practices of the early church. They, too, rejected oaths and private property. Some of them apparently taught a dualistic theology with Manichean overtones. The true church, in their view, consisted of pure Christians dedicated to lives of holiness. It was not the church of Rome, which in fact persecuted true Christians. Consequently, the Cathars rejected Rome's authority and established religious rites of their own, including rigorous catechesis followed by a kind of "spirit baptism" (*consolamentum*) that supplemented the water baptism received at birth. None of this endeared them to the dominant church authorities, of course, and the Cathars were quickly branded heretical. After several unsuccessful attempts to re-convert them or to suppress them with inquisitions, Pope Innocent III authorized a crusade to exterminate the Cathars in 1208. Because the pope promised to give the Cathars' lands to anyone who killed them, there was no shortage of volunteers. Thousands of Cathars were massacred along with thousands of normal Catholics who happened to live near them—and whose land was attractive to the mercenaries. While a handful of Cathars survived to face the Inquisition, the movement was crushed.

The ideals of apostolic poverty could not be suppressed entirely, however. In fact, the age of Humiliati, Waldensians, Cathars, and similar movements also produced two religious orders who overcame initial suspicions and established themselves as durable voices within the institutional church: Franciscans and Dominicans. The Franciscans had a lot in common with the other movements. Their founder, Francis of Assisi (c. 1182–1226), owed his considerable wealth to the emergent cloth industry, much like Waldes of Lyons. Like Waldes, too, Francis, a layperson, experienced a dramatic conversion that caused him to renounce wealth and property and to embrace a life of evangelical poverty and humility. Assembling a small community of "brothers," Francis drafted a simple rule and in 1210 sought its papal approval. Innocent III, who was better than most popes at recognizing a need to integrate such voices if possible, rather than suppress them indiscriminately, welcomed Francis' proposal. A new order was born. Having secured papal endorsement, the Order of Friars Minor launched a missionary movement that spread over Europe within a decade.

The Dominicans were an indirect product of the Cathars. They were founded by Dominic de Guzman (c. 1170–1221), a Spanish priest dispatched by Innocent III to convert the Cathars. While Dominic's successes in this regard were modest, the "heretics" made a profound impression on him. Combining ideals of apostolic poverty with a powerful commitment to preaching, Dominic laid the groundwork for a new order, based on the *Rule of Augustine*, and approved by the pope in 1216. Though their views on property were less radical than those of the Franciscans, the enormous subsequent success of the Dominicans further underscores the widespread yearning for a Christianity patterned on a more primitive apostolic example. Clearly, these mendicant orders had struck a nerve.

Such developments of the twelfth and thirteenth centuries recall a basic tension between Western Christianity's institutional and political demands, on the one side, and its spiritual needs, on the other. While that dynamic had been present in the West in one form or another from the beginnings of post-imperial Christianization, it now developed a specific focal point: the role of wealth and property. It is no accident that a deep suspicion of wealth and property arose as a counterpoint to the political rise of the papacy. It gained strength as popes abandoned the Gregorian reform-ethos. Soon, even those advocates of apostolic poverty who had been approved by Rome found themselves in conflict with the papacy.

In 1323, Pope John XXII, residing in the papal palace of Avignon, defined as heresy the assertion that Christ and his apostles owned no property. Anyone who claimed that Christ and his apostles owned no property would henceforth be subject to excommunication. This was a hard blow to the mendicant ethos. It was also a direct hit on the more rigorous members of the Franciscans, who were now forced to modify their ideals of poverty. Those who resisted—among them the theologian and philosopher William of Ockham (c. 1285–1347)—were declared heretical and excluded from the pope's church. That church, it was clear, would tolerate no critique of its financial practices. To hammer home his point, John XXII "gave" the Franciscans all the church properties that they had up to now only borrowed. The Franciscans could no longer say they owned nothing.

Deeper cultural shifts in the economic life of late-medieval Europe posed an additional challenge to the mendicant ethos. This is most evident in urban centers. As cities developed new market-based economies, they also cultivated a distinctive ideal of citizenship. It involved owning property. Those citizens who owned houses and means of production—those who had *invested* financially in the city—were considered better citizens. Correspondingly, men of means and property rose to the front ranks of those cities and became "pillars of the community," as one says today. This opened the door to a much more positive assessment of worldly possessions in general. Beautiful objects, not only those found in nature, but, more importantly, those that were crafted by artisans and sold as commodities, acquired cultural value. Desiring and owning such objects was thought ethically acceptable, and those who did so saw themselves as "life-affirming."

In such contexts, the older ascetic ideals of the mendicant tradition had no place. They were dismissed as old-fashioned or even as socially dangerous. Only a few of the mendicant friars resisted these shifts. Most accommodated themselves to the new spirit and made compromises with its property-based ethos. The few who did not were ridiculed and marginalized. Others retreated to the countryside, where their ministry had more resonance. In the cities and among the educated elite, anti-fraternalism, hostility toward mendicants in general and Franciscans in particular, became a prominent feature of Renaissance society. Theirs was not a message anyone wished to hear.

Conclusion

The preceding text has lifted up several narrative strands from a grand and convoluted medieval tapestry. Obviously, one could say much more. But these strands were not selected at random. They were chosen to illustrate and explain some of the important issues facing Western Christianity on the eve of the Reformation. Most importantly, Christianity in Western Europe found itself in a long-term mission setting. Even if the Christian religion had reached the last corners of the continent by 1500, "Christianization," the process by which religious and cultural behavior became regulated by Christian norms, was far from complete. Arguably, it never is. From a historian's perspective, though, it is important to note that most Christian leaders were aware of this need and sought consciously to advance the progress of Christianization. It was a driving force of their vocations.

Even as most medieval leaders agreed that Christianization needed to go on, they disagreed on how that should happen. Several of these disagreements are important because they shaped the way medieval history played itself out and because their lack of resolution set the stage for the sixteenth century's Reformation.

One of the most basic unresolved issues concerned the definition of "church." Two perspectives were prominent in this debate. At times they were complementary, at others, they were at odds. The first concerned Christianity's need to organize its people, to make tangible the notion that Christians comprised "one body." There were a variety of approaches to that challenge. One drew on notions of sacral kingship, arguing that, in a Christian kingdom, the religious and political bodies were one and the same, and best governed by a king. As time went on, an alternative vision gained traction. It was based on a sharp distinction between spiritual and temporal spheres, and argued for a priority of the spiritual, governed by a priestly, or "clerical" class. By the eleventh century, its defining feature became centralized hierarchical organization with the Roman pope as head. After a brief period of dominance, the papal model succumbed to schism. Its failures helped inspire a third model, advanced during the fourteenth and fifteenth centuries, that sought to supplant (or in some views augment) the pope's authority with that of a broadly representative council of Christian laypeople and clergy. At the year 1500, all three of these options remained in contention and none had achieved a durable victory.

A second perspective focused on the church not as institution, but as a group of people seeking to live Christian lives. Its guiding principles were spiritual and ethical. It was more concerned with holiness than with hierarchy. Much of its inspiration came from monastic sources. It hardly ever came from Rome. The dynamic was often guided by "restorationist" tendencies, a desire to restore the ethos and practices of the apostolic age. It almost always had an ascetic bent. In later years it contained a rigorous critique of wealth and property. At times, this endeavor seemed to take place on a different plane from that on which royalist, papalist and conciliarist elites argued their respective ideologies. Occasionally, as with the eleventh-century papal reform movement, the elites themselves took up its cause, but generally they resisted or sought to control impulses of this kind. Tellingly, the term "heresy" was applied far more often to people who seemed to try *too hard* to be Christian than to those who rejected the religion.

Attempts of leading clergy to control and define the Christian religion remained superficial. Christianity expanded, but seldom according to anyone's plan. It grew by a mix of popular practices, local traditions, compelling individual examples, and the formative power of Christian rituals and narratives. Under the influence of the mendicants, teaching and preaching became powerful instruments of Christianization during the later Middle Ages, but theology's impact was limited by the overwhelming lack of literacy that characterized the period and by the lack of formal education for clergy. Priests were supposed to be able to read, but that was no guarantee that any of them ever did. Consequently, the great minds that emerged from the Franciscan and Dominican orders— men such as Thomas Aquinas, Bonaventure, and Duns Scotus— exerted only an indirect influence on the religiosity of common people. Its impact remains poorly understood. Efforts to exert more direct control, such as the Fourth Lateran Council's mandates on annual confession and communion, generally fell short of expectations. Even the clergy themselves paid little attention to continual injunctions against concubinage or simony. None of this should suggest that the medieval church was irredeemably "corrupt," as is often maintained. It is simply meant to underscore how disorganized the church remained. Good intentions and sound Christian principles were certainly present, but they proved difficult to implement. Had one of the competing institutional models been more successful, things may have been different.

But they were not. At 1500, Christianity remained only superficially "united," and "the church" was still a work in progress.

References

The following is a list of works cited and consulted in this chapter. Though it is only a small selection of relevant literature, it is a good place to start for further reading.

O'Donovan, Oliver and O'Donovan Joan Lockwood, eds. 1999. *From Irenaeus to Grotius: A Sourcebook in Christian Political Thought.* Cambridge/ Grand Rapids: Eerdmans.

Tierney, Brian. 1988. *The Crisis of Church and State 1050–1300.* Toronto: University of Toronto Press.

Further Reading

Baron, Hans. 1938. Franciscan poverty and civic wealth as factors in the rise of humanistic thought. *Speculum. A Journal of Medieval Studies* XIII(1): 1–37.

Bloch, Mark. 1961. *Feudal Society.* Transl. from the French by L. A. Manyon. London: Routledge.

Freedman, Paul. 1999. *Images of the Medieval Peasant.* Stanford, CA: Stanford University Press.

Fried, Johannes. 2008. *Das Mittelalter. Geschichte und Kultur* [The Middle Ages: History and Culture]. München: Beck.

Huppert, George. 1998. *After the Black Death: A Social History of Early Modern Europe.* 2nd edition. Bloomington: Indiana University Press.

Kantorowicz, Ernst H. 1957. *The King's Two Bodies: A Study in Mediaeval Political Theology.* Princeton, NJ: Princeton University Press.

Little, Lester K. 1978. *Religious Poverty and the Profit Economy in Medieval Europe.* Ithaca, NY: Cornell University Press.

McNeill, John T. and Game, Helena M., eds. 1990[1938]. *Medieval Handbooks of Penance: A Translation of the Principal* Libri Poenitentiales. New York: Columbia University Press.

Oberman, Heiko A. 1986. *The Dawn of the Reformation: Essays in Late Medieval and Early Reformation Thought.* Edinburgh: T. & T. Clark.

Swanson, Robert N. 1995. *Religion and Devotion in Europe, c. 1215–c. 1515* Cambridge: Cambridge University Press.

Ullmann, Walter. 1955. *The Growth of Papal Government in the Middle Ages: A Study in the Ideological Relation of Clerical to Lay Power.* London: Methuen.

Chapter 2

The Luther Phenomenon

Luther's "Ninety-Five Theses"

On October 31, 1517, Martin Luther, an Augustinian mendicant and professor of biblical theology at the recently founded University of Wittenberg, offered for academic consideration a series of theses, 95 in all, on the topic of *indulgences*. It was like throwing a match into a cave hoping for illumination. This cave contained explosive surprises, and when illumination came, it surpassed even the wildest expectations.

Indulgences were a well-established part of the medieval practice of penance. As was sketched in the previous chapter, private confession and satisfaction were introduced to Western Europe by Celtic missionaries and gradually institutionalized, becoming mandatory for all Christians at the Fourth Lateran Council of 1215. The practice was fairly straightforward. A person went to a priest and confessed his or her sins. The priest, acting as an earthly representative of Jesus Christ and equipped with the authority to forgive those sins, pronounced absolution. Absolution did not, however, wipe out the earthly consequences of a person's sins. If, for example, someone stole money from his neighbor, forgiveness may have saved the thief from damnation, but it did not restore the missing money. Nor, on a psychological level, did it prevent the person from repeating his or her offense at the next opportunity. To address these consequences, notions of "satisfaction"

The Reformation: A Brief History, First Edition. Kenneth G. Appold.
© 2011 Kenneth G. Appold. Published 2011 by Blackwell Publishing Ltd.

were added to confession and forgiveness. The forgiven sinner was assigned penalties and works of compensation. Though these were often fairly minor and involved prayers and contrition, the fear that penalties could accumulate to staggering dimensions was widespread. By 1500, many sinners would not expect to finish them within their lifetime; they would look forward to an extensive period of purgatory to do the rest. There were ways around this, however. Those ways often involved money.

The thought that money lessened the burden of satisfaction was not a late-medieval corruption, as is sometimes taught, but as old as the practice of penance itself. Some of the very first sixth- and seventh-century penitential handbooks made use of a pagan Germanic custom known as *wergeld*, or "blood money," a specific sum attributed to every person in society and measuring that person's "value." The spiritual penalties for killing a person could, for example, be lessened if the murderer paid his or her victim's family the appropriate *wergeld*. Similar provisions were made for deflowering virgins or otherwise compromising a person's value. Such thoughts were developed further as penance became institutionalized, and were no doubt aided by the emergence of capitalist economies and the changing role of money in that world. The granting of relief from penalty was formalized and subjected to more stringent regulation. The relief itself was called "indulgence." Only bishops had the authority to grant indulgences. Indulgences did not need to be purchased with money, but could be acquired in a variety of ways. Pope Urban II, for example, promised far-reaching indulgences in 1095 to anyone who participated in the first crusade.

Theologically, the rationale for granting indulgences was twofold. First, satisfaction, unlike forgiveness, was an entirely temporal construct. It was assigned in a pastoral context by a priest. If a priest could determine how much satisfaction to assign, he should also have the authority to lessen it as needed. The second part of the rationale was based on the notion that the church is a community sharing in some form of common life. At that time, the community was believed to include persons described as "saints," whose moral quality was so remarkable that their balance sheet of satisfaction was actually positive: they did more good deeds than they would ever need for their own satisfaction. According to a bull (*Unigenitus Dei Filius*) issued in 1343 by Pope Clement VI, the papally-led church collects the value of those supererogatory acts, adding them to a "treasury" of Christ's own works, and distributes them as the pope and his representatives see fit. In this way, other Christians receive the benefits of that treasure and have it applied to their own "debt" of satisfaction, lessening their temporal punishment. While modern readers accustomed to individualized notions of guilt and punishment might find such notions alienating, a medieval Christian would have found them no more surprising than the sharing of food or produce practiced in monasteries and other religious communities.

Martin Luther, who did live in a monastery, appears tacitly to have accepted the theology of indulgences for much of his early career, though he did complain occasionally about its abuses—as did many of his theologically alert contemporaries. In 1517, however, a particular development caused him to think more thoroughly about the practice and its theological rationale.

Albrecht (Albert) of Brandenburg (1490–1545), second son of the elector of Brandenburg, had social ambitions that exceeded his inheritance. While his older brother received the electorate, Albrecht took aim at a career in the church. In 1513, just 23 years old, he saw a chance to become archbishop of Magdeburg. There were two obstacles: he was not a priest, and he was much younger than the required age of 30. Both problems proved soluble: he quickly let himself be ordained, and he agreed to pay curial officials for an exemption from the age limit. Barely a year later, Albrecht added an even bigger prize, becoming archbishop (and elector) of Mainz, the most powerful ecclesial position in Germany. This required yet another dispensation, because canon law prohibited bishops from occupying more than one see, and Albrecht now had two. Here, as well, money had a way of solving problems. On the other hand, lack of sufficient money creates other problems—and this was the case for Albrecht. Since he had not nearly enough funds to buy all the desired dispensations from the curia, he did something quintessentially modern: he took out a loan. Turning to the immensely wealthy Fugger banking family of Augsburg, Albrecht secured the monies to pay off Rome and the emperor—and to become archbishop of both Magdeburg and Mainz.

Albrecht now needed a way to pay off his debt to the Fuggers. Happily, a golden opportunity presented itself: Pope Leo X (1475–1521) was busy raising funds for the construction of a splendid new papal church in Rome, the St. Peter's Basilica, and announced a general indulgence, available to qualified customers. The proceeds would go towards his basilica. Sensing an opening, Albrecht offered to help the pope; in return, he would be allowed to use half the income thus generated to pay off the Fuggers. It was a deal (albeit a secret one). Albrecht commissioned a team of indulgence preachers to travel his dioceses and market the papal offer.

The most famous of these preachers was a Dominican friar named John Tetzel (c. 1465–1519). Tetzel was an extremely skilled manipulator of religious anxiety. Because indulgences could be purchased not only for one's own use, but also on behalf of those who had already departed and were presumably at that very moment suffering away in purgatory, Tetzel and his cohorts capitalized on concerns for those loved ones, as well. Traveling from town to town, his highly emotional sermons painted graphic pictures of purgatorial suffering capped by personal appeals to his listeners: "Do you not hear the voices of your dead parents and other people, screaming and saying: 'Have pity on me, have pity on me!'" All the listener had to do was drop a few coins in the box at the rear of the church—and that suffering would be relieved: "As soon as the coin into the box rings, a soul from purgatory to heaven springs!" (Lindberg, 2010: 71).

Many found Tetzel's tactics repugnant. Elector Frederick the Wise, who ruled Luther's Saxony, banned Tetzel from entering the state. But quite a few Saxons, including residents of Wittenberg, were still lured to the neighboring territories where Tetzel was active. Word of his actions reached Luther, who was prompted to take a deeper look not only at the Dominican's methods, but also at his theological premises. The result was Luther's *Disputation on the Power and Efficacy of Indulgences*, commonly known as "The Ninety-Five Theses" (*Luther's Works*, 1955– (hereafter LW): vol. 31, 25–33).

The indulgence sellers' most obvious theological offense lay in their clever insinuations that salvation itself could be bought. There had always been an ambiguity at the heart of penitential practice, a blurring of the lines between absolution and satisfaction. Tetzel's made-for-profit preaching took advantage of this confusion and marketed the indulgences as "tickets to heaven" (Lindberg, 2010: 72). To an innocent listener, the indulgence bought not only relief from temporal penalties, but salvation itself. Tetzel, along with any church official involved in the indulgence trade—including the pope—would have been well aware of this. Even in retrospect, such cynical exploitation of common people by their church leaders is disturbing, and the fact that Tetzel was a mendicant adds irony. From the perspective of economic history, though, such behavior simply mirrored the values of a burgeoning commercial age. The ascetic ideals of the early monks and first mendicants, so often a corrective to such behaviors, had all but vanished from the church's public face.

Luther's disputation attacks the commercialization of indulgences head-on: "Christians are to be taught that if the pope knew the exactions of the indulgence preachers, he would rather that the basilica of St. Peter were burned to ashes than built up with the skin, flesh and bones of his sheep" (Th. 50). Interestingly, Luther often seems to assume that the pope is unaware of the more egregious abuses; though such words certainly carry a paraenetic undertone, they are not a direct critique of the papacy. Tetzel and his cohorts, on the other hand, lie squarely in the line of fire: "They preach only human doctrines who say that as soon as the money clinks into the money chest, the soul flies out of purgatory" (Th. 27).

Other theses aim to correct erroneous teaching, reminding the reader, for example, that indulgences only grant relief from temporal—not eternal—punishment. Similarly, Luther observes that penitential canons only apply to the living, not the dead. Temporal punishment, therefore, ends at death: "The dying are freed by death from all penalties ..." (Th. 10). That, of course, puts limits on the pope's power over souls in purgatory. While Luther does not yet criticize the notion of purgatory itself (that would come later), he does wish to make clear that the pope cannot impose or grant indulgence from purgatorial punishment. All he can do for them is pray, like any pastor for his flock.

Luther's text goes well beyond these more topical concerns, however, and calls for a fundamental reconception of penance itself. In words reminiscent of the early Celtic monks, Luther's first thesis sets the tone: "When our Lord and Master Jesus Christ said, 'Repent', he willed the entire life of believers to be one of repentance" (Th. 1). Repentance is all-encompassing. Such repentance, clearly, could not be bought with money. It is also more encompassing than the sacrament institutionalized by the church: "This word [repentance] cannot be understood as referring to the sacrament of penance, that is, confession and satisfaction, as administered by the clergy" (Th. 2). Luther returns to a pre-sacramental, pre-institutional understanding of penance, something broader and more basic than what was being administered—even in the best cases—by the clergy. In that regard, his theses do more than address abuses of a system; they reveal the beginnings of a positive program of reform that seeks to restore an earlier and purer ideal of Christianity.

Luther's concerns are primarily pastoral, rather than polemical. He seeks to redirect penitential practice, to return it to its religious moorings, and use it to transform Christian life. Subsequent theses shed further light on his vision. Luther wants to see "true repentance," and "true contrition," neither of which, in his view, are achieved by granting people reprieves from penitential penalties. These are precisely the attitudes that penance, properly understood and accompanied by sound preaching of the Word, should evoke. True repentance, furthermore, leads to works of charity. In a remarkable thesis that both supports this specific vision and at the same time undercuts the commercialization of penance, Luther argues that a Christian improves more by doing works of love than by buying indulgences: "Christians are to be taught that he who gives to the poor or lends to the needy does a better deed than he who buys indulgences" (Th. 43). Works of love allow love itself to grow—and this is the measure of a good Christian.

Rome's Response

On October 31, 1517, Luther wrote a letter to Archbishop Albrecht of Mainz, advising the bishop to reassess the indulgence trade and enclosing a copy of his "Ninety-Five Theses." Similar letters were sent to other nearby bishops. It is highly likely that Luther also posted a copy of the theses that same day on the wooden door of Wittenberg's Castle Church, which served as the university chapel. In any case, the theses soon reached a wider public. Both actions—the mail to Albrecht and the theses' broader publication—set events in motion that Luther could hardly have foreseen. They launched the Reformation.

Albrecht, whose financial complicity in the indulgence trade was unknown to Luther, saw the Wittenberg professor's texts not as an invitation to theological debate, but as an existential threat. The archbishop forwarded the material to Rome, along with a note complaining about its author, an irksome and presumptuous monk whose views would lead unsuspecting sheep astray—if allowed to spread.

This is exactly what Pope Leo X and his allies now sought to prevent. High-pitched replies by Tetzel and others aimed to derail Luther's theses by calling them "heretical." The papal curia launched an inquiry against Luther in early 1518, hoping to bring him to trial in Rome in the near future. To prepare for this, yet another Dominican, the seasoned inquisitor Sylvester Prierias (c. 1456–1523), drafted an opinion on Luther's theses. A revised version of that document entitled *De potestate papae dialogus* ("Dialogue on the Power of the Pope") was published for a wider audience and reveals how Rome's response was taking shape. For Prierias, the debate was not primarily about indulgences, but about the pope. While he comments on most of the 95 theses, his line of argument inevitably ends with an appeal to papal authority: the indulgences are defensible because the pope says they are. Luther's critique of indulgences, in Prierias's words, was an attack on the pope.

When faced with such responses, Luther was exasperated. He had hoped to open a discussion about truth—about distinguishing between true and false doctrine. This was his right and duty as a professor of theology, and this is what disputations were for. Instead, he was confronted with an authoritarian attempt to silence debate and to crush the quest for truth. Luther could not accept the papal line that truth is defined by the pope and a heretic is anyone who disagrees with the pope. Again and again, he countered that someone should *prove* to him that his positions are heretical. How should they do that? By using Holy Scripture. If, Luther argued, the pope can demonstrate to him that his theses contradict the Bible, then he will be happy to withdraw them. It is this appeal to the authority of Scripture over an inherent authority of the pope that—while not part of the "Ninety-Five Theses" themselves—now began to define Luther's position.

By responding to a question that Luther had not intended to raise, Rome shifted the focus of the debate. That was a perilous blunder. A controversy initially limited to indulgences now became a public referendum on the papacy itself.

Unwittingly, Luther had tapped into a deep pool of insecurity in Rome. The papacy's overly defensive reaction betrayed its greatest fear: the last thing the curia wanted was a challenge to papal authority. Its political position in 1517 was precarious. Memories of the fifteenth-century councils still haunted men such as Prierias, and the notion that they all sought so hard to establish—that the church was an institution centered around the pope's authority—was far from firm in the minds of their contemporaries. Ironically, Luther had had no intention of challenging the pope. But by overplaying its hand, the curia now conjured up the very danger it wanted so much to evade.

Of all the factors that caused unease in Rome, conciliarism had the deepest ideological foundation. The disastrous schism of the fourteenth and early fifteenth centuries not only wrecked the papacy's credibility, it also invigorated the search for an alternative constitution of the church. The line of argument that extended from *Dictatus papae* (1075) to *Unam sanctam* (1302) and depicted a quasi-monarchical institution in which salvation itself depended on "subjection to the Roman Pontiff," always controversial, was now simply untenable in the face of parallel papacies. Progressive thinkers drew inspiration from the polities of the early church, where bishops made decisions collectively in synods or councils.

This more "representative" vision of the church gained support from political theorists such as Marsilius of Padua (c. 1275–c. 1342), whose democratic conception of sovereignty, delineated in his famous work *Defensor pacis*, called for rulers to be elected by "the people." Any authority attributed to those rulers came not "top-down" from God, but "from below," from the people. Such theories were useful to scholars who needed to define an authority above the pope(s) in order to overcome the schism. That authority rested in the church *as a whole*, represented as broadly as possible by a council.

After much negotiating among scholars and clergy, the Council of Constance (1414–1418) finally put those notions into practice. The council passed its first test by removing all three competing popes and electing a single successor, thus healing the schism. Furthermore, it laid the foundation for future conciliar governance by decreeing that representative councils should be held every 10 years. The conciliarists hoped that councils would prove better than popes at reforming the church. Success was short-lived, however. Subsequent councils in Siena (1423–1424) and Basel (1431–1449) saw a dissipation of conciliarist energies and a reassertion of papal power. Exploiting disagreements among council members in Basel, Pope Eugene IV hamstrung the conciliar movement by disbanding the council and, in 1441, by decreeing papal superiority.

While the papalists had scored an important success over their conciliarist rivals, that victory proved superficial; the cultural legacy of Constance was hard to negate. French kings, in particular, were disinclined to accept a papalist restoration. With the Pragmatic Sanction of Bourges (1438), King Charles VII drastically limited the pope's authority over French clergy and created a largely independent Gallican Church. Tensions continued, however, as the papacy resisted those moves. The French kings used the threat of conciliarism to keep the popes off balance. Things came to a head in 1511, when King Louis XII organized a council in Pisa without papal blessing—and the assembled clergy suspended Pope Julius II. Not surprisingly, Julius rejected the legitimacy of that under-attended council, but he was sufficiently alarmed to convoke one of his own in Rome: the Fifth Lateran

Council (1512–1517). While Lateran V outwardly strengthened the pope's position, French maneuvering paid off. Louis' successor, King Francis I, negotiated the Concordat of Bologna (1516) with the pope, a modified version of the earlier Pragmatic Sanction. The Concordat carved out an astonishing degree of autonomy for the royal French church and gave the king wide-ranging powers over the clergy in his country. According to some, the French church had declared independence with a stroke of the pen—and without a Reformation. It was not a proud moment for papal supporters. Pressed into compromise by the lingering specter of conciliarism, the pope had agreed to a painful reduction of his powers.

The French were not alone in seeking greater ecclesial autonomy. All across Europe on the eve of the Reformation, similar trends were underway. In Spain, where the joint monarchy of Fernando and Isabel united the kingdom and a successful though bloody program of *reconquista* drove the remaining Jews and Muslims from its soil, Christianity underwent a rigorous reorganization at the hands of the monarchs and well beyond the reach of Rome. While king and queen took responsibility for the Spanish church, Spain's primary reformer was an Observant Franciscan named Francisco Ximenes de Cisneros (1436–1517). Cisneros applied Franciscan ideals to the Spanish church, demanding poverty, celibacy and regular preaching from the friars and, with the aid of the Inquisition, forging a consolidated Christian culture unique in Europe. Because of these successes—which acquired an entirely new dimension as Spain began to expand into the New World after 1492—popes were little inclined to interfere. And they had little success whenever they tried.

The Swiss gained *de facto* independence from the Holy Roman Empire in 1499, and though it would take two more decades before many of them extended that autonomy to their churches in a formal manner, they already enjoyed considerable powers of local self-determination. The Germans, resistant to centralization on principle, jealously guarded their local privileges and took a dim view of papal incursions. They were also frustrated by the continued absence of reform-initiatives, and their leaders regularly compiled lists of grievances that called for comprehensive political and ecclesial restructuring. Next to disputes over taxes and other financial issues, one particularly important conflict involved legal jurisdiction. German rulers sought the right to try clergy and others who violated church law in courts at home rather than turning them over to ecclesial authorities. Similar efforts had occupied church–state relations in England for centuries, and both kings and archbishops of Canterbury had a long history of rivalry with Rome. Few people had taken the quest for freedom as far as the Czechs. The great Bohemian reformer Jan Hus, a fierce critic of ecclesial corruption who was burned at the stake as a "heretic" at the Council of Constance in 1415, became a martyr and inspiration to his countrymen. For the Czechs, reforming the church and achieving political independence now went hand in hand.

The trend toward local political autonomy was particularly pronounced in Western Europe's powerful cities. Northern Italian city-states and the free imperial cities of the Empire, most of whom owed their rise to trade, had secured considerable independence during the Middle Ages and generally governed themselves (see Chapter 3). During the fifteenth and early sixteenth centuries, Renaissance humanism helped create an urban cultural elite that in addition to being wealthy was intellectually self-confident and willing to question traditional authorities. Here, as in the larger kingdoms and principalities, more and more local magistrates felt responsible for the churches in their domain.

Some cities were also homes to universities. The explosive proliferation of European universities between the fourteenth and sixteenth centuries deserves an account of its own (and has, indeed, produced several), but can be illustrated with a few figures. Prior to 1348, there were only a handful of universities in Europe: Paris, Bologna, Oxford and Cambridge are the best-known examples, with Salamanca and Coimbra further south. Between the founding of the University of Prague in 1348, and the Reformation, nearly 40 new universities were established. The next century would add many more. While early universities were founded by popes and often supervised by bishops, they were increasingly built and managed by secular rulers interested in acquiring centers of learning in their own territories. One can hardly overstate the cultural significance of these intellectual centers, with their powerful ethos of academic freedom, their ability to attract a diverse and cosmopolitan faculty and student body, and their unique cultivation of a life of the mind. On top of this, they were a reservoir of specialized knowledge in fields such as theology and law, often consulted for expert opinions. All these factors impacted the church. The University of Paris played a central role in the conciliar movement, for example, and Luther's position at the University of Wittenberg gave him the freedom to articulate his views. It also gave him a community of colleagues who stimulated and supported him.

While all of these cultural, political and social-historical factors presented new difficulties for centralizing church leadership in Rome, the most profound challenge to papal authority came from the papacy itself. In a nutshell, the papacy's authority was undermined by its inability to provide reform. It is easy, in this respect, to point to the poor moral quality of the Renaissance popes, whose unabashed worldliness reached new heights in the decades leading up to the Reformation. But the papacy's failure to instigate reforms was not simply caused by bad popes. Its system of supporting structures was also suspect. One can often measure an institution's quality by looking at the leaders it produces. The fact that the Roman curia could, in 1492, elect no one better than the decidedly unapostolic Rodrigo Borgia (Pope Alexander VI) says something about the underlying values of that body. One wonders how history would have turned out if it had selected someone like his countryman Ximenes Cisneros instead.

Christians interested in a more apostolic church seldom looked to the pope for leadership. While the "vicar of Christ" was cavorting in Rome, dedicated laypeople and clergy began taking such matters into their own hands. Thousands of new spiritual communities cropped up across Europe during the fifteenth and early sixteenth centuries and were dedicated to activities ranging from devotional practice and Bible study to charity work and communal living.

One particularly successful example was a movement known as "Modern Devotion," inspired by the Dutch preacher Gerhard Groote (1340–1384). Groote founded religious communities of laypeople known as Brethren and Sisters of the Common Life.

Alienated by the dissolute morals around them, these Christians committed themselves to a more earnest life of penance, askesis, mystical reflection, and, significantly, of learning. One of Groote's followers, Thomas à Kempis (c. 1380–1471), wrote the immensely influential devotional work *Imitation of Christ* (1418). One of the most widely-read books in Christian history, this spiritual guide and meditation on the life of Christ serves as a blue-print for the devotional approach adopted by the movement. The Sisters and Brethren founded numerous houses for women and men, and scores of schools in the Netherlands and Germany. It has occasionally been called a "Renaissance north of the Alps"—though it is marked by a thirst for holiness and a monk-like "contempt for the world" seldom associated with the Renaissance further south. Several key figures of the Reformation were either followers of the movement or otherwise had contact with it, including the great humanist scholar Erasmus of Rotterdam, Pope Adrian VI, the Swiss Reformer Heinrich Bullinger, and even Martin Luther, who spent a year with Brethren as a schoolboy.

Dedicated laypeople and clergy came together in other kinds of confraternities, as well. Many of these were small and local, and were especially common in cities and towns. Their members came from all walks of life. Most did not live together but met regularly to pursue activities that included particular devotion to Mary, penitential exercises, prayer, or caring for the sick and poor. In Genoa, for example, Caterina Fieschi Adorno (1447–1510), later known as St. Catherine of Genoa, a deeply pious noblewoman who devoted herself to work in the local hospital, inspired a small group of laymen to form the Oratory of Divine Love in 1497. Its Roman offshoot, founded between 1514 and 1517, included a number of men who would go on to play important roles in the Catholic reform movement. Guided by Gregory the Great's dictum "the test of love is seen in action," these and many similar Oratories committed themselves to works of charity, in particular to service in hospitals, and often ministered to victims of the recurring plague.

Movements such as these were part of a broad, grassroots religious revival that went hand in hand with a resurgence of a mendicant ethos. The traditional mendicant orders, especially the

Franciscans, played a part in that development as well. Though the order was split by differences in rigor, a reform wing, led in the early stages by men such as Bernardino da Siena (1380–1444) and Giovanni da Capistrano (1386–1456), began to assert itself during the fifteenth century. The Franciscans sent itinerant preachers across Europe, wandering from place to place much as their Celtic missionary forebears had done nearly a thousand years before. Even the message, calling for repentance and askesis, was similar. Now, however, that vision of a purer Christian life came in the context of a profit-based commercial economy, where the mendicant message of voluntary poverty had a particular cutting edge. This went beyond preaching in some cases. In the Hungarian Peasants' War of 1514, for example, Observant Franciscans took up arms and led peasants into battle against the nobility—including their own bishops.

Some historians have described the decades prior to the Reformation as a time of unrest and discontent, marked, in particular, by widespread hostility to the clergy. Such views are misleading. As the examples already mentioned show, the fifteenth and early sixteenth centuries were bursting with an enormous degree of spiritual energy. This was not fueled by anti-clericalism, but by a quest for a more meaningful Christian life. It was, broadly speaking, a dynamic driven by a powerful monastic, and often mendicant, ethos—even when, as in the case of most confraternities, the communities were not bound by monastic vows. These groups broadened monastic and fraternal ideals and adapted them to a non-cloistered context, mostly for laypeople. To the extent that such movements manifested hostility, it was directed against "the world" and its exploitative, hollow values. Clergy became targets mostly when they were seen as part of that world. Far more troublesome for the clergy was the realization that they were being left behind as Christianity moved ahead into a new era. Not only did many aspects of the new spirituality take their initiative from lay sources, but the practices themselves often emphasized non-sacramental, "spiritualized" activities that did not require clergy. In fact, the very distinction between "clergy" and "laypeople" became blurred as the latter were energized by the new range of religious experience that they themselves initiated and controlled.

Such emerging forms of community, spirituality and Christian action amounted to a grassroots reform of the church itself. They were not so much anti-clerical as they were *non-clerical*.

The greatest challenge to papalist ideology at the dawn of the Reformation may well have been the papacy's irrelevance to that grassroots reform process. It is intriguing to consider the sale of indulgences from this perspective. Indulgences were one way the pope could make himself "relevant" even to the lowliest and most remote parishioners. People who would otherwise never have thought of the pope could now identify him with relief from spiritual punishment and as a benefactor to their departed loved ones. To the anxious men in Rome, Luther's "Ninety-Five Theses" undercut this image as much as they threatened the financial system it engendered. Not only did the theses argue for a more limited understanding of the pope's spiritual authority, they also drew attention to the simony and financial corruption that the pope had failed to reform. Once Luther's critique became popularized and recast in polemical woodcuts and pamphlets, it acquired a much more hostile tone. Gone was the image of a benevolent *papa*. It was replaced by a picture of impotence and, even worse, suggestions of complicity. The pope seemed very much "of the world."

Luther the Reformer

In 1523, the famous shoemaker-poet Hans Sachs, a Nuremberg Meistersinger, penned a remarkable poem of 700 lines entitled "The Wittenberg Nightingale" (*Die wittembergisch Nachtigall*). The poem was about Martin Luther. Sachs describes how Luther, the nightingale, heralds a new dawn, an awakening from a bitter night of falsehood and deception into the light of God's pure truth. The creatures of the night, a lion (the pope), wolves (the clergy), and frogs (scholars) all try their best to silence the bird, who sings bravely on. Sachs's poem opens a window onto an exceptional time. The poet himself finds it apocalyptic, an "end-time." Howling horrifically is the old order, slipping away as day begins to break. Throughout the poem, Sachs's dualism is consistent: on the one side are forces of man, characterized by invented doctrines, rituals and canon laws, corruption, profligacy, and profiteering; on the other is God's word, proclaimed by Luther. Luther saves the sheep from the night's predators and restores them to the fold. It is almost impossible to put oneself in the shoes of someone who experienced the Reformation first-hand. Yet poems such as Sachs's "The Wittenberg Nightingale" afford a glimpse of that distant reality. Beneath the apocalyptic clouds sensed by men such as Sachs, one sees the figure of Luther—magnified into heroic proportions by a poet who has keenly felt the pulse of his day. It is, today, unfashionable for scholars to use categories such as "hero" to describe historical personages, and caution is particularly warranted in the case of Luther, to whom previous eras attached the term all too promiscuously. On the other hand, there is something truly remarkable about the way Luther, in a very short time, captured the imagination of so many of his contemporaries. Their fascination was much deeper than that accorded to typical persons of power and fame. These people were inspired. In their ears, Luther was a "voice from the unseen Heaven" (Carlyle, 1993). Far below their feet, the plates of the earth were responding—and things were about to be made *right*.

The printing press, a new technology in the early 1500s, played a formidable role in giving Luther's case such wide public resonance, launching "the West's first large-scale media campaign" (Edwards, 1994: 21). Sachs's "The Wittenberg Nightingale" is a good example of how Luther's story could be told, and his theological ideas distilled into terms for a mass audience. Of course, poets such as Sachs, and artists such as Lucas Cranach and Albrecht Dürer, who all sympathized with the Reformation, added an agitational edge to such depictions. End-times are times of urgency, times to make a decision, and these men did their part to make that happen.

In addition to such elevated media, presses churned out smaller fare, as well. Thousands of pamphlets (*Flugschriften*) were printed in the years after Luther began his contest with Rome. Many were written by laypeople, some published in secret, but together they made an impact. They were a call to arms, wrapped in end-times urgency and mobilizing thoughts and emotions for the cause. While their styles and contents varied—and included satires ridiculing the clergy, allegories depicting the pope as the Antichrist, mock dialogues featuring theologically savvy peasants, and short doctrinal tracts—most such pamphlets used verses from the Bible. The Bible, long unavailable to most laypeople, was emerging not only as an authority, but as a source of liberation. Another important characteristic was the frequency with which Luther's conflict with the pope served as the dominant theme. Here, again, the papacy's strategic miscalculation in its initial response to the "Ninety-Five Theses" becomes evident. The conflict lent itself wonderfully to the mass medium of pamphleteers: one man fighting heroically against a huge and dark conspiracy. Importantly, many people felt he was fighting on their behalf. Even with the very low literacy rates of the time, the demand for pamphlets was astonishingly high (and more than a few printers earned a small fortune from them). Luther had become larger than life.

Luther's own works made up a significant part of the published material. In fact, Luther was far and away the most popular writer in Germany during much of the Reformation. Most of his published works were in German, rather than the academic language of Latin; his intended audience lay beyond the walls of the university. While propaganda certainly played a role in Luther's output, it was overshadowed by a much greater interest: roughly 40 per cent of Luther's German publications before 1530 consisted of sermons (Edwards, 1994: 27). Their purpose, clearly, was edification. However much pamphlets and other media had begun to stylize the early Reformation as a personal struggle between Luther and Rome, the Reformer himself remained focused on theological content. His interest was pastoral; his mission was to teach.

The Reformation was caused by a great many historical factors that were beyond Luther's control. At the same time, though, his role in that Reformation is undeniably unique. Luther's singular position at the helm of the early Reformation is due to factors rooted in his person. Without Martin Luther, there may well have been some sort of Reformation, but it would have been very different. He, to a degree unlike any of his contemporaries, placed his personal stamp on this remarkable era. He did so by sheer force of personality, charisma, profundity of thought, and an undeniable bit of luck. Some historians have described Luther as a "religious genius." That may be. But Luther was also one of the most *multi-dimensional* geniuses in the history of Christianity, a man whose accomplishments included theological and devotional writings that became classics of their genre, a monumental (and linguistically brilliant) translation of the Bible into German, musical compositions and hymns of enduring quality and popularity, broad-based educational and social reform, and an astonishing ability to provide leadership through a time of epochal transformation. Luther the individual fascinated his contemporaries, and he continues to fascinate—and mystify—students of his life and thought to this day.

Genius comes in earthen vessels, and the earth that made Martin Luther merits a closer look. Born on November 10, 1483, in the successful mining town of Eisleben, Luther found himself part of the rising bourgeoisie. While his grandparents had been peasants, his father Hans owned an interest in a local mining initiative. Together with Luther's mother Margareta, he fostered the kinds of ambitions for his children that were typical for an up-and-coming member of his class. Martin was sent to school, leaving home as a teenager for Magdeburg and then Eisenach. In 1501, Luther enrolled in the University of Erfurt, earning a Master of Arts degree in four years and then beginning studies in law. That was his father's wish. That, however, was not to be. According to his own account, which echoes the conversion story of St. Paul, Luther found himself alone on a road on a midsummer day in 1505 when a thunderstorm rolled in over the hills. With lightning crashing around him, he threw himself to the ground and prayed to St. Anne, pledging to become a monk if allowed to survive. He survived. Two weeks later, on July 17, 1505, and to the consternation of his father, Luther gave up his studies in law and entered the Erfurt cloister of the mendicant Augustinian Hermits.

Luther's decision was an about-face—leaving "the world" and its careers for an altogether different, ascetic path of introspection, study and religious service. Luther was ordained to the priesthood in early 1507, and celebrated his first mass in the Erfurt cloister on

May 2 of that year. After ordination, he continued his studies of theology in Erfurt, interrupted by a trip to Rome in 1510–1511. Sent on official business by their order, Luther and a fellow monk walked the entire way—a voyage lasting a good six weeks and becoming as much a pilgrimage to the Holy City as a business trip. During his four-week stay in Rome, Luther did his best to take in as many religious sites as possible, but was also taken aback by the cynicism and dissolute living he encountered there (prostitution and pederasty are often mentioned in later accounts). The effect of these mixed impressions was evidently sobering, but does not seem to have inspired a deeper-lying break with Rome. Luther returned to Erfurt to resume his studies, transferring to the University of Wittenberg in the fall of 1511. Residing in the local Augustinian cloister, he received a doctorate of theology in October of 1512, and began lecturing in Wittenberg shortly thereafter, taking the professorship vacated by his spiritual advisor, Johannes von Staupitz (c. 1468–1524).

There has been much speculation about when, and under what circumstances, Luther had the intellectual "breakthrough" that made him into a Reformer. By most accounts, the process came in stages and was anchored in the kind of critical self-examination and penitence that characterized his Augustinian experience. In all of these exercises, Luther encountered God primarily as a God of judgment and punishment. God was *just* in that God meted out justice—by saving the righteous and condemning the rest (analogously, one could say a policeman is just insofar as he punishes criminals and protects the innocent). For Luther, this was deeply unsettling since, in his own eyes, he was far from certain that he would measure up to God's standards at the Last Judgment. As far as he could tell, he would likely experience the destructive, punitive force of God's justice. A profound shift in Luther's thinking occurred, however, when he reinterpreted the Bible's passages about God's justice (above all Rom. 1,17). In this new light, justice (or righteousness) is not only something that God "has," but something that God bestows onto others. Specifically, God *makes just* those who are faithful to him. Here the focus is on God's infinite mercy—on God's willingness to change those who believe in him. God's justice is not so much a standard by which people are measured (and against which most inevitably fall short), as a quality that God shares.

As Luther himself recounted late in life (especially in a preface to the 1545 edition of his Latin works), this theological insight had enormous existential implications for him and changed his entire theological outlook. He leaves open when, exactly, that breakthrough took place—but that is less important than the fact that it did, and the circumstances that shaped it. For one thing, one notices how deeply personal this insight was for Luther. It was more than an abstract point. At stake was Luther's *own* relationship to God, and this was something he experienced intimately and at the cost of considerable personal anguish. Furthermore, the insight came while reading and reflecting on the Bible. Of course, he was prepared for this rediscovery of the biblical message both by the Augustinian teaching that his particular order cultivated (his interpretation owes a lot to Augustine), and to conversations with his mentor Staupitz, but the discovery remained very much his own. In other words, the biblical message spoke to his own faith in a profoundly personal way. Aside from the value of the theological insight itself, this gave him enormous confidence in his reading (he had experienced its truth first-hand), as well as a lasting appreciation for the Bible's ability to speak as a "living voice." These factors help explain Luther's unshakeable sense of certainty as he entered his more public conflict with Rome. He had experienced an authority that was more than merely human.

Luther's early lectures at the University of Wittenberg focused on biblical exegesis. His interpretations were more theological and also more experiential (that is, concerned with how the biblical message affected one's experience of God) than those of his scholastic predecessors, a trend already conspicuous in the first surviving lectures of his tenure, on the Psalms (1513–1515). Those were followed by lectures on Romans (1515/16), Galatians (1516/17), and Hebrews (1517/18). In addition to his university duties, Luther also preached regularly in Wittenberg's City Church.

The man who wrote the "Ninety-Five Theses" in late 1517 was, by most appearances, an earnest Augustinian monk and Bible scholar teaching at a remote, provincial university. Founded by

Elector Frederick the Wise in 1502, the University of Wittenberg was barely 10 years old when Luther joined the faculty. It was—unlike, for example, Paris or Oxford—hardly the kind of name that commanded instant respect in Rome. To the curia, Luther was a "little monk" with a thin resumé and no reputation. The theses themselves, while certainly provocative, only scratched the surface of the much deeper theological energies that had begun to occupy Luther. This may partly explain Rome's half-hearted pursuit of the matter. They underestimated Luther.

Political considerations also slowed the papal response. After beginning an investigation of Luther in early 1518, the pope and his advisors sought to put him on trial in Rome itself. This proved difficult. Frederick the Wise was reluctant to hand Luther over to the Romans and insisted on having the trial—if indeed it proved necessary—in Germany. This revived a long-standing disagreement over jurisdiction: German princes wanted to try their subjects at home rather than yield authority to Rome. In other words, Frederick saw value in taking a stand on sheer principle. He was well-positioned to do so. Of all the German princes in 1518, Frederick the Wise was the most powerful, and the pope very much desired his support in matters of imperial politics. Rome accommodated Frederick's wishes and, instead of insisting on Luther's extradition, agreed to a more informal hearing in Augsburg, where both Frederick and a papal legate, Tommaso de Vio, otherwise known as Cajetan (1469–1534), were attending an imperial diet.

On October 12, 1518, Cajetan, a Dominican, summoned Luther to his private quarters (which, appropriately enough, happened to be in a house owned by the Fuggers). The conversation appears to have been polite but firm. Cajetan called upon Luther to renounce his errors, desist from further error, and to refrain from activities that could damage the church. Luther answered by saying that he was not aware of any errors, and asking that Cajetan point these out to him. Cajetan obliged, citing two questions raised by the "Ninety-Five Theses." Luther requested time to consider and returned the next day, accompanied by witnesses, to submit his answer: He remained unconvinced that he was in error and, while he fully respected the church's teaching authority, he found himself unable to recant until his positions were given a full hearing—and he was proven wrong. At a third meeting on October 14, he also submitted a written rebuttal of Cajetan's two critiques. Cajetan, exasperated, raised his voice and ordered Luther out of the room, threatening him with excommunication unless he recanted.

The pope did eventually excommunicate Luther, but it took him more than two years to do so. Again, imperial politics retarded the process. Emperor Maximilian died in January of 1519, precipitating an election and a frenzy of diplomatic maneuvering. Opposition to Luther's extradition hardened among the German princes, who saw the case as an opportunity to increase their jurisdictional authority, and used the imperial negotiations to strengthen their position. Rome, for its part, had an interest in seeing Frederick the Wise crowned emperor and carefully avoided offending him by pursuing Luther too vigorously. Frederick, on the other hand, did not want to be emperor, but played along and extracted important concessions from the eventual victor, Charles of Spain. While Luther's case was overshadowed by all of these affairs, he benefitted from the conflict of agendas and gained valuable time.

The period between Cajetan's interview in October 1518 and the pope's bull of excommunication in January 1521 opened a decisive window during which Luther's personal case became a public affair that animated much of Europe. It was here that a Reformation program began to take shape. On the question of indulgences, Luther and the curia continued to talk past each other, though the exchange did prompt a reduction of the indulgence trade in Germany. Luther's desire for a public debate over his views finally bore fruit in the summer of 1519, when Duke George of Saxony (a cousin of Frederick the Wise and ruler of an adjacent territory), organized a disputation in Leipzig between Luther, his colleague Andreas Bodenstein von Karlstadt (1486–1541), and one of their sharpest opponents, the Ingolstadt professor John Eck (1486–1543).

Though the official theses covered a number of topics, including differences over grace and free will, the Leipzig Disputation was most memorable for its exchanges between Luther and Eck over papal authority. This, of course, was the raw nerve that Luther's actions had plucked in Rome. Eck's plan of attack aimed at linking Luther with the views of John Wyclif and Jan Hus that had been condemned by the Council of Constance in 1415—where Hus was burned at the stake. In this, Eck succeeded. Luther boldly redoubled his position that the pope has no God-given primacy in the church, and that salvation does not depend on subordination to the pope. In Luther's view, he was simply affirming the doctrine of the early church, as well as that of Greek Christianity to this day. If that happened to be what Hus had also said, then so be it—Hus must have been right. "Does that mean that even councils can err?," continued Eck. "Evidently," replied Luther. Eck rejoiced and thought he had won the debate. Only the consequences turned out differently than he expected. Luther was not burned at the stake; Frederick the Wise did not suppress Luther's writings; and the debate over papal authority was not ended. On the contrary, it now picked up speed. An avalanche of pamphlets swept through Germany, an alarming number of them supporting Luther. While Eck thought he had convicted Luther by invoking the authority of popes and councils, Luther's supporters argued that Eck had failed to prove his position by Holy Scripture—and was simply gathering human sentences. The gulf between papalism and its opponents began to widen. In the wake of this publicity, Luther's very survival now seemed like an affront to the pope's authority. And not only was Luther surviving—his cause was growing daily.

After the Leipzig Disputation, Luther entered a period of extraordinary productivity, publishing some of the most important works of the Reformation. His theology (treated in greater detail in the section "Luther's Theology") was maturing, and his focus was broadening. The question of papal authority was a fairly minor aspect of these efforts. Luther's works of this period show little interest in theories of church governance. He is far less concerned with defining the "church universal" than he is in reforming—and improving—the church locally. He even questions whether the term "church" (*Kirche, ecclesia*) is all that useful, preferring the less ambiguous (and more concrete) "congregation" (*Gemeinde*). In that regard, he has more in common with earlier missionary figures in the history of Western Christianization—the Celtic monks, the early Franciscans, the Waldensians, and others—than with those reformers who targeted institutional ills (for example, Leo IX, Gregory VII, the conciliarists). His instincts are pastoral, and his aim is to educate and edify.

In the summer of 1520, the Roman curia finally found time to draw its proceedings against Luther to a close, and published a bull (*Exsurge Domine*) that extracted 41 exceptionable propositions from Luther's works and threatened Luther with excommunication if he did not recant publicly within 60 days. Luther's response marks a turning point in Reformation history. On December 10, 1520, Luther, his faculty colleagues, and a group of students gathered outside Wittenberg's city gate and built a bonfire. Into the flames they tossed a copy of the *Corpus Iuris Canonici* (the standard book of canon law) and similar writings. Luther personally burned the bull *Exsurge Domine*, along with a few choice works of John Eck, who had agitated furiously for the bull's execution. Afterwards, Luther published a short tract in German explaining their actions. It was a deliberate act of defiance against the pope's jurisdictional claims, and a rejection of the legal system that, in Luther's view, the papalists had used to buttress their ideology. Luther would not stand by as institutional force was used to suppress a search for truth. He insisted again on an impartial hearing of the theological issues at stake.

With this bonfire, Luther also burned any bridges that may have remained to Rome. He was willing to accept—and disregard—the pope's excommunication, which followed on January 3, 1521, with the bull *Decet Romanum pontificem*. Given the circumstances, the pope's step may seem inexorable, but it was also fateful. By drawing a line between itself and Luther, Rome created a limit around its own authority. Whatever Luther did next, it would be outside the pope's purview. And Luther now set about building a church. It would be a church without a pope.

Had the pope's bull of excommunication worked as intended, none of this would have happened. Normally, declaring a person a heretic gave both civil and ecclesial authorities the right to arrest him—in fact, it ordered them to do so. Luther should have been sent to Rome forthwith; there he would have been executed. Again, however, Frederick the Wise protected him. The elector continued to insist on a hearing before impartial judges in Germany—agreeing with Luther on that point, and resisting pressure from Rome. Furthermore, Frederick obtained the support of the recently crowned Holy Roman emperor, Charles V, and both agreed to have Luther testify at the upcoming imperial diet in Worms, in April 1521, before taking further action. In this clash between papal and temporal authorities, Rome was losing ground.

Luther left Wittenberg for Worms on April 2. The trip took two weeks, in part because Luther accepted numerous invitations from magistrates, universities, and churches along the way to speak or preach. On April 17, having arrived in Worms the previous day, he was summoned to appear before the emperor and a court of princes and officials, the most powerful men in the Empire. Before them lay a stack of Luther's publications. He was asked two questions: (1) did he admit that these were his own writings? and (2) was he willing to reject the views they contained? Luther's answer would determine his fate. Someone in the audience called out to have the works' titles read out loud. One by one, they were enumerated. Luther now gave his answer. The works, he conceded, were his own. As to their contents ... here he would like more time to reflect. The emperor gave him one day.

On April 18, Luther returned to the court. Asked again whether he was prepared to reject the contents of his works, he gave a carefully nuanced answer. His pastoral works he could not repudiate, as even his opponents found them edifying. He also stood by those works that criticized the papacy's abuse of power and its use of human laws to tyrannize Christian consciences. Experience and countless complaints of his countrymen bore him out and called for him to stand fast in this matter. The third group included writings that attacked individual opponents and their theology. Here, Luther conceded, he may have been a bit too harsh. But because the contents of these works defended the teachings of Christ, he could not renounce them either. If the emperor or someone else could produce biblical evidence against his teachings, he would be happy to recant, but until that happened, he was unable to do so. A restless murmuring began to spread in the hall as the speaker asked Luther once again to recant—in plain and simple language. Luther gave his final answer:

> If I am not refuted by Scriptural witness or clear reason, I cannot. Popes and councils both have erred and contradicted themselves, and so their testimony alone will not convince me. I am bound by the words of Scripture which I have cited. And as long as my conscience is held captive by the words of God, I cannot and will not recant, as it is unsure and imperils salvation to do anything against one's conscience. God help me. Amen. (Author's translation; see LW: 32, 112)

After several days of deliberation, the emperor gave Luther his verdict. He would prosecute Luther. This meant that Luther would be arrested and executed. Because he had been given a guarantee of safe passage before traveling to Worms, though, he was, for the time being, allowed to leave. Keeping in mind what had happened to Jan Hus in Constance, Luther and his companions departed promptly for Wittenberg. As their coach passed through the Thuringian forest on May 4, a group of armed riders appeared out of the shadows, held up the entourage and rode away with Luther. Word of Luther's death spread quickly.

Luther, however, was not dead. The riders had been dispatched by Frederick the Wise and took the Reformer to an undisclosed location. Not even the elector could say where he was—which was convenient, given the political pressure Frederick now faced.

A few days after Luther's disappearance, Charles V promulgated a decree of prosecution, the Edict of Worms, which declared Luther an outlaw of the Empire. The first provision stated that, if found, he was to be apprehended and turned over to imperial authorities. The same held for his supporters. Second, Luther's writings were to be confiscated and burned. The third provision mandated episcopal censorship for all religious publications in the Empire. Because the German princes were responsible for the edict's enforcement within their territories, much now depended on them. Several had been impressed by Luther's courage at the diet, and began to take an interest in the little monk. Frederick's own interest had by now grown into full-fledged support. He was beginning to think that Luther just might be right. Luther, for his part, rested incognito in one of Frederick's hunting castles, the Wartburg. Here he spent the next 10 months, from May 4, 1521 to March 1, 1522. Despite the Edict of Worms, his writings continued to circulate; if anything, demand for them now escalated and their popularity soared. Luther himself was busy with his next project: a German translation of the New Testament. He wanted to give the Bible to the people.

Luther's Theology

In the Reformation, theology *mattered*. Much of the early energy of the reform process was driven by ideas. Ideas had been important before in the life the church, but the degree to which they mattered now was unprecedented. There are several reasons for this.

The most significant factor was cultural, and it came as a result of the printing press. Europe was becoming *literate*. Even if a majority of its inhabitants still could not read or write in 1520, the availability of the printed word inspired a broad-based change in cultural values. "Writing," argues the philosopher Walter Ong, "restructures consciousness" (Ong, 1982: 78ff). As societies make a transition from oral to written culture, people begin to think differently. In particular, interest in—and capacity for—abstraction develops. Texts allow development of intellectual complexity in ways that oral discourse does not. That can have a liberating effect. Dependence on spoken tradition and its conservation gives way to independent engagement with texts. The rise of Renaissance humanism and its famous motto *ad fontes!* ("back to the sources") signals this shift at the level of cultured elites. Scholars sought to discover ancient texts, including the Bible, on terms entirely their own, rather than adding just one more layer of commentary to the readings of their immediate predecessors. The impact of such a shift in values upon broader cultural strata outpaced the increase in actual literacy rates. Even people who could not yet read and write seem to have understood that books were important—and valuable—things. They also appeared much more eager than earlier generations to discuss abstract ideas. One of the remarkable features of Reformation history concerns the *breadth* of involvement in theological discussion. Suddenly, members of all social strata, not just clergy and academics, took an interest in these topics. A shoemaker-poet such as Hans Sachs, who left school at age 14, wrote detailed expositions of Luther's theology—in verse. Anecdotes abound of common peasants offering opinions on eucharistic theology, clerical marriage, or even on free will and justification. The demand for pamphlets laying out dogmatic theology also testifies to a widespread interest in such matters. Some contemporary theologians like to argue that common people could hardly have grasped the complexities of Luther's thought, but that is beside the point. Far more significant is the mere presence of such an interest, because it indicates a fundamental historical shift.

That shift set the stage for one of the Reformation's most durable cultural achievements: the establishment and proliferation of schools. Luther himself was a forceful advocate for building schools—and, in a step that was even more revolutionary, for enrolling girls alongside boys in those schools. The capacity to read and write, and to engage in advanced theoretical discussion was to be made available to as many young people as possible. While enthusiasm for education typically lagged behind in rural areas (for reasons that will be discussed), even villages soon had their own schools. In Luther's mind, education and literacy, while important for their own sake, also equipped future parents to lead religious households, reading out loud from the Bible and devotional or catechetical literature to their children and farmhands. In this way, too, the base of literacy and literate culture continued to expand.

Higher education also changed. Not only were many more universities built during the fifteenth and sixteenth centuries, but the number of people enrolled in those universities increased exponentially, as well. Aggressive scholarship programs in states such as electoral Saxony reveal a desire of rulers to make higher education available to as many of their subjects as possible. That desire was not only limited to rulers. In Wittenberg, for example, citizens established a scholarship fund specifically for children of *Handwerker* (workers and craftsmen).

University curricula incorporated humanism's values, especially its dedication to primary texts and eloquence of language. The move to include subjects such as rhetoric and poetry, as well as Greek and Hebrew, began in the 1420s and 1430s in the universities of northern Italy, gradually drifting across the Alps as the century progressed. Luther's studies in Erfurt introduced him to elements of this change, and the University of Wittenberg, which sought to position itself as a cutting-edge institution, embraced humanism enthusiastically.

This had an impact on Luther's own development. In 1518, the university made one of the most auspicious appointments in the history of higher education, calling a 21-year-old rhetorician named Philipp Melanchthon to its faculty. Melanchthon would become Luther's most important collaborator—and one of the greatest educators in German history, eventually earning the nickname *praeceptor Germaniae* ("teacher of Germany") for his enormous influence on students. As a discussion partner, Melanchthon, who soon committed himself to the Reformation cause, brought precision to Luther's thought. In contrast to Luther's penchant for verbal broadsides, Melanchthon's writings are concise, composed and to-the-point. In 1521, he wrote the first textbook of Protestant theology, *Loci communes*, which remains a classic of its genre. As a faculty colleague, Melanchthon was just as valuable, helping to orchestrate a full-scale humanistic reform of the university's curriculum. Wittenberg was becoming an exciting place to study—and enrollment figures reflect this. It was also an immensely stimulating place to think, and thus formed a vital context for the development of Luther's theology.

The cornerstone of Luther's thought was his doctrine of justification. *Justification* refers to the process by which humans are made just in God's eyes. In that sense, it touches the very core of the Christian religion, describing how people are reconciled with God and begin to lead God-pleasing lives. In the Latin West, reflection on justification became particularly intensive during an exchange between Augustine and his adversary Pelagius (c. 355–c. 420). The latter held that humans can freely choose either to sin or to do works of righteousness. Augustine rejected that position, arguing that humanity's basic orientation favored sin and that a person required God's assistance—grace—to turn instead towards righteousness. Humans, in Augustine's view, contribute nothing toward their justification, but depend entirely upon God's grace.

While Augustine's position prevailed theologically, Pelagian tendencies continued to resonate in the practical context of medieval mission and Christianization. The notion that people are free to choose a more moral life fits more conveniently with the kinds of exhortations to discipline that marked the mission effort. Further opportunities for confusion arose when medieval theologians began linking justification with penance, since penance emphasized human actions. In time, Christian thinkers developed models of justification that sought to account for the human aspect of the process in ways that went beyond a strict Augustinianism. Acknowledging that people required some sort of "preparatory grace" from God to point them in the right direction, they also felt that God had given humans enough natural sense of right and wrong to make a positive effort towards righteousness on their own. At the very least, by simply "doing what is within oneself" (*facere quod in se est*), people could remove obstacles to God's grace. God would then be more likely to follow up with justification. Such views were anchored in the practice of penance. Late-medieval theologians such as Gabriel Biel (c. 1420–1495) wanted to argue that if a person comes to confession with a proper attitude of contrition, then God will be more inclined to help him or her by bestowing the grace of justification.

Luther regarded such views as a creeping Pelagianism. In his mind, people were being taught that they could earn justification. Not only was that theologically wrong—since it undercut both the power of God's grace and an awareness of human dependence on God—but it was also bad pastoral practice. How could anyone know if he or she were truly contrite? How could persons know if they had done enough of "what is within them"? If these were conditions for receiving grace then no one could ever be certain to have met them; reconciliation with God would forever be out of reach and the Christian life would be one of perpetual insecurity. Christians who were being taught these things were being held captive in a never-ending hamster wheel of human effort and anxiety. It also made them vulnerable to manipulation by men such as Tetzel, as they sought to "buy" the security they lacked in faith.

Luther returned to a rigorously Augustinian view of the human condition, a thought-process grounded by his readings of St. Paul, particularly Romans and Galatians. While people could certainly do individual deeds that seemed morally good, Luther argued, they did so out of self-interest. They were incapable of loving God above all else. That was human nature. And only an act of God could break that pattern and waken the human heart to loving God. The human role in the process is entirely passive. We "do" nothing at all; we simply receive. Receiving the news of God's saving grace means trusting God, and that in turn is called "faith" (Luther frequently uses the term *fiducia*, which emphasizes the element of trust). One simply trusts and believes that the message is true—and therein lies one's certainty. It is a certainty based not on one's own efforts, but on the promise of God; the believer can be certain that God tells the truth. Put in more theological terms, Luther argues that people are "justified through faith alone, by the grace of God alone" (*sola fide, sola gratia*).

In a 1520 treatise entitled *On the Freedom of a Christian*, perhaps his most eloquent exposition of justification and its implications for the Christian life, Luther explores this notion of faith more deeply (LW: 31, 327–377). Because it was Christ who through his self-sacrifice merited, or "earned" salvation on our behalf, faith involves a relationship with Christ. In faith, the believer is "united" with Christ. Using language with strong mystical over-tones, Luther describes that union more closely. It is a kind of exchange: Christ takes the guilt of our sins upon himself and gives us his righteousness. This is the basis of our justification. But Christ does more than that. Christ also takes up residence in the believer, working good. In this regard, Luther speaks of an "alien righteousness" of the believer: the Christian becomes more righteous and begins to behave in a genuinely righteous, God-pleasing manner—not by his or her own power, but by virtue of Christ's presence within. Justification therefore does more than put the believer right with God, it also initiates a life-long process of transformation. In Luther's eyes, that process expresses itself both in increasing love of God, and in selfless service to one's neighbor. Justification frees one *from* being concerned with one's own salvation and *for* service to one's fellow humans. It would be wrong, therefore, to say that works of charity are irrelevant to Luther's notion of faith, as is sometimes supposed. Luther simply argues that such works are not the *cause* of one's justification; they are its *effects*.

Luther repeated and re-emphasized the basic principles of this doctrine of justification in countless of his writings. It remained central to his thought. Regrettably, by the time it emerged in a complete and mature articulation, relations between Luther and Rome had already become so polarized that a balanced assessment of these teachings was impossible. Today, many scholars agree that, while Luther certainly offers a clear corrective to the prevailing doctrines of his day and introduces a fresh conceptual language, his formulations were by no means "heretical," and could likely have been included within the considerable doctrinal diversity of the time. Politics, however, prevented that from happening.

Luther's teachings on justification emphasize "the Word." By this he means primarily the word of God as encountered in Scripture.[1] It is "the Word" that teaches us that we are saved through grace by faith in Christ (that message is also called the *euangelion*, or "the Gospel," and contrasted with "the Law," by which we are accused and our shortcomings revealed). Because Luther did not find this message in the church's preaching of his day—and in fact saw it contradicted by the church's preaching—he placed a strong emphasis on the authority of Scripture. That had two important consequences for his thought. First, wherever a conflict between the church's traditions and the words of Scripture arose, Scriptural authority prevailed. In that sense, one can speak of a "Scripture principle" in Luther's thought. Second, Luther placed a premium on preaching. Preaching, when done by someone trained in Scripture and focused on Scripture, was the ordinary means by which people encountered the Word. For all his emphasis on the Bible's authority, Luther was not a

---

[1]   In theology, "the Word" is also a synonym for Christ—and Luther uses this sense of the term, as well.

"fundamentalist" in the modern sense. Not all parts of the Bible were equally valuable, in his view, and both readers and preachers needed to be trained to discern the "center"—that is, "find Christ"—in Scripture. That task typically required a sound theological education, and Luther and Melanchthon soon established ordination exams in Wittenberg to ensure that their graduates were properly equipped. The Word of God should not be smothered by a lot of inane human words.

It is easy, given Luther's emphasis on the Word, to overlook the importance he attached to sacraments. He devotes particular attention to Holy Communion. Here, his theological development was more gradual than in the case of justification. Luther retained much of the deep eucharistic piety that was cultivated in the monastery and he remained profoundly reverential toward the mysteries that, in his experience, were at the heart of the sacrament. Still, he argued for changes in eucharistic practice. In another 1520 treatise, *The Babylonian Captivity of the Church*, he describes three ways that the Roman church has "held the sacrament captive." Luther's critique of the first, Rome's long-standing refusal to distribute wine to laypeople at communion, takes up the defining cause of the Bohemian reform movement. Named "Utraquists" for their demand that the eucharist be given "in both kinds" (*sub utraque specie*), the followers of Jan Hus had seen their position rejected (and their leader executed) at the Council of Constance, whose decision Luther here opposes. Both because of this historical background and because the practice itself signaled a qualitative distinction between clergy (who received bread and wine) and laity (who received only bread), the issue was highly political. For Luther, it also had another facet: the Bible clearly describes Jesus giving his disciples both bread *and* wine. The decision to limit lay communion to one kind, on the other hand, not only had no biblical basis, even its "human" rationale seemed weak. In Luther's view, the Council of Constance had simply invoked "custom"—and then given itself the authority to legitimate the practice, claiming inspiration by the Holy Spirit. Playing this self-ascribed authority off against the testimony of Scripture, Luther argued, was hubristic and it burdened the consciences of laypeople by undermining their trust in the Bible.

Luther's second critique aimed at the use of Aristotelian philosophical terminology to define what happens in the eucharist. The notion of "transubstantiation," used in official documents since the Fourth Lateran Council (1215), sought to explain how the elements of bread and wine change into Christ's flesh and blood—while remaining empirically unchanged. Luther found transubstantiation unpersuasive and preferred other explanatory models, but his real concern lay with imposing unnecessary conceptual baggage on a process that remained a mystery and could only be grasped properly in faith. This was another example of clerical arrogance, and it subverted people's experience of the sacrament. Even worse, in his view, was the third "captivity": regarding the mass "as a good work and a sacrifice." Here Luther attacks the erroneous notion that celebrating a mass is a human act of sacrifice or propitiatory offering, rather than a divine act promising salvation. Such thinking was connected to the frequent endowment of private masses on behalf of the deceased or for other personal purposes—a practice analogous to the sale of indulgences.

As subsequent disputes with inner-Protestant adversaries such as Huldrych Zwingli (see Chapter 4) indicate, Luther's sacramental theology remains relatively conservative. He insists, for example, that Christ is truly and physically (not just spiritually or symbolically) present in the eucharistic celebration—a notion of "real presence" that hews close to the line taken by Rome. Again, Luther's critiques have a strong pastoral subtext. He is guided by the needs of parishioners. With such people in mind, his reforms aim at restoring a purer, more biblical experience of God—not by reinventing Christianity, but by reasserting its hidden (and suppressed) strengths.

This kind of moderate biblicism has implications for how Luther envisions religious community. His primary focus lies on the spiritual bonds that connect people who are affected by—and respond to—God's grace. The "true" Christians are not always visible as such, but are scattered among the mixed group of people that makes up the institutional church. Unlike many other reformers in Christian history, though, Luther does not advocate a separation or withdrawal from the institutional church. In fact, to the end of his life, he always insists on the indispensability of that visible, external structure. It alone provides the preached word and proper sacraments upon which all true Christians depend. That creates an ongoing, irreducible tension for Christians who must live in such a mixed community. It also makes institutional reform imperative.

If popes and bishops fail to provide the kinds of reform the Christian people need, committed Christians need to turn to other leaders. Luther himself does this in a third major treatise of 1520, an appeal *To the Christian Nobility of the German Nation Concerning the Reform of the Christian Estate*. The address begins with a focused and often vehement critique of papal ideology, attacking the "three walls" behind which "the Romanists" seek refuge from reform: (1) the assertion that spiritual authority is superior to the temporal; (2) the claim that only the pope has authority to interpret Scripture; and (3) the insistence that popes alone have the power to call councils. Rejecting all three propositions, Luther calls upon the secular nobility to take charge of church reform. His justification for doing so is more than merely pragmatic. He bases his appeal on an underlying theological conviction that the distinction between clergy and laypeople was simply functional; each had different tasks in the public life of the church, but both share equally in the church's spiritual authority:

> [T]here is no true, basic difference between laymen and priests, princes and bishops, between religious and secular, except for the sake of office and work, but not for the sake of status. They are all of the spiritual estate, all are truly priests, bishops, and popes. (LW: 44, 129)

How can that be? "[B]ecause we all have one baptism, one gospel, one faith, and are all Christians alike" (LW: 44, 127). In this respect, the Christian people form a *priesthood of all baptized believers*: "[W]e are all consecrated priests through baptism" (LW: 44, 127).

Having called the nobility to action, Luther now follows with a list of desired institutional reforms. Many of these aim at limiting the pope's income and power, curtailing the payment of taxes to Rome, restricting the pope's claim on German benefices, and ending the pope's involvement in temporal affairs, particularly as ruler over

Italian territories. On the other hand, Luther advocates strengthening episcopal autonomy, absolving bishops from swearing oaths of obedience to the pope. Addressing the long-standing medieval controversy between papalists and imperialists, Luther sides with the latter when he says, "the pope should have no authority over the emperor, except the right to anoint and crown him at the altar ..." (LW: 44, 164). In no way may the pope regard the emperor as his vassal or demand homage from him, much less make him kiss the pontiff's feet.

Other reforms aim at ending questionable religious practices, such as pilgrimages to Rome—which, according to Luther and likely based on memories of his own trip 10 years earlier, are more likely to scandalize than edify the pilgrim. The proliferation of private masses, veneration of saints, but also the abuse of excommunication for political ends—all of this should stop. The clergy, too, need reform. Most importantly, no priest should be required to take a vow of celibacy: "Restore freedom to everybody and leave every man free to marry or not to marry" (LW: 44, 176).

Luther's reform proposals stretch beyond the church and its clergy. He also calls for revising university curricula, and for reforming society as a whole. Gluttony, excessive drinking, and prostitution are to be banned—as are the excesses of commercial culture: conspicuous consumption of food and clothing, and the hoarding of wealth. He even takes aim at the financial practices of bankers such as the Fuggers, wondering whether it can be moral to earn so much by charging interest and engaging in other "unproductive" activities. But "I know full well that it would be far more godly to increase agriculture and decrease commerce" (LW: 44, 214). Interestingly, Luther does not see the mendicant orders as a corrective to that commercial culture, in part because their ethos is exceptional rather than societally comprehensive, and in part because they have not remained true to their vows: "It is far more important to consider what the common people need for their salvation than what St. Francis, St. Dominic, and St. Augustine, or anyone else has established as a rule [for mendicants], especially because things have not turned out as they planned" (LW: 44, 172).

This treatise became the most popular of Luther's early writings. Some of it is also populistic, catering to widespread resentments and long-standing desires for German autonomy. Many of the political points—reducing taxes to Rome, strengthening temporal powers, and lay control of clergy—had already been achieved by the kings of France and Spain, and so Luther's demands tugged at the Germans' cultural pride. The mix of populism, pragmatism and theological rationale proved compelling, however, and the German princes began to take notice. It would not be long before they answered Luther's appeal. The results, as we shall see, were mixed. Luther may have been the focal point of the early Reformation, but that does not mean he was in control.

References

The following is a list of works cited and consulted in this chapter. Though it is only a small selection of relevant literature, it is a good place to start for further reading.

Carlyle, Thomas. 1993. *On Heroes, Hero-Worship, and the Heroic in History*. The Norman and Charlotte Strouse Edition of the Writings of Thomas Carlyle. Berkeley/Los Angeles/Oxford: University of California Press.

Edwards, Mark U. 1994. *Printing, Propaganda, and Martin Luther*. Berkeley: University of California Press.

Lindberg, Carter. 2010. *The European Reformations*. 2nd edition. Oxford: Wiley-Blackwell.

Luther's Works. 1955–. (LW). *American Edition*, vols. 1–55. Philadelphia: Fortress Press.

Ong, Walter J. 1982. *Orality and Literacy: The Technologizing of the Word*. London/New York: Methuen.

Further Reading

Brecht, Martin. 1985–1993. *Martin Luther*, 3 vols. Minneapolis: Fortress Press.

Febvre, Lucien. 1928. *Un Destin: Martin Luther* [Martin Luther: A Destiny]. Paris: Presses Universitaires de France.

Hendrix, Scott. 1981. *Luther and the Papacy: Stages in a Reformation Conflict.* Philadelphia: Fortress Press.

Kaufmann, Thomas. 2009. *Geschichte der Reformation* [History of the Reformation]. Frankfurt/Leipzig: Verlag der Weltreligionen, 2009.

Kolb, Robert. 2008. *Martin Luther: Pastor, Professor, Confessor.* Oxford: Oxford University Press.

Leppin, Volker. 2006. *Martin Luther.* Darmstadt: Wissenschaftliche Buchgesellschaft.

Minnich, Nelson H. 2008. *Councils of the Catholic Reformation: Pisa I (1409) to Trent (1545–63).* Aldershot, England; Burlington, VT: Ashgate.

Oberman, Heiko A. 1989. *Luther: Man between God and the Devil.* New Haven, CT: Yale University Press.

Reformation Christianity. 2007. Ed. Peter Matheson. Minneapolis: Fortress Press, 2007.

Sachs, Hans. 1523. *Die wittembergisch Nachtigall.* Bamberg.

Schwarz, Reinhard. 1998. *Luther.* 2nd edition. Göttingen: Vandenhoeck & Ruprecht.

Scribner, R. W. 1981. *For the Sake of the Simple Folk. Popular Propaganda for the German Reformation.* Cambridge: Cambridge University Press.

Tierney, Brian. 1988. *The Crisis of Church and State 1050–1300.* Toronto: University of Toronto Press.

Wicks, Jared. 1978. *Cajetan Responds: A Reader in Reformation Controversy.* Washington, DC: Catholic University Press.

Chapter 3

Reformation Reforms

The Politics of Reform

As Luther sat in the Wartburg, events down below began unfolding at a rapid pace. Prior to Worms, Luther had already become a public figure who captivated wide-ranging audiences across Europe, with Germans especially fascinated. His confrontation with the emperor at Worms in April of 1521 put him on a new stage, however. Whereas the earlier conflict with the pope and curia was dominated by a dispute over ideas, his cause now entered into the domain of high politics. Here, ideas also mattered, but they were often judged by their political usefulness—not just by their intellectual persuasiveness. Luther's courage in Worms impressed some of the attending princes. His continued survival after Worms raised their eyebrows even further. They began to think he may be useful.

Luther's attack on the centralized ecclesial authority of Rome and his defiance of the emperor's power animated long-standing ambitions of many European rulers. In Germany—or, more properly, the Holy Roman Empire—his 1520 appeal *To the German Nobility* (see Chapter 2) struck a particularly resonant chord, since this region was not a party to the extensive liberties granted to national rulers such as the king of France in the 1516 Concordat of Bologna. Both territorial princes in the Empire and magistrates of the free imperial cities desired similar privileges and greater

The Reformation: A Brief History, First Edition. Kenneth G. Appold.
© 2011 Kenneth G. Appold. Published 2011 by Blackwell Publishing Ltd.

local autonomy. With respect to the papacy, those aims attached themselves to a number of specific grievances, such as the "export" of church taxes and other monies to Rome, the pope's "interference" in the appointment of German bishops, and the dispute over church-legal jurisdiction. But there were also purely political agendas, aimed more squarely at the emperor and focused largely on a desire for greater representation and decision-making powers at the imperial level, as well as autonomy from the Empire at the local level. Because Luther's appeal catered to these grievances and ambitions, many German politicians saw him, at the very least, as a welcome tool for gaining additional leverage against their opponents. Some developed sympathy for his reforms, as well.

In Luther's absence, his colleagues in Wittenberg began to introduce practical reforms. Leading the way were Philipp Melanchthon and Andreas Bodenstein von Karlstadt from the university, and Gabriel Zwilling from the Augustinian cloister. Central to their efforts were reforms to the mass. Overjoyed at news of his survival, they soon found ways to correspond with the hidden Luther, and his views certainly figured in their decisions. At services for the university faculty in the early fall, Melanchthon had communion distributed in both kinds, began eliminating language of sacrifice from the liturgy, and celebrated in German rather than Latin. This was still a relatively private context. In October, though, the Reformers' actions grew louder. To begin with, many of the Augustinians—Luther's brothers in the cloister—refused to perform private masses and began renouncing their monastic vows. Karlstadt stirred things up further by offering a public disputation on the mass—where he, of course, advocated the changes that he and Melanchthon had already implemented in smaller circles. Opposed to all of this was a group of conservative clergy that served as canons in the Castle Church of All Saints. Because Wittenberg was very small—about a 10-minute walk from the Augustinian cloister on one end to the Castle Church on the other—pressures mounted. No resident could have remained oblivious to the developments, and in fact most took an avid interest. Even Frederick the Wise took notice and issued warnings, calling for caution and calm. Instead, the townspeople grew more restless. In early December, mobs stormed the churches, disrupting services and assaulting the clergy. A number of citizens were arrested. In an odd twist to the story, Luther himself arrived in Wittenberg on December 4, dressed in a disguise, to see first-hand what was happening. He seems to have missed most of the action, though, because he left again quickly, saying that he was "pleased with the reforms." No one seemed to know exactly what that meant. In any case, the shouting continued. The townspeople submitted a list of demands for reform to the city council, calling also for the release of their imprisoned cohorts. Frederick ordered the Wittenbergers to refrain from going ahead with the reforms. Concerned about the political implications and unsure about the measures themselves, Frederick wanted to preserve the status quo. Interestingly, this put him at odds with Wittenberg's more progressively minded city council. It also disappointed the Reformers in town.

The crisis proved far from resolved, however. Undeterred by the elector's call for restraint, Karlstadt orchestrated a riotous Christmas Day mass in the Castle Church. The church was packed. Karlstadt, dressed in everyday clothes, preached in German and offered communion in both kinds. Parishioners crowded around the altar, grabbing the cup with their own hands like a punch bowl. Few of the people had been to confession or fasted; some were evidently drunk. The shock value for more sensitive souls was astronomical. Pieces of the host—Christ's own physical body—fell from the plate, landing on the floor to be trampled by grubby Wittenberger feet. For some, Karlstadt had defiled the eucharist. To others, though, he had made an important statement, giving Christ back to "the people."

By now, even Melanchthon began to fidget. Unsettled by the arrival of a small group of apocalyptic "prophets" from nearby Zwickau on December 27, Melanchthon wrote an anxious letter to Frederick, begging him to bring back Luther. The All Saints canons fired off more lengthy missives, filled with complaints about Karlstadt's Christmas mass and other offenses. Soon Karlstadt gave them more to fret about. On January 5, 1522, he announced his upcoming marriage (which took place two weeks later), publishing the invitation along with a brief theological rationale. Zwilling and the Augustinians also joined in the fracas.

Released from their vows by their general chapter, the monks dragged altars and sacred images out of their cloister chapel and burned them.

Wittenberg's city council took steps to create order—albeit on evangelical terms. On January 24, 1522, the council issued the "Wittenberg Ordinance," which established communion in both kinds, mandated the removal of images from churches, and revised the liturgy of the mass. It also implemented wide-ranging economic reforms, which included consolidating church revenues and confiscating some church properties to create a "common chest," a centrally administered fund for poor relief and one of the pioneering efforts of evangelical social ministry. Connected to this was a prohibition against begging—both by mendicant friars and by able-bodied laypeople who "should be put to work." Karlstadt contributed to the Ordinance.

Confronted by the council's measures, Frederick took action. A few days earlier, he had received a letter from imperial authorities demanding an immediate halt to all religious "innovations" in Electoral Saxony. That, of course, was aimed at him. Feeling the pressure, he dispatched court officials to negotiate a settlement between the warring Wittenberg factions and to end the reforms. He also demanded that the city's new Ordinance be revoked. Results were slow in coming. On March 6, Luther himself returned to Wittenberg and preached a series of eight sermons (the "Invocavit Sermons") in which he both reasserted his personal leadership and rebuked the Reformers for having taken things too fast: "It was done in wantonness, with no regard for proper order and with offense to your neighbor" (*Luther's Works*, 1955– (hereafter LW): 51, 73). Surprisingly to many, Luther objected to the city's establishment of communion in both kinds, arguing that it was well to make this an option, but not to make it a requirement. Doing so turned evangelical liberty into a law, "making a 'must' out of what is 'free'." Reiterating Frederick's demands, Luther called for the suspension of the Ordinance. He also singled out Karlstadt as the main instigator of the movement—overlooking the contributions of Melanchthon and Zwilling. Karlstadt's preaching was curtailed, and his writings confiscated and destroyed as authorities began to line up behind Luther. Alienated and defeated, Karlstadt left Wittenberg.

The Wittenberg events of 1521–1522 provide an interesting case study in the politics of reform. Here, much of the energy for reform came "from below"—from common people demanding action. But that energy needed to be organized and translated into public policy. It was at this level that a conflict emerged between the city magistrates and the elector. Who would have the right to establish reforms? The more local authorities—the city council—took the initiative. In this instance, they were unquestionably better positioned to do so; they were on site and able to feel the pulse on the ground. The elector was not. And yet the elector—with Luther's help—prevailed, overturning the council's actions. That would become the pattern throughout the German territories as the Reformation advanced: princes took charge of the reform process and used it to consolidate their authority over their subjects. As for Luther—here, too, a lesson is learned. By returning from the Wartburg and intervening in the Wittenberg events, Luther established his own personal leadership over the reform process: "Follow me ... I was the very first whom God called to this work," he tells the Wittenbergers on Invocavit Sunday (LW: 51, 72ff). Ironically, a year later, many of the 1522 provisions (except the iconoclasm) were reinstated—only this time the reforms bore Luther's signature. His concern about turning Christian liberty into a law was surely genuine; it was consistent with other positions he took. But his stand in March of 1522 also smelled of less principled motives. This was not Luther fighting against the vastly superior powers of pope and emperor; this was Luther fighting for control.

As Luther and Frederick, each in his own way, took charge of the reform movement, they also set the stage for its internal division. Tensions between local authorities and princes would return—and not all city officials were as easily cowed as those of Wittenberg. The dispute over who had the right of reform (*jus reformandi*) continued, and it sharpened wherever local and princely agendas conflicted.

Connected to this was the case of Karlstadt. Driven out of Wittenberg, Karlstadt began to identify ever more closely with the common people. Renouncing his professorship and doctoral title, he took a parish in the small Thuringian town of Orlamünde, where he introduced many of the reforms that had been thwarted in Wittenberg. Irritated, Luther began a preaching tour of the region, even visiting Orlamünde itself. This time, however, his personal presence was not well received. Karlstadt had a lot of support among the local laypeople and clergy, and Luther was distinctly unwelcome there. When the two Reformers met privately in an inn to discuss their differences, the conversation broke down under the weight of mutual recriminations. They were now more than opponents; they were personal enemies.

The feud between Karlstadt and Luther had to do with political sympathies—Karlstadt identified with the common people much more intentionally than did Luther. But it was also theological. Karlstadt's thought had more overt mystical tendencies than Luther's, which led him to emphasize spiritual rebirth and an attitude of self-abnegation (*Gelassenheit*) more than justification. His belief that the Holy Spirit addresses believers through a kind of "inner testimony" distinct from the external word provided a theoretical basis for his confidence in lay church leadership. Karlstadt's reform program was congregationalistic: the local members themselves were responsible—and had the spiritual authority—for instituting reform. Karlstadt's rejection of sacred images had its roots in both the Ten Commandments (forbidding idolatry)[1] and in a suspicion of "externals" shared by many humanists. It was his eucharistic teaching, however, that created the sharpest and most durable theological conflict with Luther. After their meeting in August of 1524, Karlstadt published five tracts on the Lord's Supper, in which he advocated a symbolic understanding of the sacrament. Luther accused him of "spiritualism" and of denying Christ's presence in the eucharist. Soon after, and thanks to Luther's

---

[1] Both Luther and Melanchthon understood the prohibition against idolatry in more spiritual terms: idolatry is what happens when we love something more than God (see Luther's explanation of the First Commandment in the *Large Catechism* [see *The Book of Concord*, 2000: 377–480]). They were unconcerned about sacred artwork or crucifixes in church—and in fact welcomed them.

warnings, Karlstadt was expelled from Electoral Saxony. He spent the next decade wandering through Germany and Switzerland, finally settling in Basel as a professor of Old Testament in 1534. Long dismissed by historians as the man who "lost to Luther," Karlstadt has recently seen something of a reassessment. Particularly significant is his influence on lay Christian movements such as the Swiss Anabaptists (see the section "The Anabaptist Alternative"), with whom he communicated frequently and whose views against infant baptism he shared. Some also regard Karlstadt as a forerunner of Lutheran Pietism. His most important legacy, however, may have been the launching of an alternative Reformation trajectory from Wittenberg foundations. The Reformation, Karlstadt reminds us, was not only about Luther.

Zurich, Zwingli, and the Cities

Other cities had more success than Wittenberg in asserting their local right to reform. That was particularly true of free imperial cities—cities that were independent of princely control and subject directly to the Empire. Many of these cities had a vibrant cultural life of their own, an educated and self-confident citizenry, considerable trade-based wealth, and fairly democratic structures of government. Geographically, many were clustered in the southern parts of Germany, northern Switzerland, and Alsace. In his classic study, *Imperial Cities and the Reformation* (1987), Bernd Moeller notes that the Diet of Worms counted 65 free imperial cities in 1521; of these, more than 50 came to embrace the Reformation at least partly—a figure of nearly 80 per cent. Added to these are a number of other cities who enjoyed many of the same liberties and privileges, such as the powerful Hanseatic trade centers of Hamburg, Bremen, Brunswick, and Danzig. Most of these also accepted Protestantism. Why, asks Moeller, were these cities so supportive of the Reformation?

The answer has to do with a corporate mentality specific to these largely closed urban settlements. Walled off against intruders and highly suspicious of outsiders, Moeller argues, they understood themselves as sacral entities—communities fused together into a religious whole. In such societies, politics and religion are hard to distinguish. The salvation of all (understood both in worldly and other-worldly terms) depended upon cooperation and unity. Catastrophes such as the plague, fires or bad weather were often explained as God's retribution for sins of the city. City leaders sought ways to reduce the presence of sin and thereby ward off calamities—and this gave them a strong interest in controlling as much as possible of the city's religious life. It also indicates why religious outsiders such as Jews so often figured as scapegoats and were expelled from many cities during the fourteenth and fifteenth centuries. But outsiders did not need to be non-Christian in order to arouse suspicion. Similar hostility was aimed at bishops and other religious authorities who tried to dictate religious life from beyond the city walls. During much of the fourteenth and fifteenth centuries, city magistrates did their best to secure as many rights of patronage over local churches as they could, which enabled them to appoint and pay their own clergy—and to require oaths of allegiance from them as well. The presence of humanist culture in most such cities also made them receptive to the Reformation's thought. By the day's standards, these were literate societies. They had their own printing presses, gathered in learned societies, read books, and discussed ideas. They were naturally interested in theology. They also tended to be dismissive of church rituals that seemed either arbitrary or superstitious. And since they were well versed in commerce, they were keenly sensitive to financial manipulation—such as they saw in the sale of indulgences. In short, given the right opportunity, they were ready for change.

Within this spectrum of free cities, Zurich was something of a special case. Though it had received its imperial immediacy (*Reichsunmittelbarkeit*, making it an imperial free city) in 1218, Zurich's subsequent development took it a step further. By 1500, it was, by most practical standards, no longer part of the Empire at all. Another political alliance had superseded its imperial ties: the Swiss Confederation.

Much of Switzerland is famously mountainous. Its alpine peoples are tucked away in remote nooks and crannies that are hard for outsiders to penetrate—much less rule. Independence is their reward. In order to protect that autonomy and to facilitate trade among themselves, several Swiss territories (known as *Orte*, and later called "cantons") swore an oath of allegiance and formed a confederacy (*Eidgenossenschaft*, or "oath association"). Originating in the most mountainous regions of central Switzerland and later adding the prosperous city-states of the valleys and plains, the Confederation came to include eight *Orte* by the 1350s, one of which was Zurich; it grew to 13 in the decades leading up to the Reformation. Relations between the states was not always harmonious—and Zurich proved particularly irksome to the others because of its territorial expansionism—but they were hard as rock when faced with common enemies. By most accounts, the Swiss fielded the most formidable fighting men in all of Europe. Their soldiers were so renowned, in fact, that mercenaries were Switzerland's most significant export for many years. Even the pope preferred Swiss guards. In 1499, the Confederation fought—and won—a pivotal war against the Swabian League of southern Germany and the Austrian Habsburgs, whose leader Maximilian I was the Holy Roman Emperor. The subsequent Peace of Basel (1499) granted the Swiss independence from imperial jurisdiction.

Switzerland differed from the German territories not only by its level of independence from the Empire, but also by its affinity for democracy. Zurich, for example, was governed by a representative body of officials and councils who were elected by their peers. Though there had once been a duchess (she was, in fact, abbess of the Fraumünster convent, promoted by the emperor), citizens rebelled and began electing their own leaders in 1336. Instrumental to that process were Zurich's craftsmen, who had organized themselves into guilds and demanded political representation. The ensuing structures of government gave that to them. Craftsmen dominated Zurich's Great Council, of whose 162 members 144 came from the 12 major guilds, the remaining 18 from a guild of patricians and urban noblemen, known collectively as "constables." Next to the Great Council was a Small Council, which ran most of the day-to-day business of the city and was presided over by the mayor. Here, too, the guilds gained considerable influence, though their numbers were balanced more effectively by the constables (of 50 councilmen, 24 came from the craftsmen's guilds, 24 from the constables and two were elected freely). In matters of great importance, both bodies convened together, forming the Council of the Two Hundred. While it would be misleading to describe this form of government as "democratic" in the pure sense of the word since the councilmen were not elected by the population as a whole, its inclusion of the craft guilds (which was common in late-medieval cities) made it more broadly representative than the patrician oligarchies of some cities, and much more so than the hereditary monarchies that dominated most of the rest of Europe. That would prove very significant for the Reformation in cities such as Zurich, because here the adoption of reform was not decided by a single person—that is, a prince or king—but by the votes of a representative council. Swiss city Reformers needed good political skills.

On the eve of the Reformation, Zurich's religious life was concentrated in three major churches: the Grossmünster (Great Minster), with 24 canons, 32 chaplains and one *Leutpriester* (people's priest); the Fraumünster (Minster of Our Lady), with seven canons and three chaplains; and the Church of St. Peter, with a dozen clerics. The city also included cloisters of the three major mendicant orders—Franciscans, Dominicans (with houses for both male and female members) and Augustinian Hermits. Though the Fraumünster was attached to a convent for Benedictine nuns, only the abbess remained in residence at the time of the Reformation. All of these religious institutions belonged to the diocese of Constance, whose seat lay across the border in the German city of that name, but whose bishop at the time, Hugo von Hohenlandenberg (c. 1457–1532), happened to hail from a town near Zurich. Because the diocese was enormous, administering a huge area with more than 15,000 priests, Zurich's city officials had an easy time taking over many of the bishop's supervisory functions, and sidestepped the bishop in regulating church incomes and properties, and in administering the cloisters. In addition, the magistrates had an eye on the city's moral life, passing legislation against gambling, dancing, and cursing, and taking action against derelict clergy. The Great Council even secured the right to appoint several of the highly endowed canons at the Grossmünster and Fraumünster. The magistrates' move to require oaths of loyalty of the clergy further underscored the city government's growing influence over Zurich's church life in the decades leading up to the Reformation.

In 1518, the most prominent preaching position in Zurich became vacant. It was that of the people's priest at the Grossmünster. Responsible for filling the post were the church's 24 canons. They were looking for a man with preaching ability and charisma; those who were reform-minded also wanted someone who was compatible with their interests. Because not every canon had the same notions of reform, however, the process was bound to be conflicted. In the end, they found a man and elected him by a vote of 17–7, after airing some nagging questions about his personal morals. That man was Huldrych Zwingli (1484–1531). Within a few years, he would launch the Swiss Reformation.

Zwingli was born only seven weeks after Martin Luther, on January 1, 1484. Apart from that and a life-long fascination with the Bible, however, the two could hardly have been more different, both in social background and temperament. Zwingli's family were peasants. While Luther's parents were eager to distance themselves from the peasant roots of their forebears, Zwingli and his relatives were proud of their heritage. Of course, peasants in Switzerland, where their emancipation from feudal servitude was fairly advanced, were not the same as peasants in Germany. In addition, Switzerland's rural regions were the most democratic parts of the country. Zwingli's family profited from this. His father was an *Ammann*, similar to a mayor, in their town of Wildhaus in the Toggenburg, about 40 miles east of Zurich. The family had influence and means. Huldrych's uncle, abbot of a Benedictine monastery, supervised the boy's early education. By most accounts, Zwingli was a conspicuously gifted pupil, and soon left for a cosmopolitan tour of Swiss and Austrian schools and universities that steeped him in biblical humanism and culminated in a Master's of Philosophy degree in Basel in 1506.

Aged 22 and freshly consecrated, Zwingli took his first parish in Glarus, a town with a strong mercenary culture and ties to the pope. Many of the young men of Glarus fought for the pope (against the French) and Zwingli accompanied them on at least one campaign in Italy. While economically profitable for towns such as Glarus, the mercenary business also had a corrosive effect on morals and community life; aside from the obvious horrors of war, soldiers from one and the same town often found themselves hired by opposing armies. Zwingli began to preach against mercenary culture—his first taste of the pulpit as a site of political controversy. He warmed to the experience, and his exhortations grew more frequent and more forceful. At the same time, Zwingli immersed himself in study of the Bible. That gave wind to his reforming instincts, and it was here, in the parish of Glarus, that he began to find his voice. At the core of his emerging vocation lay a commitment to biblically based preaching, emphasizing a literal rather than spiritual interpretation and frequently aiming at ethical applications. This was formed further by intensive readings in Patristics, study of Greek, and by his avid correspondence with other Swiss humanists, a circle of friends and like-minded colleagues that eventually secured him an introduction to the most celebrated humanist of the era, Erasmus of Rotterdam, whom he met in 1516.

Whether Zwingli experienced a kind of "Reformation breakthrough" during this time remains unclear. Zwingli himself gives rather vague accounts of his intellectual and spiritual development. That may not be surprising. Unlike Luther, whose guiding insights were born in an environment of intense introspection, Zwingli's sense of direction appears to have drawn much more heavily from his interaction with the outside world. Zwingli was by nature a political animal, thriving in the raw air of personal confrontation and interaction, not the humid dankness of a monk's cell. His vision became clearer as those interactions continued. Unlike Luther again, Zwingli's early reforming efforts did not involve a conflict with the pope. On the contrary, within the context of Swiss mercenary politics, Zwingli counted as a supporter of the pope and cultivated good relations with Rome—which paid him an annual stipend. As the mood in Glarus shifted more heavily toward supporting France, both Zwingli's connection to Rome and his critique of the mercenary business made his position untenable. In late 1516, he left for the pilgrimage town of Einsiedeln, site of a largely defunct Benedictine monastery whose few remaining residents spent more time hunting and fishing than contemplating. That spoke to Zwingli's tastes, as well, and he threw himself into the pastoral analog of those activities, visiting parishioners and preaching. But the last wisps of the site's meditative spirit seem to have inspired him at least slightly. He intensified his scholarship and readings of Scripture, and flirted briefly with the thought of chastity.

Like many clergymen of his day, Zwingli made little effort to conceal his fondness of women. It was this, along with reports of past relationships, that gave ammunition to those canons of Zurich's Grossmünster who opposed his appointment in 1518. Much of their concern was hypocritical and simply a pretext for more political issues. Their own candidate had six children. More broadly speaking, the diocese of Constance counted roughly 1500 illegitimate children fathered by clergy—each year. Nor was it inclined to take action against these activities: the fees collected for legitimating such offspring provided a source of income as inexhaustible as the priests themselves. Besides, even Bishop Hugo kept a concubine. As an impediment to Zwingli's appointment, the issue therefore carried little weight. If any of the canons remained undecided, he put the matter to rest with a letter expressing contrition for "youthful sins" and promising improvement. That promise, of course, did not last long. But the Reformation's commitment to ending concubinage by allowing priests to marry affected Zwingli, too. A subsequent long-term relationship would culminate in his marriage to the widow Anna Reinhart in 1524.

Zwingli's preaching at the Grossmünster did not shy away from controversy. In fact, the *Leutpriester* reveled in it, taking particularly enthusiastic aim at the "lazy" mendicants in the city. As we have seen, however, such rhetoric was not unique in his day. It belonged to the conventional repertoire of every urban elite from Florence to provincial Wittenberg. Criticizing mendicants—whose message of Christian poverty did not square well with the property-owning ethos of a rising bourgeoisie—was as commonplace as modern-day politicians' rants against taxes. It was similarly effective. The local mendicants were predictably upset; but the message played well with Zurich's councilmen, who began to like what they heard from the new people's priest.

An even more mundane issue sparked the Zurich Reformation. It was a debate about sausage. On the evening of March 9, 1522, the printer Christoph Froschauer offered a plate of *wurst* to a small group of friends in his shop. That seemingly banal event was made remarkable by its timing: it took place at the beginning of Lent. Church law prohibited eating meat during Lent. Froschauer knew this, as did those who partook of the unholy communion. One of those in attendance was Zwingli. Politically astute as always, Zwingli remained in the room but did not eat the sausage. That allowed him, as news of the event spread and quickly caused a city-wide scandal, to defend the fast-breakers' principles without needing to acquit himself. With debate raging in the streets, Zwingli stepped up to the pulpit and gave a rousing sermon in support of breaking the fast. Salvation depends not on man-made rituals, he proclaimed, but on faith. Lenten fasting is a human invention; it is not prescribed by the Bible, and it has no impact on salvation. Zwingli's sermon, entitled *Von Erkiesen und Freiheit der Speisen* ("On Choice and Liberty of Foods"), was published a few weeks later, on April 16.

Reactions to both the provocative dinner and Zwingli's sermon came promptly and involved nearly every level of civil and church authority. Zurich's city council approached the Grossmünster canons and the city's three *Leutpriester*—one of whom, of course, was Zwingli—and requested a formal opinion. The opinion that followed was mixed, softening principle with pastoral concern: Zurich's clerical elite conceded that fasting was a human tradition, but advised against provoking further uproar by suspending the practice. In the meantime, though, Bishop Hugo of Constance heard about the controversy and sent an episcopal delegation to meet with the council and the local clergy on April 7–9. Using his contacts in the Great Council, Zwingli arranged to appear simultaneously with the bishop's men, thereby gaining an opportunity to rebut their views and to present his own. His tactics paid off. While the Great Council agreed to affirm the laws on fasting, it did so provisionally—on the condition that the bishop provide biblical support for the regulations. Hugo's response, dated May 24, was livid. He had no intention of providing explanations of any sort and demanded that the council enforce the law.

While the council thought this over, Zwingli followed up with a letter sent directly to Hugo on July 2, now demanding the right for priests to marry. Two weeks later, he redrafted the letter in German, addressed it to "all Swiss" and published it. By now, Zwingli's opponents in Zurich had heard enough. Konrad Hoffmann, a Grossmünster canon who was skeptical of Zwingli from the start, had, over the course of three observant years, meticulously catalogued the people's priest's offenses. He now submitted that list to the council. Hoffmann was joined by some of the local mendicants, whose animus against the Reformer was hardly surprising, in calling for action against Zwingli. Tipping its hand, the council sided with Zwingli, endorsed his style of "preaching according to the Gospel," and created the new position of *Prädikant* (city preacher) for him. This made Zwingli accountable to the magistrates and shielded him from episcopal discipline. The skirmish over Lenten sausages was turning into a full-blown conflict between episcopal and magisterial authorities over church-legal jurisdiction.

Deflecting calls to have Zwingli extradited to stand trial in Constance, the city council decided instead to have a public disputation in Zurich, at which both sides would be challenged to present their positions and the standing accusations of heresy against Zwingli would be aired. The event, known as the First Zurich Disputation, took place on January 29, 1523, and became a defining moment for Zurich's Reformation. In all fairness, the outcome was probably decided before the disputation began. The councilmen made two preliminary decisions that were determinative: the council would judge the disputation and decide who won, and it would use Scripture as its norm. It thereby reduced the episcopal party to Zwingli's equal while raising itself above both, and it accepted Zwingli's biblicist methodology. None of this was lost on the bishop, who hesitated to send his emissaries and complained bitterly afterwards that the deck was stacked against them. Zwingli, however, did not behave as if the conclusion were foregone, and hastened to assemble a summary of his positions, collected in 67 articles and drawn from his sermons and other writings.

More than just a summary, the "Sixty-Seven Articles" are a theological *tour de force*, affirming Zwingli's belief in a Gospel that derives its power and authority from its God-inspired biblical content—and not by virtue of the church's secondary authorization. Central to that content is the message of salvation through Christ—and through nothing but Christ, certainly not through any rules or rites of human making. Based on these two principles—*sola Scriptura, solus Christus*—Zwingli assesses concrete issues in the life of church and society. These include the status of the pope (Christ is the only "highest priest"), the mass (is not a sacrifice, but a memorial), church properties (God is against the hording of goods), clerical marriage (is not prohibited by God, and must therefore be proper), excommunication (cannot be pronounced by individuals—that is, bishops—but only by the congregation together with its pastor), and the status of temporal vs. spiritual power (spiritual power's pomp has no basis in Christ's teaching, while temporal power does; its jurisdiction is therefore superior, provided it base its laws on God's will). Though some of Zwingli's thoughts resemble Luther's—and Zwingli had both read Luther and defended his teachings against accusations of heresy—they also show considerable distinctiveness. Even the core concept of "the Gospel" carries a different accent with Zwingli; Christ's role as "leader," and the resulting ethical implications for Christian society receive stronger emphasis. Less important for Zwingli is the spiritual dynamic of justification proper. Still, the two Reformers hold views that are largely compatible—with one exception: Luther would not have described the mass as a "memorial." That seemingly small difference would come back to haunt the two.

More than 600 people attended the disputation. Bishop Hugo's representative, an eminently capable theologian named Johannes Fabri, centered his attacks on the proceedings' methodology, arguing that the council had no authority to decide what remained a matter of episcopal jurisdiction. Zwingli's articles never entered the debate. Not surprisingly, the council was not persuaded by Fabri's rejection of its authority—and quickly declared Zwingli victorious, thereby clearing him of charges of heresy.

By siding with Zwingli in the First Disputation, the city council established itself as Zurich's ecclesial authority. Historians have noted that this effectively marks the beginning of a new church polity: not only did the council replace the bishop as primary instrument of ecclesial oversight in Zurich, but the disputation itself took on the character of a churchwide assembly or synod, its attendees involved collectively in ascertaining truth. Bishop Hugo had little choice but to resign himself to the new reality. Since he had no means of enforcing his laws apart from the city council (and organizing military action was not, in the wake of the 1499 Swabian War, a viable option at that time), he could do little more than wage a war of the pen. Relations between Zurich and the bishop would end formally with an exchange of correspondence in August 1524.

The council took the additional step of declaring that all the clergy in the *state* of Zurich, not just the city, would henceforth be freed from episcopal jurisdiction and subject to the city magistrates. That was an interesting move because Zurich's rural people outnumbered city residents by a factor of 10 to 1 (c. 50,000 to c. 5,000). And while the rural congregations seemed happy to gain independence from the bishop of Constance, they had mixed feelings about seeing him supplanted by urban magistrates. If they resented sending their hard-earned tithes to Constance, was it any better to send them to Zurich instead? Wouldn't it be best of all to keep them in the village? Tensions between rural and urban interests were a longstanding problem, not only in the city-state of Zurich, but in all of Switzerland. These conflicts would now become part of the Reformation's internal dynamic and affect its practical course—all the more so since the council only declared Zwingli formally victorious, but said nothing about the material contents of his "Sixty-Seven Articles." These material issues would now need to be contested one by one on the field of local and regional politics.

That process began almost immediately, helped along by Zwingli's published explanation of the 67 articles, the *Ußlegen und gründ der schlussreden oder artickeln* ("Explanation and Grounds of the Conclusions or Articles"). Priests began to marry publicly (though Zwingli himself waited another year before marrying Anna Reinhart, with whom he had been living for some time). The Dominicans' cloisters were secularized, and most of their inhabitants left. Protests against tithes cropped up, especially in rural areas. None of these changes took place smoothly, since there remained a powerful minority who opposed them. The most controversial issues, though, dealt with removal of images and reform of the mass. Images were sacred artwork, but they were also property, and sometimes valuable. Because they were often connected to the families of wealth who sponsored them, images pricked social sensibilities of the poor as much as they inspired theological outrage against perceived idolatry. Few actions symbolized a break with the past—both religiously and socially—as satisfyingly as "cleaning house" in a church, throwing out all that offended and returning the space to some semblance of austerity. Removing and destroying "idols" was a hallmark of popular reforms throughout Europe and took place in virtually every cultural context. Whatever one may have thought of the activity itself, however, it clearly caused legal complications. To the sponsors of sacred artwork, who often remained its legal owners, forceful removal of such objects constituted theft. This, and the understandable offense taken by non-iconoclastic persons at seeing works of art destroyed, meant that political authorities felt pressure to protect the images. In the Zurich region, several notable incidents of iconoclasm in the wake of the First Disputation forced the magistrates to take action.

An additional impetus was supplied by Konrad Hoffmann, whose previous attempts to oust Zwingli had fizzled out, but who now felt his conscience compromised by the latest changes to the eucharistic liturgy. Zwingli and his fellow Reformer Leo Jud, a longtime friend and now *Leutpriester* at St. Peter's, were busy redefining the mass as a service centered around the Word—Scripture reading and preaching. Often, eucharistic celebrations were simply left out, and when they were not, the liturgy was modified to avoid language of sacrifice. Zwingli's eucharistic theology stressed a spiritual communion over the physical, and expressed this by defining the sacrament as a "remembrance" of Christ's sacrifice on the cross—rather than as a re-enactment of that sacrifice. Traditionalists such as Hoffmann felt that Christ's presence was being denied and the sacrament itself destroyed (as we shall see, this was a concern also shared by some Reformers—notably by Luther).

The city council sought to resolve these issues—on images and the mass—with another disputation. The Second Zurich Disputation took place on October 26–28, 1523, and drew more than 900 attendees. Neither Hugo nor the bishops of Chur and Basel, who were also invited, sent representatives. The disputation's outcome was somewhat unexpected. The council did declare Zwingli victorious, which dealt a final blow to Hoffmann and the remaining traditionalists. But Zwingli also made a number of important concessions, arguing that the pace of reform should slow. He favored an incremental approach that combined religious change with education. Images of Christ in churches should only be removed once Christ was planted firmly in the believers' hearts, argued one of his colleagues. A significant group of Zwingli's associates now felt abandoned, however. In their eyes, Zwingli was compromising God's word for political calculus. He was pandering to the council rather than following his conscience. This group, led by Zwingli's younger ally Konrad Grebel (c. 1498–1526), began to question the wisdom of delegating religious authority to a political instrument such as the council. Images were idolatrous because God had decreed them to be so—and that was true regardless of what the city council decided. God's Word would not be put to a vote. Zwingli's path, that of a "magisterial Reformation" (Reformation by the authority of magistrates) was no longer a path they were willing to take. And so the Second Disputation succeeded in thwarting Zwingli's Catholic-minded opponents in Zurich—but it also split the reform movement into two factions. Grebel and his allies began to organize their efforts apart from Zwingli and in a little over a year would form the core of a new community known as Anabaptists.

While Zwingli's reforms in Zurich continued, Zurich itself became a model for other cities. Initial reactions within the Swiss Confederation remained skeptical, however. The other *Orte* criticized Zurich's neighbors for failing to enforce the bishop's laws and, by extension, for harboring revolutionaries. Criticism was most pronounced in the rural, alpine states of central Switzerland: Lucerne, Schwyz, Uri, Unterwalden and Zug. These five suspected, not entirely without justification, that urban Zurich was more interested in expanding its political influence at their expense than it was in any kind of genuine religious improvement. Their main instrument of reaction were the Confederation's diets (*Tagsatzungen*), which provided opportunities for joint decision-making. At diets in 1524, they sought measures to suppress the "Zwinglian-Lutheran-Hussite heresy," but failed to secure universal approval. Hopes of putting Zwingli and Jud on trial at the diet also fell through, but the Catholic traditionalists did apprehend three other men, two officials and a pastor, for removing images; all three were put to death. Two years later, in May and June of 1526, another diet convened in the Swiss town of Baden and organized a public disputation at the federal level. Arguing for the Catholics was none other than John Eck, who seven years earlier had faced Luther in Leipzig. Zwingli was slated to oppose him, but concerns for his safety kept him in Zurich; his friend Johannes Oecolampadius (1482–1531), the leading Reformer of Basel, appeared instead. In the eyes of the majority, Eck trounced Oecolampadius. As a result, and in an act analogous to the imperial edict of Worms (see Chapter 2), the diet voted to condemn Zwingli, regard him as excommunicated, and to ban publication of his works. The Baden diet's actions backfired, however. Instead of consolidating opposition against Zwingli, it polarized the Swiss *Orte*, effectively pushing the powerful city-states of Basel, Schaffhausen, and Bern, all of whom were receptive towards Zwingli's ideas but whose magistrates had not adopted the Reformation, into Zurich's corner. Within a few years, all three would be Protestant.

Guided by Zwingli and the city magistrates, Zurich's reforms effected a comprehensive restructuring of public life. Cloisters were taken over by the city government, some converted into hospitals. The Grossmünster chapter was allowed to keep its wealth, but now focused its attention on education. Zwingli, who had been promoted to canon, was put in charge of the Latin School, soon hiring teachers for Greek and Hebrew. His efforts to make Bible study a regular part of the city's educational landscape led to the creation of a special instrument, the *Prophezei*, which met daily and gathered the city's clergy, the canons, students of the Latin School, and guests. Its work contributed to the *Zurich Bible*, a Swiss-German adaptation of Luther's High German translation, with part of the Old Testament supplied by Zurich itself. One of the most important areas of reform put marriage laws, previously defined by the bishop, into the city government's juris-diction. Marriage, no longer considered a sacrament, was now a civil act and subject to civil courts. Among other things, this made the dissolution of marriage easier—though that does not seem to have had immediate repercussions in Zurich. Substantial liturgi-cal reforms were enacted as well. Images were removed in an orderly fashion. Services would be in German, readings could be done by laypeople as well as clergy, and communion would be served in both kinds in wooden vessels and from a real table. It would only take place four times a year. Rather than kneeling around an altar in a posture of subordination, the parishioners would pass the bread and wine among themselves in the nave. This new way of experiencing Christian community had parallels in social reform: the old feudal order was abolished and Zurich's peasants declared free.

Other European cities embraced the Reformation in ways that often resembled the Zurich process at least outwardly. Events were typically set in motion by individual clergymen, whose preaching provided the necessary spark for a larger movement. That preaching often drew on Luther's thought. As mentioned in Chapter 2, Luther's works made up an enormous proportion of printed material in German-speaking Europe, and his Latin writ-ings traveled even further. In northern cities such as Hamburg, Brunswick, and Lübeck, Luther's influence clearly led to a desire for restructuring the church and civil society. New ordinances were drafted by Johannes Bugenhagen (1485–1558), Luther's associate and head pastor of Wittenberg's City Church. In the cities of southern Germany, Alsace, and northern Switzerland, though, Zwingli's influence, along with that of the Strasbourg Reformer Martin Bucer (1491–1551), was more obviously domi-nant. Theologically, both Zwingli and Bucer owed a lot to Luther—and the early reception of Luther's works in those cities had an undeniable impact on the reform movements there—but their style of implementing reform was recognizably different, stressing greater lay involvement, congregational discipline, and austerity in worship. Whether the preachers' theological profile owed more to Luther, Zwingli, or Bucer, their preaching efforts most often created a groundswell of support in parts of the community and eventually precipitated magisterial action. That action did not always come right away. In Strasbourg, for example, it took the city council more than a decade to ratify a complete Reformation program, which happened in 1534.

Accounts such as these tend to give the impression that the Reformation of the Empire's cities was inexorable, driven by a desire for autonomy and "progress." Such conclusions would be misleading, however. The mere fact that so many city magistrates took so much time in adopting the Reformation calls for greater nuancing. If the political gains promised by the magisterial Reformation were so obvious, why were they not grasped more quickly? Why were they resisted by many councilmen? There is no single answer to these questions, since every city has its own story. In some cases, as in Danzig, Lutheran Reformers such as Pankratius Klemme (c. 1475–1546) found support in the council, but the council was not free to act; in Danzig, it was pressured both by the bishop and the Polish king, and it took the city until 1557 to prevail. In other cities, magistrates were simply afraid of revolution—and sought above all to guarantee peace and stability. That was especially true of places where the magistrates came from well-established patrician classes who had more to lose from instability than up-and-coming groups such as craftsmen (for example, Basel and Bern). It needs to be noted, too, that embracing political progress and adopting the Reformation were not the same thing—and that is especially evident once one leaves the cities. The most democratic and socially progressive parts of Switzerland, for example, were the five inner *Orte*—and they all stayed Catholic.

At least some urban authorities also reacted negatively to the Reformation's ideas. The urban reform movements were about more than power and politics. They were also motivated by missional impulses, a quest for more authentic holiness in a new social and cultural context. Not surprisingly, there were different opinions on how to achieve that. For Zwingli, it had to do with paring the Christian religion down to its essentials, carving away "human traditions" and other externals in order to emphasize an inner, spiritual core of faith. Even among reform-minded Christians, there was genuine disagreement over the value of externals, however. Zurich's Konrad Hoffmann was not alone (and not just reactionary) in objecting to changes in eucharistic practice. Some—including even Luther—felt that fasting, understood properly, could be a useful spiritual exercise. There were also many who sincerely believed that marriage was incompatible with a clerical ethos. Others found iconoclasm repellent and saw the visual arts as an important educational tool. And, of course, there were some who simply took sober stock of the Reformers' theology—and remained unconvinced.

Still, the great majority of imperial cities did come to embrace the Reformation and bore considerable responsibility for its eventual success. The story of the countryside, on the other hand, was quite different.

Rural Revolution of the 'Common Man'

The vast majority of Europe's inhabitants did not live in cities; Europe was mostly rural. For these people, the Reformation was a more ambiguous event, as much a source of disappointment as it was of hope. These are the people who figure most sparingly in traditional accounts of Reformation history—but theirs are the stories by which the Reformation's success and legacy needs also to be assessed.

Most of Europe's rural people were peasants. Many of these lived in some form of feudal servitude. By most indications, the quality of their lives had taken a marked turn for the worse in the fifteenth and early sixteenth centuries. Almost all peasants remain nameless to history; they could not write their own life-stories, nor were their individual lives so exceptional as to warrant documentation by those who could write. But exceptions did occur. During the fifteenth century, Europe's peasants began to complain. And at least some of those complaints found their way into writing and were submitted to authorities. Still nameless for the most part, the peasants now, at least, left a record. Someone took notice; the nameless were finding a voice.

Peasants' grievances almost always focused on loss of traditional freedoms and privileges. Their access to "common lands"—forests, fields, and waters not restricted by feudal arrangements—was suddenly being denied by the lords. That meant they could no longer hunt, gather firewood, or fish in those areas. Landlords also denied them the right to travel freely, or even to marry whom they wished. Other complaints documented a significant increase in the financial burdens placed on peasants by the lords. Rents were raised, as were both the size and number of other payments. The lords took more and more produce and livestock, they took the clothing of deceased fathers from their heirs, they even charged widows of murdered men a fee to find and try the murderer. To make matters worse, peasants were often prohibited from selling their goods at the market. In bad years, they had no guarantee of making it through the winter. As the grievances make clear, the peasants experienced these conditions not only as oppressive, but also as something new: the lords were changing the rules, "ancient tradition" was being violated, and it seemed to be happening arbitrarily.

Even if no one bothered to give the peasants an explanation for these changes, they were far from arbitrary. The lords, too, felt pressure. After the Black Death of the 1340s decimated Europe's population, something unprecedented happened: there was too much food. Farming was as inefficient as always, but now there was suddenly more grain in the fields than hungry mouths could eat. As a consequence, prices plummeted. Rural landowners saw their incomes plunge, as well. To protect their lifestyles, they max-imized control over their resources—and in an agrarian economy, the main resource was land. They also sought to expand their control over additional resources—and these were the people who worked on that land. The results are easy to trace in the peasants' complaints: lords took control of the "common areas" and declared them private property; peasants who continued to hunt there were arrested for "poaching." The lords raised rents, increased other fees and taxes, and otherwise sought to compensate for their lowered earnings. In addition, they built a fence around their "human capital"—the peasants who worked for them. Rental agreements were structured to last lifetimes and even to exceed lifetimes by binding the original tenant's heirs to the property. Once agreed, neither the tenants nor their descendents would ever again be free to leave those grounds—unless they were sold by the lord. Step by step, serfs were drawn into a bondage akin to slavery.

An illustrative example of how this process could work in detail comes from the land of Kempten, in the south-German Allgäu region. While the city of Kempten had gained free imperial status in the late Middle Ages, the surrounding lands were ruled by powerful prince-abbots of the Benedictine order. Their agenda since the early fifteenth century aimed at consolidating the various types of peasants in their territory and increasing their control over them. By a variety of means, they sought to pressure free and tenant farmers into serfdom (*Leibeigenschaft*), the lowest and most slave-like condition of peasant bondage. Those means included flagrant perjury. When the peasants filed a formal complaint against the prince-abbot in 1423, the man of the church forged a letter, allegedly written by Charlemagne, that purported to show that Kempten's tenant farmers had always been serfs. As was typical in such conflicts, the court sided with the abbot and endorsed his continued persecution of the farmers, whom it deemed "rebellious." Interestingly, the peasants then appealed to the pope—and succeeded in convincing Martin V to expose the forgery and reprimand the abbot. A generation later, though, the same patterns of oppression returned. The new prince-abbot did not resort to forgery, but abused his ecclesial position in other ways to pressure the peasants, excommunicating those, for example, who married spouses from territories not his own. Free farmers who questioned his extortionate tax increases simply had their lands confiscated—a straightforward act of larceny. Finding no support in local courts, the peasants appealed to the emperor, who saw merit in their case. There would be no time for justice, however, as soldiers of the Swabian League descended on the "insubordinate" farmers, destroyed their homes, and plundered their villages. From here on, conditions for the Kempten peasants worsened steadily. And their lot was by no means atypical. Peasants throughout Swabia, Bavaria, Austria, and Alsace experienced similar circumstances and filed similar protests. Prior to 1525, they did not argue for an end to serfdom (unlike many of their Swiss counterparts, who did so successfully), but simply for a restoration of their rights according to "ancient tradition." As in Kempten, courts of law generally sided with the rulers. There was a reason for such judicial bias. Courts were staffed by members of the ruling class and typically acted in the interests of that class. That pattern was reinforced by the political agenda of the German princes, which aimed at transforming loosely organized territories into centralized "absolutist" states. To do so, they created professional bureaucracies and filled judicial courts and administrative offices with men who shared their views. For the common people's hopes for justice, this spelled disaster. Old-style village courts, where peasants may have had some representation, were supplanted by new structures, where they had no voice at all and where their interests were not likely to find a sympathetic hearing.

Frustrated by the lack of response to their grievances—and seeking to defend themselves against the lords' armies—peasants began to take more drastic measures. They withheld payments, they went on strike, and they took up arms in rebellion. Accounts of uprisings occur all across Europe during the fifteenth and early sixteenth centuries. The most successful of these took place in Switzerland, where peasants often bettered their circumstances in the long run. The longstanding Hussite revolt in Bohemia brought mixed results. Most of the rest, however, failed. Uprisings in Hungary and Slovenia in 1514 and 1515 were crushed mercilessly, while smaller-scale efforts in Austria, Alsace, and southern Germany occasionally resulted in short-lived compromises but gained little long-term traction. Still, the unabated frequency of such uprisings unnerved the nobility. There was a basic instability in the lands that no amount of intimidation or even outright force seemed able to suppress. Landowners were particularly rattled by the increasing tendency of peasants to organize across jurisdictional boundaries. The peasants chose an unusual symbol for such gatherings: a shoe with long leather straps that wrapped around the calves where the shaft of a rider's boot would be. Called *Bundschuh* (from "bound" and "shoe"), this was a peasant's footwear and easily distinguished from a nobleman's riding boot. The point was obvious. Placed on a flag, the image became a symbol of organized peasant revolt and a call to arms. Its appearance signaled trouble.

In May of 1524, trouble came on a scale that no one could have imagined. The first tremors seemed harmless. Deep in the Black Forest, a small group of peasants denied allegiance to their lord, the Benedictine abbot of St. Blasius. About the same time, the villagers in Eschbach, a bit further west, declared their desire to be free of taxes—and to strangle their lords and clergy. A few weeks later, on June 23, a group of peasants in the county of Stühlingen and Lupfen went on strike. To amuse herself, the local countess had ordered them to interrupt their harvest to collect empty snail shells for her yarn. They refused. A whole litany of long-suppressed grievances now broke to the surface and fueled the strike. These events appeared unconnected at first, but they were local sparks of what turned out be an all-encompassing conflagration.

The initiators came from the Stühlingen group. Led by a charismatic speaker and former mercenary named Hans Müller of Bulgenbach (c. 1490–1525), they opened negotiations with the count. When these broke down, they organized protest marches through the Black Forest, recruiting supporters from other disgruntled peasant communities such as those near St. Blasius. Isolated local conflicts quickly grew into something much larger—and, importantly, something coherent. Townspeople from Waldshut, an evangelical city led by the theologian Balthasar Hubmaier (c. 1480–1528), pledged their support, and even Zurich sent soldiers across the border to protect the rebels. For the moment, though, there was no violence. Unsettled by the scale of organized protest they were witnessing, and remembering that most of their troops were off fighting in the Italian Wars, the lords bought time with further negotiations. Though these lasted most of the winter, they were fruitless. The lords typically demanded outright surrender, which the peasants found unacceptable.

In the meantime, though, the unrest had spread much further. Peasants all across southwestern Germany, including the long-suffering farmers of Kempten, joined together in regional alliances. Early in 1525, their rhetoric began to feature appeals to Scripture and the Word of God. Their exposure to the Bible led them to discover a far more potent legal principle than that of the undependable "ancient tradition"; they now called for "divine right" (*Göttliches*

Recht). With the help of a local Zwinglian pastor, Christoph Schappeler (1472–1551), and the lay preacher Sebastian Lotzer (c. 1490–?), the peasants drafted a new program: a series of political demands supported by Scripture and called *The Twelve Articles*.[2] Written in late February 1525, in the imperial city of Memmingen, the *Twelve Articles* became something of a declaration of independence to the wider peasant movement, calling for the abolition of serfdom, congregational election of pastors dedicated to the Gospel, local retention of tithes, and a restoration of traditional rural rights. Motivated by a sense of divine justice, the southwest German peasant alliances held a peasant parliament in Memmingen on March 5, and formed a broader "Christian Union" (*Christliche Vereinigung*) as a counterpart to the Swabian League of the lords.

The parliament discussed a common platform, based partly on the *Twelve Articles*, and aimed at a comprehensive reform of church and society according to "divine right." In early March, they began to implement this program, halting payment of taxes and tithes (which essentially ended the lords' superiority), opening castles to the common people, restoring peasants' fishing and hunting rights, and replacing hostile clergy in the churches. In Memmingen itself, the reforms went further, abolishing serfdom completely and establishing the free congregational election of pastors. At a subsequent meeting of parliament on March 15, members agreed to create a new judicial system, composed of judges who would decide in matters of divine law. Luther, Melanchthon and Zwingli topped the list. Representatives of the Swabian League continued to negotiate with the peasant leaders, seeking above all to gain time for organized retaliation. They rejected the list of proposed judges, by the way.

---

[2] The formal title reads: *Dye Grundtlichen Vnd rechten haupt Artickel, aller Baurschafft vnnd Hyndersessen der Gaistlichen vnd Weltlichen oberkayten, von wölchen sy sich beschwert vermainen.* ("The just and fundamental chief articles of all peasants and subjects of ecclesiastical and secular authorities in which they consider themselves aggrieved"). For an English translation of the text, see Scott and Scribner, 1991: 253–257, or LW: 46, 8–16. The document's contents will be discussed further, below.

As the negotiations dragged on fruitlessly, peasants began to lose faith in their leaders and take matters into their own hands. That meant violence. On May 26, peasants stormed a castle near Ulm and set it ablaze. Others soon followed. Not surprisingly, the abbey of Kempten loomed large in their sights, and the peasants took it over, confiscated its enormous treasure, and distributed it while the prince-abbot scurried to safety. In fact, few noblemen resisted, prompting one observer to compare them to a bunch of shivering old women. But the peasants' successes were short lived. Taking advantage of a respite in the Italian Wars, the Swabian League finally got back a good number of its troops, and these veterans now marched, led by the seasoned commander Jörg Truchsess von Waldburg (1488–1531), against the common people. Thousands died and were captured before Jörg—whose bloody campaign earned him the nickname *Bauernjörg* ("Peasant-George")—met a force that gave him pause. About 12,000 peasants had assembled near the cloister of Weingarten. Outnumbered, he weighed his options and decided to negotiate. The resulting Treaty of Weingarten (April 17, 1525), by which the peasants laid down their arms and disbanded for promises of future arbitration, effectively ended the rebellion in this part of Germany. Given its ambitious reforming program, which amounted to a religiously motivated social revolution, the Swabian Christian Union's abrupt end was a serious blow to the German peasants' cause. To this day, scholars are baffled by the peasants' willingness, given their military advantage, to sign such a treaty.

Meanwhile, though, peasants in other regions banded together and sought to acquire by force the rights they had been denied by negotiation. Many of these also saw initial success. The Black Forest bands, still led by Hans Müller of Bulgenbach, gained control over considerable expanses of territory and began to impose the *Twelve Articles*. In mid-May, Müller laid siege to the city of Freiburg with an army of 12,000 men, forcing its surrender on May 23. Now the peasants' political inexperience became evident. Once they captured the city, they had no idea what to do with it—and went home. They won a moral victory but failed to make strategic use of it. Such mistakes proved costly, and within a few months Habsburg troops had suppressed the rebellion violently and executed Hans Müller and other leaders.

In Franconia, peasants aided by rebellious townspeople took over Rothenburg ob der Tauber, and continued their march from there. Another band occupied the city of Weinsberg. Here bitterness toward the nobility vented itself in a brutal display of revolutionary vengeance. Count Ludwig of Helfenstein, son-in-law of the emperor, was in charge of Weinsberg's defenses. Accustomed to command, he disdainfully ordered the rabble to disperse, threatening to burn their villages and hunt down their women and children if they refused. The peasants not only refused, they attacked the castle and captured the count. One by one, he and members of his noble entourage were made to run the gauntlet, beaten and stabbed by the rows of assembled peasants until they were dead. A piper accompanied the spectacle with a tune. The Franconian bands next occupied the important city of Heilbronn, where they, too, set up a peasant parliament and drafted a program for an "imperial reformation" (Scott and Scribner, 1991: 259–264). They even pressured the powerful Archbishop of Mainz to accept their conditions. Their string of victories came to an end in Würzburg, however, where they took charge for several weeks and forced the bishop to flee, but remained unable to defeat the city's garrison. In early June, various armies converged on them from the outside and put an end to the Franconian rebellion.

As the Weinsberg massacre illustrates, the peasants were capable of considerable violence. Rarely, however, were the results that extreme. Far more often, it was the peasants themselves who were massacred. One of the most infamous of such cases took place on the evening of May 16, 1525, in the Alsatian city of Saverne. A huge force of peasants occupied the city when it was besieged by the arch-Catholic Duke of Lorraine. Known as "Antoine the Good," the duke bitterly hated anything that smelled of Protestantism—and his nose was particularly piqued by the peasants' revolt. Realizing they had no hope of escape, the peasants accepted Antoine's offer of surrender, gave up their arms and marched out of the city carrying a white flag. The duke's forces mowed them down, murdering more than 16,000 unarmed Alsatian farmers while Antoine looked on.

Recovering from their initial shock, the princes were regaining the upper hand. Their most celebrated victory—and one of the worst defeats for the peasant cause—came near Frankenhausen, in Thuringia. The theologian Thomas Müntzer (c. 1489–1525), who had been inspired by Luther in Wittenberg but whose subsequent course became both more political and more mystical, served as a military preacher for a peasant army organized in the imperial free city of Mühlhausen—where Müntzer was pastor. Thomas Müntzer remains one of the most controversial figures of the Reformation. Vilified by Luther and his followers ever since a highly polemical public exchange between the two in the summer of 1524, Müntzer was rehabilitated by Friedrich Engels in the nineteenth century and became something of a hero to the Marxist movement—which only made him more suspect to Western Lutherans. Unfortunately, little is known of the "real" Müntzer's background and early development, except that he likely stemmed from a bourgeois milieu similar to Luther's, and occupied himself with questions of social justice and a critique of feudal society early on. Müntzer also had a strong mystical streak that informed not only his theology but also his politics. For him, the two were closely connected. Like many Reformers, Müntzer believed that the true church was composed of the elect. He differed, though, in how he understood those elect and their calling in the world. Central to Müntzer's belief system was a conviction that the Holy Spirit illumines a believer's heart, and that that experience eclipses any external information provided by Scripture, the institutional church and its clergy. Müntzer did value these "externals," however: he put together a reformed liturgy in German, wrote hymns, and commended regular Bible-reading. A proper liturgy and true preaching could facilitate the more important mystical experience.

Unlike many mystics, Müntzer saw the Spirit's illumination as something directly pertinent to the world—and not as a means to other-worldly transcendence. Müntzer's mysticism does not cause the mystic to "leave" the world, but empowers him or her to change it. Illumined, the elect become agents of God's transformative will in human society, working for good and against evil. Given Müntzer's commitment to justice for the common people, his views easily assumed a revolutionary tone. That was particularly evident in a pivotal sermon Müntzer preached to two future Saxon electors, Duke John and his son John Frederick, on July 13, 1524, in the castle chapel of Allstedt, Saxony. Based on the story of Daniel's interpretation of Nebuchadnezzer's dream in Daniel 2, Müntzer casts himself as a new Daniel, called to preach the truth to the rulers before him. That truth prepares the way for complete social transformation—a world in which godlessness, fraud, and exploitation cease, and the elect govern according to their values. Tellingly, it is the poor laypeople and peasants who recognize God's will most clearly. They form the cornerstone of the true church. But if the princes are on God's side, they will make themselves his instruments and join the cause. Ominously, Müntzer continues: "If, however, they do not do it the sword will be taken from them" (*Spiritual and Anabaptist Writers*, 2006: 68). Where Luther preached obedience to temporal powers for the sake of order, Müntzer envisions a higher order that relativizes—and even destroys—temporal powers that stand in its way. Whatever else one may think of Müntzer's theology, this was a courageous thing to preach to that particular "congregation." Within weeks, Müntzer was summoned to a hearing. Egged on by Luther, the authorities were reining him in. He fled to the free city of Mühlhausen.

Twice the size of Zurich, Mühlhausen was one of Germany's largest cities. It had gained its wealth during the Middle Ages through textile production and trade, but had in recent years seen economic stagnation. Socially stratified, it was governed by a city council that drew heavily on the upper classes and marginalized a significant part of the remaining population. That was about to change. In 1523, a former Cistercian monk named Heinrich Pfeiffer (?–1525) began to preach inflammatory sermons and organize popular resistance against the council. The protesters' demands included greater political representation as well as reform of the churches; if they were not supplied with evangelical preachers, they would elect their own. An armed insurrection forced the council to accept the demands, which temporarily restored a brittle peace. This was the situation Müntzer, who quickly befriended Pfeiffer, found in August of 1524. Müntzer's preaching animated the common people and revived their previous grievances—now articulated in sharpened terms. Müntzer and Pfeiffer called not only for greater representation for the common people, but for a complete replacement of the old council with a new one dedicated to divine justice and elected for life. This went too far for many, however, and the preachers had to leave Mühlhausen in September. Müntzer traveled to southwest Germany and Switzerland, where he met with peasant leaders, as well as with the theologians Balthasar Hubmaier of Waldshut and Johannes Oecolampadius of Basel. By February of 1525, however, both he and Pfeiffer were back in Mühlhausen. This time, their program gained acceptance and the city was turned into a "Christian democracy."

Mühlhausen became a source of inspiration for peasants throughout Thuringia, and in April and May of 1525, these, too, began to rise up like their counterparts in Swabia and Franconia. In Müntzer's eyes, this was the apocalyptic moment of truth when the God-fearing would at last prevail over the wicked. He organized troops to come to the peasants' aid. All in all, 7000–8000 peasants gathered near Frankenhausen on May 12 to battle the princes. Müntzer took the role of military chaplain and fired them up with his eschatological message. Initial skirmishes went in favor of the rebels, but by May 15, the full forces of Landgrave Phillip of Hesse and Duke George of Saxony were assembled and began their attack. Panicked peasants ran for the city walls; most were slashed and gored by riders on the fields, others hunted down and killed in the streets of Frankenhausen. Six-thousand peasants died; the princes lost six soldiers. Müntzer managed to hide in the city, but was found, tortured, and held captive. The princes now marched on Mühlhausen, which they accused of fomenting the rebellions. They forced its surrender, stripped it of its free imperial status, and exacted debilitating reparations. Both as a prominent economic center and as an experiment in Christian government, Mühlhausen was finished. The same was true of the Thuringian peasant movement and its leaders. Heinrich Pfeiffer, who had stayed behind during the battle, was found and executed on May 27. Müntzer was brought to town and decapitated on the same day.

Though local uprisings continued throughout the summer, the German peasants' rebellion was effectively over, crushed by the lords and princes. The Reformation had reached a turning point.

Up until 1525, common people saw in the Reformation a reason to hope for greater justice. That had several causes. On the one hand, the general feeling of fundamental, even apocalyptic change energized the common people who had so much to expect from any promise of change. Luther and Zwingli stirred those expectations with their rhetoric of Christian freedom and their personal stances against clerical abuse of power. Some of the Reformers' teachings gave the people particular cause for hope. Any peasant, Luther and Zwingli each had said, could read and understand at least as much of the Gospel as a priest or bishop—if not more. For a German peasant, such words had a significance that transcended their original theological context. In the peasants' experience, priests and bishops were not only religious authorities, they were also—and much more tangibly—oppressive landowners. Anti-clericalism was an ever-present motif of the peasant uprisings, and thanks to Luther and Zwingli, it now seemed to gain theological underpinnings. Rural people began to hope that they, too, would benefit from the ecclesial restructuring that the Reformation had launched. They thought they would have something to say about how it happened—a *jus reformandi* of the common people. In all of this, the Reformers were an inspiration. It is almost touching to see how naïvely the Memmingen peasants, for example, called upon Luther, Melanchthon, and Zwingli to be their judges—their helpers in the quest for divine right.

As they would soon learn, those hopes were misplaced. Zwingli did support the peasant cause in part, but Luther and Melanchthon turned their backs on the common people, each issuing a stinging refutation of the *Twelve Articles*, with Luther even imploring the princes to kill the "robbing and murdering hordes of peasants." For the Lutheran Reformation, the consequences were bitter. Never again would Luther's thought resonate with the same force in rural Germany. Abandoned, the peasants grew sullen and lost interest in what now seemed simply like a religion of the rulers. Luther complained about their intransigence and stupidity for the rest of his life—and never seems to have grasped the cause.

Apart from their political losses, the peasants' defeat meant the end of an important vision for reordering church and society. That vision did not have time to reach optimal coherence, but several features already stood out by April 1525. At the very least, the peasants argued for greater political representation within the existing system and communal control of tithes and taxes. As time went on, however, many began to argue for an entirely new, post-feudal order. Their emphasis on common ownership of properties and distribution of wealth according to need flew in the face of the old order. It also proved irreconcilable with the commercial values that dominated the cities. Many of the peasants were headed toward a prototypical form of communism. With respect to the church, two aspects of their demands—articulated in the *Twelve Articles*, but more and more common thereafter—stand out: the authority to elect their own pastors, and the right to use their own tithes to support that pastor. This meant a significant change in how clergy and laity related to each other. These measures would put an end to the identification of priests with feudal lords; the priest would not come to the village as landowner and out-sider, but as servant—one to whom the peasants were proud to pay a salary with their own incomes and of their own volition.

To understand why Luther objected to this vision, it is worth taking a closer look at his response to the *Twelve Articles*, written in April of 1525.[3] Luther's rejection of the peasant cause—and especially his vitriolic language in later writings—has long lacked a satisfying explanation. Some historians put it down to the Reformer's political naïveté, or to a concern that "his" Reformation, dependent on princely support, would be lost if identified with insurrection. Others speak of Luther's social conservatism. Such judgments are no doubt partly true. But there may well have been deeper reasons. If Luther was "conservative," what, exactly, was he trying to conserve? What, conversely, was he struggling—however naïvely—to prevent?

Surveying Luther's writings prior to 1525, one is struck by the paucity of references to peasants and rural life. It is likely that Luther had only a very vague conception of the conditions that motivated the peasants' revolt—and he admits as much in his response to the articles. Of the 12, he only addresses the first three,

---

[3] *Admonition to Peace. A Reply to the Twelve Articles of the Peasants in Swabia* (LW: 46, 17–43).

passing over the legal issues concerning taxes and access to common lands. These were the issues that caused the rebellion in the first place, but Luther concedes that he is unqualified to address them. He focuses on those matters that came later, the notions of "divine right" that linked the uprisings with the Reformation. After chiding the lords for failing to live up to their Christian duties and for exploiting the peasants, he proceeds to distance himself from the peasants' own appeal to "the Gospel" to legitimate their demands. They have not understood the Gospel at all, he exclaims, but teach something entirely different: "The Gospel, however, does not become involved in affairs of the world, but speaks of our life in the world in terms of suffering, injustice, the cross, patience, and contempt for this life and temporal wealth. How then, does the Gospel agree with you?" (LW: 46, 35ff). One could take issue with this, of course, and it is a position that Luther himself contradicts elsewhere, but he is not interested in a sustained discussion of the matter. He has made his point: the peasants may invoke the Gospel and divine right, but they do so in a way that is not Luther's.

Clarifying "the Gospel" is not Luther's primary concern. As he turns to a refutation of the first three articles ([1] The entire community should have the power and authority to choose and appoint a pastor; [2] Tithes should be used locally to pay that pastor; and what is left over distributed to the poor and needy; [3] Serfdom should be abolished), another issue emerges. Luther is far more preoccupied with the question of *property*. Congregations should only elect their own pastor as a last resort—but then make sure to pay him "from their own possessions," not from money they owe the lord (that is, their regular tithes). Doing otherwise constitutes "robbery and theft." Withholding tithes from an overlord in order to pay a pastor directly is also "nothing but theft and highway robbery." Even abolishing serfdom "absolutely contradicts the Gospel"—not because it has nothing to do with justification by faith, but because it "proposes robbery, for it suggests that every man should take his body away from his lord, even though that body is the lord's property" (LW: 46, 37–39).

Luther does not seem prepared to consider the possibility that existing property rights or feudal relations may themselves contradict God's teaching. In other words, he has not understood the theological intent of the *Twelve Articles*—nor is he inclined to try. That is probably not surprising. The *Articles'* position aims at a communal definition of property—ultimately, a sharing of possessions and resources—that puts it at odds with the property-owning ethos not only of the feudal lords, but also of the urban bourgeoisie. Even though the peasants' positions were not developed fully at this stage (and there was a considerable variety of positions and agendas within the peasant movement), their implicit threat to the regnant understanding of property and its corresponding social order was quickly evident to Luther. Unwilling to take their views seriously as a prelude to an alternative social model, he rejects them out of hand as an endorsement of "robbery."

That is not simply conservatism; it is in some ways a progressive position. The principles of property ownership Luther defends were the foundation of the new order that began to assert itself on European society during the late Middle Ages, beginning with the cities but affecting rural feudal structures as well. His reaction to the peasants' communal spirit has much in common with the Florentine citizens' rejection of the Franciscans discussed above. It is an established type of argument. Even Luther's invective against the peasants—accusing them of acting out of "self-interest," of wishing to "rob" and "steal" what is not theirs, and so on—simply echoes hackneyed slurs uttered against protesting peasants everywhere in Europe for 200 years. One is tempted to say that Luther was behaving true to his (middle) class—but that is a bit facile. In any case, Luther's statements do more than affirm princely authority; they fit into a broad stream of Renaissance thinking that defends the new order of wealth and private property. It is hostile not only toward incursions like those of the peasants, but also to the more advanced theological critiques offered by the Franciscans.

While it is easy today to criticize Luther's attitude toward the peasants, one needs to remember that the property-owning principles he defends, while arguably extortionate, became the cornerstone of contemporary Western culture. Most Western Christians share his assumption that private ownership is worthy (and are unenthusiastic about its alternatives); nations enshrine the defense of property in their constitutions. Those who profit from these values seldom question the price that others pay for them. Far from "conservative," Luther's response to the *Twelve Articles* is in that regard perhaps unwittingly "modern."

The Anabaptist Alternative

Whether today's commentators regard Luther's refutation of the peasants as "conservative" or "modern," a good number of his own contemporaries thought his commitments un-Christian. While these people were rarely part of the peasants' movement, they shared some of its values and developed them further. They sought to restore a more purely Christian life patterned after the apostles. They were the heirs to the great medieval reform traditions embodied, though in different form and habit, by the wandering Celtic missionaries or the early mendicant friars. Loosely organized, they went by a variety of names, but their enemies called them "Anabaptists."[4]

The Anabaptist movement sprang up from a variety of sources. One of these lay in a conflict between the city of Zurich and its rural dependencies over tithes. Tensions between the rural and urban populations of Switzerland—and of Zurich in particular—were nothing new, but in 1522 and 1523, they were animated by Zurich's Reformation and the spirit of change it radiated. Zwingli himself had written critically of tithing practices, and though he targeted old-church abuses rather than the system itself, his rural followers understood his words as a more sweeping critique. Their interests were similar to those of many rural people in such circumstances, and anticipate demands formulated two years later by the German peasants: they wanted to use their tithe-payments

[4] "Anabaptist" comes from the Greek word for re-baptism; it was a polemical term that seized on this group's practice of believer's baptism—which in the early years often resulted in "re-baptizing" persons who had already been baptized as infants. Today it is used by Mennonites and other heirs to the Anabaptist tradition to describe themselves.

directly to support a priest of their choice rather than send them to a far-away agency that, aside from pocketing a percentage itself, sent them a clergyman of its own choosing. A direct challenge to the tithing system came from the village of Witikon, outside Zurich, which elected its own pastor—an energetic Reformer named Wilhelm Reublin—in December 1522, without securing permission from the Grossmünster chapter in Zurich. The chapter agreed to let the matter pass if Witikon continued paying its tithes—and supported Reublin from additional funds (anticipating Luther's response to the first of the *Twelve Articles*). Witikon complied, but a sense of injustice remained in the air. Reublin began agitating against the wealthy—including "indolent" clergy. Other villages joined Witikon in asking Zurich's city council to suspend the tithe payments. The council refused. Zwingli supported the council's decision and wrote one of his best-known works, *Divine and Human Righteousness*, in June 1523 to defend the tithing practice (Zwingli, 1984). While not a matter of "divine justice" it is a legitimate part of "human justice," Zwingli argued—something governments may impose to maintain civic order. Not only the villagers, but also part of Zwingli's own circle in Zurich—including Konrad Grebel—were disappointed. Grebel spoke of a new "tyranny."[5]

This conflict over tithes set the stage for the much deeper split in Zurich between the Grebel circle and Zwingli after the Second Disputation in October 1523 (see the section "Zurich, Zwingli, and the Cities"). Here, Grebel and others saw their worries confirmed as Zwingli once again deferred the Reformation's agenda to Zurich's councilmen, slowing down reforms to the mass and suspending the removal of images. In their view, Zwingli had subordinated God's word to human interests—and this they could not do. Grebel, Felix Mantz, and others began to organize on their own, meeting in small circles in private homes to study Scripture. They brought to their Bible studies the same urgency that had driven their opposition to Zwingli, and began to sharpen their

---

[5] Historians have long argued about how and where the Anabaptist movement began. A recent and richly detailed account, to which I am indebted here, is provided by Snyder (2007: 51ff).

emerging vision of a more apostolic church. Given the voluntary nature of their own association, one issue particularly caught their attention: *baptism*. Infants who are baptized have no choice in the matter; their membership in an institutional church is therefore non-volitional and, these Reformers argued, merely nominal. More importantly, there is no explicit mention of infants being baptized in the New Testament. During the summer and fall of 1524, Grebel and Mantz began developing their conception of baptism as an "outward sign" of an "inner reality" coupled with a public commitment to live in the community of believers. Practically speaking, this called for adult believers' baptism and the construction of a voluntary "free" church, a position Grebel and Mantz began to take openly. At around the same time, Reublin again attracted attention—this time by advising parents in Witikon not to baptize their infants. Controversy ensued and escalated when Zwingli, challenged by Mantz to defend infant baptism, did so—by arguing that infant baptism is neither commanded nor prohibited by Scripture. Its closest analog, according to Zwingli, comes in the Old Testament practice of circumcision, also a rite of initiation, and also performed on infants. The controversy continued.

On January 17, 1525, Zurich's city council held a disputation between Grebel, Mantz and Reublin on the one side, and Zwingli on the other. Perhaps not surprisingly, the council sided with Zwingli and issued two mandates on January 18 and 21 that effectively outlawed their opponents' notion of believers' baptism. The first decreed that all infants should be baptized "as soon as they are born"; those parents who had delayed baptizing their children had eight days to comply or be banished. The second decree expelled Reublin and all members of Grebel's circle who, like Reublin, were not citizens of Zurich. Those allowed to remain—such as Grebel and Mantz—were banned from public speaking or even from meeting to discuss the issue further. In other words, the Anabaptist Bible studies were closed down.

What happened next has come to transcend mere history; its account, recorded by the *Hutterian Chronicle* some time later, has become something of a foundational narrative for the Anabaptist tradition. It describes the movement's religious genesis. On

January 21, the evening the second decree was published, Mantz, Grebel, and others, most likely including Reublin and Johannes Brötli, a priest in nearby Zollikon, withdrew to the house of Mantz's mother. Joining them was a fairly new member of the group, Jörg Blaurock, a former priest. They prayed together.

> After the prayer, Blaurock stood up and asked Konrad Grebel in the name of God to baptize him with true Christian baptism on his faith and in recognition of the truth. With this request he knelt down and Konrad baptized him. Then the others turned to Jörg in their turn, asking him to baptize them, which he did. (*Hutterian Chronicle*, 1987: 45)

A new church was born. Already the next day, members of the circle continued baptizing adults in the surrounding villages. According to the city council's accounts, 80 adults were baptized within the following week.

Why was adult baptism so popular? A number of factors were involved. On one level, lay Christians were reclaiming their church. This was a moment that harkened back to the earliest days of Christian community, when people responded spontaneously to the call to faith, experiencing inspiration and the start of a "new life." This, the participants could tell each other, is what it must have been like in the book of Acts. There must have been something deeply moving in that discovery of "church"—not as something defined and dictated from "above" by some external authority, but as something that sprang up from out of their midst spontaneously. On a more historical level, one can draw parallels between these events of adult baptism, which were coupled with highly emotional acts of repentance, and the long Christian tradition of penance. There was a popular craving for such rites, and a combination of neglect (through absent priests and a lax culture) and corruption (through the indulgence trade) had frustrated it. Now, in something resembling a revival, the people's religious needs began to resonate—they were finding an answer. Beyond that, some people were simply convinced by the Scriptural arguments—and believed they were finally doing God's will.

Whatever the reasons for adult baptism's spread, Zwingli and the Zurich council were intent on stopping it. Throughout history, authorities have tended to take a dim view of religious revivals and the seemingly anarchic energies they release. Zurich was no exception. Theological reasoning may also have played a role in their decision-making, though the issue was probably a bit fuzzy to most; even Zwingli needed time to convince himself that he supported infant baptism. More pressing was the Anabaptists' open defiance of the council's authority. This was worrisome. The council's authority over religious affairs was still shaky and could not afford a public failure. In addition, many had come to link the rural Anabaptist movement with the peasant uprisings, and that made them even more unwelcome. Such anxieties may help explain the severity of the magistrates' subsequent reaction. Within days of the offending baptismal services, Mantz and others were arrested. For the moment, no one seemed to know what to do with them, though, and they were released again with an admonition to cease their illegal baptizing—which they of course did not heed.

Within a year, Zurich's councilmen discovered a long-neglected provision of Roman Law that defined re-baptism as a capital offense. On March 7, 1526, and with Zwingli's active encouragement, the magistrates decreed that subsequent re-baptisms would be punished by death and—no doubt licking their lips at the irony—specified death by *drowning*. Undeterred, the Anabaptists stayed the course. Felix Mantz was the first to be captured under the new law. On January 7, 1527, he was taken down to the river Limmat, hauled out to an abandoned fishing hut and drowned. He became the first Anabaptist martyr. He would not be the last. It was a remarkable development for a Reformation that had begun by preaching freedom from ecclesial tyranny, but had now come to execute its own.

The remaining Swiss Anabaptists went underground. Most of the leaders were captured and executed anyway: Johannes Brötli left to continue his ministry near Schaffhausen and was burned at the stake in 1528; Jörg Blaurock could not be executed legally in Zurich because he was a foreign citizen, so the authorities took whips and drove him out of the city—he was burned at the stake in Austria in 1529; Ludwig Haetzer, another member of the circle, was beheaded in Constance in 1529; Konrad Grebel was captured but escaped execution by succumbing to the plague in August 1526.[6] The Anabaptist movement was not confined to the Zurich circle, however. Similar initiatives were forming elsewhere, and Grebel's group early on established communication with several of their theological kinsmen in other areas. In the summer and fall of 1524, Grebel, Mantz and their friends began corresponding with Karlstadt, who encouraged them vigorously, and with Thomas Müntzer. Their letter to Müntzer, written September 5, 1524, survives, and is significant for articulating two principles that would later help define the Anabaptist movement: use of the "ban" as a form of church discipline exercised by the congregation; and a rejection of violence, a point at which they differed with Müntzer.

The Grebel circle also contacted Balthasar Hubmaier in Waldshut. Hubmaier had gone through a remarkable development, beginning as a student of John Eck (!) in Ingolstadt, where he received a doctorate in theology in 1512, taking a high-profile post as cathedral priest in Regensburg, and then, perhaps alienated by the local pilgrimage business but for reasons ultimately unknown, left his post for the remote Black Forest town of Waldshut in 1520. Here, he began to rededicate himself to the study of Scripture, started reading Luther, and eventually contacted Zwingli across the border in Zurich. Like many, though, he was soon alienated by Zwingli's performance at the Second Zurich Disputation; Hubmaier desired more strenuous reforms. He had also begun to question infant baptism. His theological training and great erudition—he was the best-educated of the early Anabaptists—made him an invaluable ally to Grebel's group. His writings, cut short by the premature death he shared with so many other martyred "radicals," are the most complete and eloquent record of early Anabaptist theology.

[6] The indefatigable Wilhelm Reublin, on the other hand, managed to elude authorities in several countries, eventually renounced his Anabaptist beliefs, changed his name and rode off into history's sunset; no one knows exactly when—or if—he died.

After receiving believer's baptism from Wilhelm Reublin in early 1525, Hubmaier persuaded Waldshut's magistrates to implement an Anabaptist Reformation. His support of the Black Forest peasants indicates a desire to expand the project beyond the city, conceivably toward establishing a regional "folk church." Though the Waldshut efforts were soon crushed by Habsburg soldiers and Hubmaier exiled, the fact that an Anabaptist "magisterial" Reformation took place at all is significant. While much of subsequent history shows the Anabaptists in opposition to civil authorities and adopting a rigorously separatist form of community, Hubmaier's experience in Waldshut suggests that this separatism was at least partly a consequence of magisterial persecution. After 1525, there was no hope of achieving a comprehensive state-sponsored Anabaptist Reformation in places such as Zurich, and most Anabaptists had no choice but to be separatist. Their early "free church" emphasis may have made that step easier, but in developing such impulses further, they were also making the best out of a decidedly unfavorable situation. Hubmaier, however, never gave up hope of repeating his Waldshut success. After he left the Black Forest and settled in Moravia in 1526, he again sought to implement reforms that combined the efforts of church and civil authorities. Once more, though, Habsburg intervention cut his endeavors short; Hubmaier was apprehended and taken to Vienna, where he was tortured and finally burned at the stake on March 10, 1528. His wife Elisabeth was also executed; Austrian authorities tied stones around her neck, threw her off a bridge and watched her drown in the Danube.

Though the Anabaptist movement was spreading, persecution, coupled with the chaos of the 1525 peasant wars, threw it in disarray. Added to this was a challenge of integrating the various groups that had emerged in different geographic areas. Next to the Swiss and south German Anabaptists, there were Saxon followers of Karlstadt and of Müntzer, as well as smaller circles in regions of Switzerland, Germany, Austria, and Alsace. Efforts to consolidate these scattered fragments culminated in a conference in the northern Swiss town of Schleitheim in February 1527. Its most important accomplishment was the adoption, on February 24, of a series of seven articles of faith and order known as the

Schleitheim Articles (or *Confession*). Drawing in part on Hubmaier's theology but going beyond it on several important points, the articles were drafted by Michael Sattler (c. 1490–1527), a former Benedictine prior who became a leading Anabaptist preacher in southwest Germany and was brutally executed by the Habsburgs a few months after the conference.

The first article reaffirms believer's baptism, linking it with repentance and commitment to a new life in Christ. The second builds on that commitment by tying it to congregational discipline, drawing on Matthew 18, 15–17, where Jesus speaks to the disciples of the "ban": if a member sins, other members speak to him or her privately twice, and if that fails the matter is brought before the congregation and can result in exclusion from communion. That topic is treated in the third article, on "the breaking of bread." Importantly, communion, defined in a Zwinglian sense as something done in "remembrance" of Christ's suffering, is only permissible between members who are "beforehand united in the one body of Christ," that is, who confess the same faith and who are reconciled. Article four develops that notion of a congregation united in faith and discipline further by advocating separation from "the world" and rejecting fellowship with all those who "have not united themselves with God." While article five speaks of the election of pastors, the final two give examples of "worldly" behaviors to be avoided: any use of the sword, including participation in civil government; and the swearing of oaths.

Interestingly, one item is not included in the *Schleitheim Articles*, though one might have expected to see it there: a rejection of tithes (that is, a call for communal retention of tithes). Some historians argue that this represents a move to dissociate Anabaptism from the now-failed peasants' rebellion, in which tithe-reform had been a prominent demand. In any case, it was replaced materially with another, more comprehensive economic provision: a call to sharing possessions.

Though not mentioned by the *Schleitheim Articles* themselves, community of goods was stipulated in congregational ordinances that emerged around the same time, and was part of even earlier discussions. Based on a reading of Acts 2, 45 and 4, 32, which describe the apostles as having "sold all their possessions and distributed them according to need," and forming a community in which no one "possessed anything of his own, but they had everything in common," many early Anabaptists sought to apply this apostolic precedent to their newfound experience of church. Similar efforts toward Christian communism appear to have been fairly common in rural contexts where a strong communal ethos prevailed, and it is no surprise that the Anabaptists, many of whom had rural backgrounds, and all of whom were uncompromising in their readiness to apply biblical values to their own situation, would have adopted such models. Though it remains unclear to what extent these early groups had opportunities to put their communistic principles into sustained practice, the mere mention of such things struck a nerve with the established authorities. Equally nettlesome were declarations that income derived from interest, including interest charged on loans, is unChristian and amounts to usury. This cut to the heart of early capitalist principles. Clearly agitated, the city governments of Zurich, Bern, and St. Gallen, who were divided in so many other matters, swiftly found a common voice in attacking the Anabaptist threat to their commercial economies in 1527:

> They hold and say that no Christian, if he really wants to be a Christian, may either give or receive interest or income on the sum of capital; that furthermore all temporal goods are free and common and everyone can have full property rights to them. For we are reliably informed that they repeatedly declared such things in the beginnings of their arbitrarily created brotherhood and in this way moved the poor simple-minded souls to adhere to them. (Stayer, 1991: 96)

Such complaints were common, and were reiterated in Switzerland by Zwingli, paralleling Luther's critique of the peasant articles. Beyond the specific issue of baptism, persecution of Anabaptists was most often legitimated by charges of sedition. And while the resolutely peaceful comportment of the Anabaptists after 1525 appears to provide few grounds for such a charge, their economic teachings evidently did—at least in the eyes of their critics. Soon, too, these teachings would be put into practice. As the Anabaptist movement developed further in the decades after Schleitheim, some form of sharing possessions was almost always part of its communal life, varying in degree from commitments to "mutual aid" all the way to a rigorous renunciation of money and private property. It was one more way by which these Christians distinguished themselves from the world around them—and one more reason to separate themselves from it.

The success of the *Schleitheim Articles* was mixed. It proved useful in unifying many Anabaptist communities, especially in Switzerland. After the Zurich expulsions in 1525 and the ongoing persecution by Zwingli and his successor Heinrich Bullinger, such communities were no longer viable within the state of Zurich. But they did sprout up and even flourish in other Swiss territories, particularly those that adopted a Reformed Reformation later, such as St. Gall or Appenzell. Other territories, such as the Aargau, were subject to complicated jurisdiction—in this case shared between Zurich and Bern—and were therefore less tightly regulated, allowing greater religious diversity. Some of those early Anabaptist communities survive to the present day.

Anabaptists also gained footholds in many of the south German imperial cities, particularly in Augsburg. Here, the *Articles'* rejection of the sword and of oaths met objections from local Anabaptist leaders such as Hans Hut (1490–1527), a former follower of Thomas Müntzer who survived the massacre of Frankenhausen before moving to Augsburg and accepting believer's baptism. Hut and others argued that Christians could in fact work for temporal government, but that the state had no business interfering in the church. That position is, of course, a natural one when the only kind of state interference one has thus far experienced has come in the form of brutal persecution. But it is also interesting to note that these Anabaptists have gone through the fire of a magisterial Reformation and emerged on the other side espousing a *libertas ecclesiae* that recalls the principles of eleventh-century Gregorian reform (see "The Rise of the Papacy: Centralization and Reform" in Chapter 1). Differences between south German and Swiss Anabaptists on these issues led to a conference in Augsburg in August 1527—called the "Martyrs' Synod" because most of its participants were executed shortly afterwards (Hut died in prison). Agreement between the parties remained elusive, but the conference is also significant for authorizing a mission initiative. A new wave of persecution cut that short by decimating the Anabaptist movement in southern Germany; untold numbers of these earnest Christians were executed in cities such as Augsburg in 1527 and 1528, the men beheaded, the women drowned.

Intense and unabated persecution gave rise to an ethos of martyrdom among early Anabaptists—the conviction that steadfastness in the face of persecution, torture, and death not only confirmed the authenticity of one's faith, but also provided a witness to the greater community. Martyrdom also reinforced the Anabaptists' restorationism; parallels between their own persecution and that of the apostles underscored their closeness in spirit to the early church. Documents such as the seventeenth-century *Martyrs Mirror* catalogued these events and preserved them for the edification of future generations.

Persecution also had a negative effect on the movement's coherence, however. Losing leader after leader, the Anabaptists lacked the continuity that a gifted figure such as Luther can provide over a span of many years. The Anabaptists met the fate that Lutherans avoided when Luther survived the Diet of Worms. This, and the lack of political backing and administrative support made them naturally more diverse than the magisterial branches of the Reformation. Aside from the Swiss Anabaptists and those who survived in Swabia, there were groups that gathered around moderate figures such as Pilgram Marpeck (?–1556) in Strasbourg and southern Germany, the apocalyptic visionary Melchior Hoffman (c. 1495–1543); and radical spiritualists such as Caspar Schwenckfeld (1489–1561) and Sebastian Franck (1499–1542), whose skepticism toward the salvific value of any external rites included baptism and therefore took them beyond the bounds of the Anabaptist movement proper. Schwenckfeld, one of the most interesting figures of the Reformation, corresponded frequently with Anabaptist leaders—as well as engaging in polemical exchanges with Lutherans—and wrote a considerable body of work. He made no effort to form a church, however, and it was not until after his death that a movement of "Schwenckfelders" took shape—eventually moving to North America. The followers of Menno Simons (1496–1561), who emerged in the Netherlands, became the largest group of Anabaptists to continue to the present.

Some of the most significant Anabaptist settlements grew in the relative safety of Moravia, to which many exiled members—including Balthasar Hubmaier—fled. Moravia, located in the modern-day Czech Republic, was governed formally by the Catholic Habsburgs after 1526, but its local nobility resisted Austrian rule as much as possible. Long accustomed to harboring Bohemian Brethren and other Hussite dissenters, the Moravian lords practiced a broad-minded religious tolerance that forestalled the kind of Habsburg persecution that terrorized religious minorities in other parts of Europe. Here, the Anabaptist social model had a chance to flourish.

There were several types of Anabaptist community in sixteenth-century Moravia, some of which were divided along fault lines already present in Switzerland and Swabia (for example, disagreements over the role of government, and oaths) and competed openly with each other. The largest and most significant of these groups were also the most radical: the rigorously separatist and communitarian Hutterites.

Named after the Tyrolean lay preacher Jakob Hutter (c. 1500–1536) who initially organized them, the Hutterites emerged out of a mix of earlier groupings and more recent refugees of the 1530s. They shared classic Anabaptist views on believer's baptism, but strengthened their emphasis on congregational discipline. It was the church—understood now as an organic community rather than a hierarchical institution—that conveyed salvation to its members. These not only joined, but "yielded" themselves to the congregation, submitting to its spiritual and ethical regulations, including those on sharing all possessions. Their commitment to a communistic economy prevented them from integrating into greater Moravian society, but that, of course, was their intention. Like many other separatist Anabaptists, they believed that salvation was not available in "the world" outside the community. They therefore had no desire to mingle with it. The Hutterites' rejection of oaths also made them resolutely post-feudal, since feudal relations were based upon oaths. Trade, on the other hand, was permitted with non-Hutterite neighbors, and this was important to their economic success. Their economy was based on the production of crafts and skilled services, which they traded for grain. Most other foods and wine were produced internally. The high quality of their goods and their reputation for industriousness allowed the Hutterites to interact very well with Moravian society; in fact, their goods and services were highly desirable. From an economic standpoint, their communistic society was a success.

Paradoxically, persecution—which took place episodically even in Moravia—strengthened the Hutterites while weakening other Anabaptist groups. By the early seventeenth century, conservative estimates place their total numbers between 20,000 and 25,000— accounting for 10% of the Moravian population (Rothkegel, 2007: 200). Some contemporaries thought there were three times that many, which may say more about the scope of the Hutterites' influence than about their true size. Their communistic economy was particularly successful during the so-called "Golden Years" of the later sixteenth and early seventeenth centuries—before they were once again dispersed by Habsburg persecution. Outside Moravia, the Hutterites' considerable mission activity expanded their influence and made them one of the most notable groups within the greater Anabaptist movement.

The Hutterites were the most successful and conspicuous of the many Anabaptist groups who practiced a form of Christian communism. Sharing possessions was not an end in itself, though, and not merely motivated by a rejection of materialism. Indirectly, of course, adopting such a life implies a profound critique of the commercial and consumerist society from which the members have chosen to separate. And it goes without saying that people such as the Hutterites were more "free" than their counterparts among the peasants of feudal Europe; in Moravia, they even had their own judicial system. But their primary motivation lay elsewhere. Like the Franciscans, they were concerned with following Christ and they understood that path to be characterized by self-denial and suffering. In addition, they cultivated a particular ethos of "yieldedness" (*Gelassenheit*), an almost mystical attitude of "letting go" undergirded by trust in the community. The driving force of that yieldedness is *love*. Love "reaches out in desire to unite with all people," writes Hans Denck in his short treatise "Concerning True Love" (1527). It also involves self-denial. "We might even say that love hates itself, for love selflessly desires only the good of others" (*Early Anabaptist Spirituality*, 1994: 112). In the hands of someone such as Peter Walpot (1521–1578), a great Hutterite leader and thinker during the Moravian "Golden Age," that vision of selflessly-giving love, if applied in the context of communal life, translated into Christian communism. Walpot gave this a classic exposition in his work, "True Yieldedness and the Christian Community of Goods" (1577), an extended interpretation of the Golden Rule ("Love your neighbor as yourself"):

> This little word "yourself" contains within it the idea of true community and all works of love and mercy which one person can show another person. Indeed, to love your neighbor as yourself is the measure of true community and all good things. Where God has poured out this kind of love in the heart of a person, true community is learned through the Holy Spirit and in the bonds of peace. There one seeks no advantage over the neighbor but rather mutuality and common concern for each other. ... For to love one's neighbor as oneself is not to have part, or even half, but the whole thing in common and to give all things for the common use. Anything less is a heathen and false love, not a Christian love. (*Early Anabaptist Spirituality*, 1994: 153)

The Anabaptist reform movement is often called a "Radical Reformation." That term is problematic if it refers only in a political sense to the supposedly "extreme" notions of communitarianism the Anabaptists developed, or to their "uncompromising" rejection of established political authorities and their consequent separatism. The term "radical," derived from the Latin term for "root" (*radix*), also describes the Anabaptists' desire to return to the "roots" of Christian society. Deep within those roots lay timeless Christian notions of transformation and renewal. In the Latin West these were linked early on with the practice of penance. As it developed, that practice was largely individualized— *private* confession, absolution, and penitential actions—and clericalized—depending on the actions of a priest to be considered valid. Centuries of additive commercialization and corruption, and also more benign changes, had covered up much of the early penitential spirit, however. With a remarkable sharpness of vision, the Anabaptists shoveled away that sediment and exposed something of the original transformative ethos that had driven earlier Christians. At the same time, though, they added a new dimension that brought something of their own age. Transformation became *communal* rather than simply individual; it also lost its clerical-hierarchical add-on. The entire community engaged in a kind of collective penance—a renunciation of greed and other egotistical vices, and a commitment to charity and selflessness that would not have been sustainable on an individual level and in fact required communal solidarity to be practicable. It drew both on monastic patterns as well as on the communitarian social spirit of late-medieval villages. What emerged was a new model of "radical" Christian living. Here was a genuine Christian alternative not only to the late-medieval church, but also to the prevailing norms of secular society. It was at once post-feudal and non-capitalistic. Regrettably, it was a model for which the rest of European Christendom had little stomach.

References

The following is a list of works cited and consulted in this chapter. Though it is only a small selection of relevant literature, it is a good place to start for further reading.

The Book of Concord. 2000. *The Confessions of the Evangelical Lutheran Church*, ed. Robert Kolb and Timothy J. Wengert. Minneapolis: Augsburg Fortress.

Early Anabaptist Spirituality. 1994. *Selected Writings*, transl. Daniel Liechty. New York: Paulist Press.

Hutterian Chronicle. 1987. *The Chronicle of the Hutterian Brethren*, transl. and ed. Hutterian Brethren. Rifton, NY: Plough.

Luther's Works. (LW). 1955–. *American Edition*, vols. 1–55. Philadelphia: Fortress Press.

Moeller, Bernd. 1987. *Reichsstadt und Reformation* [Imperial Cities and the Reformation]. Revised edition. Berlin: Evangelische Verlagsanstalt.

Rothkegel, Martin. 2007. "Anabaptism in Moravia and Silesia." In *A Companion to Anabaptism and Spiritualism*, ed. John D. Roth and James M. Stayer, pp. 163–215. Leiden: Brill.

Scott, Tom and Schribner, Bob. 1991. *The German Peasants' War: A History of Documents*. Amherst: Humanity Books.

Snyder, C. Arnold. 2007. "Swiss Anabaptism: The Beginnings, 1523–1525." In *A Companion to Anabaptism and Spiritualism*, ed. John D. Roth and James M. Stayer, pp. 45–81. Leiden: Brill.

Spiritual and Anabaptist Writers. 2006. Ed. George H. Williams and Angel M. Mergal. Library of Christian Classics 25. Louisville: Westminster John Knox Press.

Stayer, James M. 1991. *The German Peasants' War and Anabaptist Community of Goods*. Montreal & Kingston: McGill-Queen's University Press.

Zwingli, Huldrych. 1984. "Divine and Human Righteousness." In *Selected Writings of Huldrych Zwingli*, ed. and trans. Wayne Pipkin, vol. 2, pp. 1–41. Allison Park, PA: Pickwick Publications.

Further Reading

Blickle, Peter. 1992. *Communal Reformation: The Quest for Salvation in Sixteenth-Century Germany*. Atlantic Highlands: Humanities.

Blickle, Peter. 1998. *From the Communal Reformation to the Revolution of the Common Man*. Leiden: Brill.

Blickle, Peter. 2004. *Die Revolution von 1525* [The Revolution of 1525]. 4th edition. München: Oldenbourg.

A Companion to Anabaptism and Spiritualism, 1521–1700. 2007. Ed. John D. Roth and James M. Stayer. Leiden: Brill.

Dennison, James T. 2008. *Reformed Confessions of the 16th and 17th Centuries in English Translation, vol. 1: 1523–1552*. Grand Rapids: Reformation Heritage Books.

Dipple, Geoffrey. 1996. *Antifraternalism and Anticlericalism in the German Reformation: Johann Eberlin von Günzburg and the Campaign against the Friars*. Aldershot/Brookfield, VT: Ashgate.

Dixon, C. Scott. 1996. *The Reformation and Rural Society. The Parishes of Brandenburg-Ansbach-Kulmbach, 1528–1603*. Cambridge: Cambridge University Press.

Edwards, Mark U. 1975. *Luther and the False Brethren*. Stanford: Stanford University Press.

Franz, Günther. 1956. *Der deutsche Bauernkrieg* [The German Peasants' War]. Darmstadt: Wissenschaftliche Buchgesellschaft.

Gäbler, Ulrich. 1996. *Huldrych Zwingli: His Life and Work.* Philadelphia: Fortress Press.

Goertz, Hans-Jürgen. 1996. *The Anabaptists*, transl. Trevor Johnson. London/New York: Routledge.

Goertz, Hans-Jürgen. 2007."Karlstadt, Müntzer and the Reformation of the Commoners, 1521–1525." In *A Companion to Anabaptism and Spiritualism*, ed. John D. Roth and James M. Stayer, pp. 1–44. Leiden: Brill.

Goertz, Hans-Jürgen. 1993. *Thomas Müntzer: Apocalyptic, Mystic, and Revolutionary*, transl. Peter Matheson. Edinburgh: T.&T. Clark.

Gordon, Bruce. 2002. *The Swiss Reformation*. Manchester: Manchester University Press.

Hendrix, Scott. 2004. *Recultivating the Vineyard: The Reformation Agendas of Christianization*. Louisville: Westminster John Knox Press.

Lindberg, Carter. 2010. The European Reformations. 2nd edition. Oxford: Wiley-Blackwell.

Locher, Gottfried W. 1979. *Die Zwinglische Reformation im Rahmen der europäischen Kirchengeschichte* [The Zwinglian Reformation in the Context of European Church History]. Göttingen/Zürich: Vandenhoeck & Ruprecht.

Müller, Nikolaus. 1911. *Die Wittenberger Bewegung 1521 und 1522* [The Wittenberg Movement] Leipzig: Heinsius.

Packull, Werner O. 1995. *Hutterite Beginnings: Communitarian Experiments during the Reformation*. Baltimore/London: Johns Hopkins University Press.

Preus, James S. 1974. *Carlstadt's "Ordinaciones" and Luther's Liberty: A Study of the Wittenberg Movement.* Cambridge, MA: Harvard University Press.

Sider, Ronald. 1974. *Andreas Bodenstein von Karlstadt: The Development of His Thought, 1517–1525.* Leiden: Brill.

Wandel, Lee Palmer. 1990. *Always Among Us: Images of the Poor in Zwingli's Zurich*. Cambridge: Cambridge University Press.

Watts, Sheldon J. 1984. *A Social History of Western Europe, 1450–1720: Tensions and Solidarities among Rural People.* London et al.: Hutchinson University Library for Africa.

Williams, George Huntston. 2000. *The Radical Reformation.* 3rd edition. Kirksville: Truman State University Press.

Wunderli, Richard. 1992. *Peasant Fires: The Drummer of Niklashausen.* Bloomington: University of Indiana Press.

Zimmerman, Wilhelm. 1891. *Der grosse deutsche Bauernkrieg* [The Great German Peasants' War]. Berlin: Dietz.

Chapter 4

The Reformation's Establishment

The Princes Take Charge

With the peasants resubjugated and the Anabaptists elbowed to
society's margins, Europe's princes took charge of the Reformation.
Those who adopted it committed administrative energy and the
power of the sword to steer it into a more settled course. Those
who rejected it committed those same resources toward keeping
it at bay.

In the Empire, a number of princes and city magistrates made
public their sympathies for Luther in August 1526, at the First
Imperial Diet of Speyer. Having survived the peasant scare, these
rulers felt free to act on their inclination to support Luther and, in
so doing, take tighter control of religious affairs in their territories. Unlike the earlier Diet of Worms (1521), Speyer I took place
without the personal presence of the emperor.

Charles V, Holy Roman Emperor, King of Spain, Lord of the
Netherlands, and head of the Habsburg dynasty, had done his
best to suppress the princes' quest for further autonomy and to
end the Reformation within the Empire, but was persistently dis-
tracted by foreign affairs of greater urgency. In 1526, those pressures came from two fronts. The Ottoman Turks, who represented
an Islamic threat to European Christendom that had rulers all
across the continent fidgeting in their thrones, were advancing

The Reformation: A Brief History, First Edition. Kenneth G. Appold.
© 2011 Kenneth G. Appold. Published 2011 by Blackwell Publishing Ltd.

northward, besieging Belgrade in 1521[1] and much of the rest of Hungary in 1526. They conquered that kingdom in the epochal Battle of Mohács on August 29, just two days after the Diet of Speyer closed. On the second front, the King of France had allied himself with several Italian city-states and with Pope Clement VII (forming the appetizingly-named League of Cognac) to declare war on Charles. This was a rather perverse twist in alliances, pitting the Holy Roman Emperor, highest secular defender of the old faith against its supreme clerical leader, the pope. Charles' troops invaded the Holy City in 1527, unleashing a "Sack of Rome" reminiscent of the fifth-century barbarians and imprisoning the pope in one of his castles. The irony was not lost on Luther, who remarked jovially that "Christ reigns in such a way that the emperor who prosecutes Luther for the pope is forced to destroy the pope for Luther." (*Luther's Works*, 1955– [hereafter LW]: 49, 169).

With Charles preoccupied, the princes sought a provisional solution to the Reformation's crisis. Those with Lutheran sympathies, led by John of Saxony and Philipp of Hesse, outnumbered the pro-Catholic representatives at the diet and were able to agree, on August 27, 1526, to a suspension of the Edict of Worms (1521), which had banned Luther, prohibited his writings and mandated the prosecution of his followers. Speyer I left it up to the princes themselves to deal with the Reformation as each saw fit. That opened the door to legalizing Lutheranism in those cities and states whose rulers supported it.

Practical reform measures could now begin in earnest, since pressures of the kind that had encumbered Frederick the Wise in 1521 (see Chapter 3) were no longer a factor. That resulted in a wide-ranging secularization of church properties, as princes took possession of church lands and buildings, which often included abandoned monasteries, in their territories. They also plucked the longstanding thorn of clerical jurisdiction, thereby subjecting clergy to the authority of civil courts. Working in tandem with the Reformers, the Lutheran princes devised a system of *visitation*—an inspection of the territory's churches and schools

[1] The Serbian city belonged to the Kingdom of Hungary at this time.

carried out by a court-appointed commission that typically included leading churchmen and lawyers. Melanchthon wrote a famous "instruction" to the visitors in 1528, outlining their duties and drafting guidelines for pastors, congregations and schools. In many territories, such ad-hoc commissions would eventually mutate into "consistories," permanent administrative offices charged with oversight of religious matters. That process took many of the functions traditionally ascribed to bishops and anchored them in the prince's court, setting the stage for a princely regiment of the church.

Not surprisingly, Charles was displeased by the outcome of Speyer I. In March of 1529, he called another diet, again in Speyer. Here, too, he was unable to attend and delegated leadership to his brother Ferdinand, who had represented him three years earlier. This time, though, Ferdinand opened the diet by reading a proclamation by Charles. The emperor revoked the provisions of 1526 and reinstated the Edict of Worms. He also called for restoring the bishops' authority and halting all Lutheran "innovations" until a council ruled on them. Now, unlike the previous diet in Speyer, the Catholics had a majority and accepted the emperor's terms. The Lutheran minority resisted. In negotiations on April 19 and 20, 1529, they submitted a formal *protestatio*—making use of a constitutional provision designed to protect minorities from unjust majority decisions. This "Protestation," endorsed by five princes and 14 imperial cities, gave rise to the initially pejorative name "Protestant." Its supporters argued that they would each have to account for their decisions before God personally, and therefore could not in good conscience assent to the emperor's repressive measures, even if they were overruled by a majority. The newly-minted "Protestants" included John of Saxony, George of Brandenburg-Ansbach, Ernst of Brunswick-Lüneburg and his brother Franz, Philipp of Hesse, and Wolfgang of Anhalt, as well as the cities of Constance, Heilbronn, Isny, Kempten, Lindau, Memmingen, Nördlingen, Nürnberg, Reutlingen, St. Gall, Strasbourg, Ulm, Weissenburg, and Windisheim. With this legal step, the Empire's estates were religiously divided. They did agree on something else, however: both Catholics and Lutherans voted to punish Anabaptists by death. If Speyer II marked the birth of

"Protestant freedom," as is sometimes asserted, then that freedom was decidedly selective.

The legal consequences of Speyer II and the Lutheran "protestatio" remained unclear. Because Charles refused to accept the protest and continued to insist on having the majority's decision implemented, the Protestants had to be concerned with military reprisals. Their primary political alliance, the "League of Torgau," formed in 1526 in response to the recently formed Catholic "League of Dessau," was defensive, with no standing army but built on pledges of mutual military aid. Among the Torgau members was the city of Magdeburg, whose residents had Lutheran sympathies but were ruled by Archbishop Albrecht of Mainz and Magdeburg. They had particular reason to be concerned.

In this vein, Landgrave Philipp of Hesse sought to expand the Protestant alliance southward to include the Reformed territories of Switzerland. There was a major obstacle to those efforts, however: a bitter and very public argument between Luther and Zwingli over eucharistic theology. The debate focused on how to interpret Jesus' words of institution at the Last Supper (Mt. 26; Mk. 14; Lk. 22; 1 Cor. 11). According to Zwingli, Jesus' words "This is my body" and "this is my blood," spoken while he distributed the broken bread and the cup of wine to his disciples, do not make sense if understood literally. Bread cannot *be* a man's body; wine cannot *be* blood. Therefore, Jesus must have been using the verb figuratively to mean something like "this represents my body," or "this signifies my blood." Luther was appalled by what he saw as Zwingli's attempt to "explain away" the mystery of Christ's presence and to raise dictates of human reason above the clear words of Jesus himself. Luther was not bothered by the apparent absurdity of those words. In his view, if Jesus says "This *is* my body," then that is how we need to understand the sacrament: Christ is truly—and bodily—present.

Neither position was entirely new. While Luther rejected the medieval notion of transubstantiation as a definitive doctrine (see Chapter 2), he retained the traditional belief in Christ's "real presence," arguing that the body and blood were there *with* the bread and wine even if they did not "replace" them. How, exactly, that could be possible, Luther did not know. Nor did he feel that further explanation was necessary. There would always remain an aspect of the inexplicable in matters of religious belief. In this respect, the mystery of eucharistic union was analogous to that of the incarnation; both united the divine with the earthly in a way that transcended human capacities for rational understanding. Zwingli's position drew on a tradition of spiritualizing interpretations of the sacraments that circulated among some humanists, particularly in the Netherlands, but were also espoused by Karlstadt after he left Wittenberg. In fact, it was probably Luther's antipathy toward Karlstadt that, at least initially, fuelled his suspicion of Zwingli.

Modern-day readers may well ask what was at stake in this apparent debate over semantics. The consequences for sacramental practice were far from trivial, however. The entire dynamic of the celebration changed depending on which side one took. Zwingli—much like Karlstadt at his famous Christmas Mass—sought to give the sacrament back to "the people," to strip it, therefore, of its "magical" connotations and hierarchical choreography, and make it a congregational rite of remembrance. Here, the focus was on the congregation; the members distribute bread and wine to each other; they are the ones who *remember*. Luther, on the other hand, emphasized the divine actions in the eucharist. For him, it is God who acts. God brings something new— Christ himself—into the worship service, and this is what the congregation *receives*. That is expressed ritually in the distribution, which continues traditional practice: the congregation comes to the altar and receives the elements from the pastor.

The two sides had been arguing about these matters for more than four years before Philipp moved to reconcile them in October 1529. He was encouraged by the Strasbourg Reformer Martin Bucer, who envisioned a mediating position and felt some sort of compromise was realistic. The Landgrave invited Luther, Melanchthon, Zwingli, Oecolampadius, Bucer, and a small number of other theologians and church leaders to his castle in Marburg, where they negotiated for four days (October 1–4), at times heatedly, at others more soberly, but without resolving their differences. Pressed by Philipp, Luther quickly assembled a list of 15 articles of faith before adjourning, and secured Zwingli's agreement to the first 14. That, at least, signaled theological consensus on a wide range of topics, including the eucharist. They could not, however, agree on that part of the 15th article that addressed "real presence." While negotiations on this issue would continue—with Bucer finally crafting a compromise, called the "Wittenberg Concord" (1536), that was accepted by all but the Swiss Zwinglians—it would remain a source of division between Lutherans and Reformed for centuries. Philipp's political plans for a pan-Protestant union were put on ice.

In the meantime, Emperor Charles V wrapped up his most pressing military affairs, reconciled with Pope Clement VII, and turned his attention to the Protestant princes in Germany. Convening a diet in Augsburg in the spring and summer of 1530, Charles summoned the Protestants to give an account of their faith. Drawing on previous documents, Melanchthon put together a series of 28 articles of faith, of which the first 21 were meant to indicate Lutheran consensus with traditional doctrine, while the remaining seven addressed reform initiatives that were contentious (for example, clerical marriage, communion in both kinds, and the temporal power of bishops); there was no mention of the pope. Called the *Confessio Augustana* ("Augsburg Confession"), it was presented to Charles in German and in Latin on June 25, and read aloud by the Saxon chancellor—in German so that the general public who were assembled outside could follow along.

The Protestants initially hoped that discussion of the Augsburg Confession would lead to some sort of reconciliation, or at least an agreement to defer resolution of the contentious issues to a general council. Such considerations may also have moved the authors to condemn as harshly as possible the Anabaptists, who figure in several of the articles. The diet took a very different course, however. Warning signs appeared early on. Prior to Augsburg, John Eck had busied himself compiling a list of no less than 380 "heresies" of which the Lutherans were said to be guilty (published, together with 24 theses of Eck's own, as *404 Articles*). After the Augsburg Confession was presented, Eck, together with Johannes Fabri, Zwingli's opponent at the First Zurich Disputation, and Johannes Cochläus, confidant of Albrecht of Mainz and one of Luther's most vehement critics, prepared a rebuttal, called the

Confutatio. The authors critized all 28 of the Lutherans' articles—including the 21 deemed uncontroversial. Reconciliation was beginning to seem unlikely. Melanchthon, who was busy negotiating behind the scenes, drafted an *Apologia* that responded to the confutation's charges. Charles refused to accept it. By now, the Protestants recognized that Charles would not be an impartial judge but was in fact siding with Rome. They began to leave. On November 19, Charles promulgated a final decree, the Recess of the Diet, mandating restoration of Roman practices and ceremonies, and demanding enforcement of the Edict of Worms. The Protestants had until April 15, 1531 to comply.

Politically, Charles's position was more awkward than his tone suggests. Augsburg had exacerbated rather than lessened the confessional division in the Empire, and Charles had few good options for reuniting it. A military strike against the Protestant estates was one possibility, but was rejected by the Catholic princes, who were concerned that the emperor's increased power would also come at their expense. The other obvious option was a general council. In fact, Charles very much desired a council and repeatedly implored the pope to convoke one. Popes were pathologically averse to councils, however, and Clement VII predictably refused—prodding the emperor to subdue the Protestants "by other means."

Faced with the possibility of a forced return to the old faith—and an end to the Reformation—the Protestants redoubled their efforts to form an effective defense alliance. Building on the League of Torgau, they began to expand their membership. Finding themselves outside the bounds of imperial law, they advanced legal theories that legitimated resistance against an unjust emperor for the protection of one's own subjects. Luther, who had not attended the Diet of Augsburg because of threats to his safety, concurred and called on the German people to "defend the Gospel." In February 1531, the Protestant estates formed the Schmalkaldic League, led by Electoral Saxony and Hesse, and comprising all estates who were willing to sign the Augsburg Confession. It fielded a standing army. The inner-Protestant differences that Marburg failed to resolve in 1529 were now lessened by the increased likelihood of war. Personal obstacles receded, as well, after Zwingli was killed in a Swiss civil war in October 1531 (see below). Those south German imperial cities that had sympathized with him (Strasbourg, Constance, Memmingen, and Lindau even presented their own confession, the *Confessio Tetrapolitana*, at Augsburg), now signed the Lutheran document and sought the Schmalkaldic League's protection. Other cities and principalities followed. Because of its defining status for the League, the Augsburg Confession was more than a mere summary of Lutheran theology; it had become the foundational document for a political movement. Furthermore, thanks to this text, that movement understood itself as "confessional." Religious affiliation defined political identity.

Despite these martial overtones, a temporary resolution proved easier than expected. Again, the emperor's political agenda forced his hand. He needed German support to ward off a renewed invasion by the Turks, and he wanted to see his brother Ferdinand elected King of the Germans—which required cooperation of the Protestant estates. These demanded suspension of the Recess of Augsburg. While Charles would not sign on to such an agreement himself, he authorized two of the Catholic princes to negotiate with the Protestants. The resulting *Nürnberger Anstand* ("Peace of Nürnberg") was signed on July 23, 1532, and restored the Protestant estates to a situation much like that created by Speyer in 1526. Their reforms could continue—at least until a council addressed them. Importantly, the treaty was left open toward potential signatories that might wish to join the Reformation at a later date. For the time being, this was a significant settlement since it returned the Protestants to imperial legality and allowed the Reformation to go forward. It was, of course, only temporary: though Charles supported the treaty, he did not sign it, which left his options open; other Catholic estates also refused to acknowledge it; and the appeal to a future council made the religious situation provisional.

For nearly 15 years, the peace held and Lutheranism expanded in the Empire. Though neither the emperor nor a church council had given final approval to the Reformation, the Reformers were by now disinclined to wait. In their view, the truth of the Reformation's basic positions could not be overturned by these authorities anyway; Scripture—and not emperors or councils or popes—grounded that truth. And so they began the process of building new church institutions in place of the papal-episcopal polity that had failed them. The key to those efforts was education.

Lutheran educational reform took on an almost staggering dimension and was one of the most ambitious cultural projects to emerge from the Reformation. Its long-term effects were profound. Schools were built in towns and villages, and made available to both boys and girls. As many children as possible were to learn how to read and write and gain competence in math and other subjects. Visitation records indicate that some rural people resisted these efforts and kept their children away from the local schoolhouses, but, over time, literacy increased markedly. The Bible was, of course, the most popular text. Similarly significant was Luther's encouragement of domestic devotional life: parents were to teach their children and households the basic tenets of evangelical Christianity. His pioneering *Small Catechism* (1529) provided instruction for this purpose, explaining the Ten Commandments, the Apostle's Creed, the Lord's Prayer, and the sacraments. At a higher level, universities took on a central role in the life of Lutheran churches. Existing universities were reformed and new ones, such as the University of Marburg (1527), founded. They not only trained future pastors, they also administered ordination examinations, thereby monitoring the quality of Lutheran clergy and contributing to its theological consistency. Melanchthon drafted guidelines for ordination exams and their topics with his *Examen ordinandorum* of 1552. All of these initiatives increased the educational level of Lutheran clergy dramatically—particularly when compared to many pre-Reformation situations in which clergy merely had to demonstrate an ability to read. In time, aggressive scholarship programs, which were particularly pronounced in Electoral Saxony, made university education accessible to entirely new social classes, as well. The Reformation was transforming German culture.

Institutional oversight of Lutheran churches passed from bishops to territorial princes and, in urban settings, to city magistrates. The transfer was not one-to-one, however. Temporal rulers typically set up commissions—like the consistories in Electoral Saxony and other territories—to monitor church life. Even here, though, those authorities generally shared their supervisory function with church "superintendents"—the evangelical successors to bishops. Wanting to redefine the episcopacy as a pastoral office rather than one mixed with temporal power and lordship over land (as was the case with prince-bishops), the Reformers in Germany renamed it—though "superintendent" was simply a Latin translation of the Greek "episkopos"; both meant oversight. Congregations played a role in church administration, as well, usually having at least some say in the appointment of their pastors, for example.

That process of church-building continued until shortly after Luther's death (of natural causes) on February 18, 1546. Almost as if on cue, Charles now decided to invade the Lutheran lands, precipitating the Schmalkaldic War of 1546–1547. His timing was dictated not by Luther's passing, though, but by his improved political fortune. Pivotal to his plans in Germany was the defection of Moritz of Saxony (1521–1553), duke of the Albertine Saxon territories, which included the cities of Leipzig and Meissen. While Moritz supported the Reformation (unlike his predecessor Duke George, who fiercely opposed it), his confessional loyalties gave way to political ambition—earning him the epithet "Judas of Meissen." Moritz especially desired the electoral privileges that were attached to the Ernestine Saxon throne and held by his cousin John Frederick I—whom he hated.

With Moritz's support, imperial armies marched through Protestant Germany and conquered the Schmalkaldic League in short order. In April 1547, Charles himself stood in Wittenberg's Castle Church and looked down on the grave of Luther—whose Reformation he had now halted. Pressed by aides to exhume the Reformer's body and put it "on trial" (a common procedure for deceased heretics, who were subsequently mutilated and burned), Charles refused. He had enough living trophies: both John Frederick of Saxony and Philipp of Hesse had been captured. Threatened with decapitation, John Frederick signed over to Moritz his electoral dignity and large parts of his territory, including Wittenberg ("Capitulation of Wittenberg"). John Frederick and Philipp remained imprisoned until 1552.

Having conquered the Schmalkaldic League, Charles now set about reversing the Reformation. Since the pope had finally convoked a council in 1545, and that body was still meeting, Charles deferred ultimate measures to its authority and sought a temporary solution instead. Passed at an imperial diet in Augsburg in 1548, this measure became known as the "Augsburg Interim." It mandated wide-ranging restoration of pre-Reformation rites and practices, though it also contained a number of concessions to the Lutherans. As a result, it was unpopular with Catholics and Lutherans alike. The former insisted that it had no application in their territories. Lutheran reactions were mixed. Many imperial cities, particularly in the south, enforced the Interim and expelled Lutheran clergy (Martin Bucer, for example, had to flee Strasbourg). Most of the cities in the north refused, however, as did a number of Lutheran princes. Others made only token efforts at enforcement. Moritz of Saxony published a weakened version with the help of Melanchthon that sought to rescue Lutheran doctrinal concerns. Known pejoratively as the "Leipzig Interim," it proved unpopular as well.

Outright resistance to the Interim was particularly pronounced in the city of Magdeburg, whose leaders cranked the presses and sent a flurry of polemical literature against the Interim sailing through the land. This was illegal, and imperial troops laid siege to the city, but the Magdeburgers stayed resolute. Fortunately for them, Moritz of Saxony led the siege and was having a change of heart. Ever resourceful, the newly-minted elector now saw political advantage in resisting the emperor—and at last stood up for his faith. He made a secret pact with Magdeburg, feigning the siege in exchange for lordship of the city. At the same time, he reconciled with the other Lutheran princes and even secured political backing from the king of France—who was as eager as anyone to see Habsburg interests thwarted. He got his wish. Moritz led a "Revolt of the Princes" that reclaimed Protestant territories, sent Charles scampering across the Alps, and culminated in the Peace of Passau in 1552. In addition to liberating the captive princes John Frederick of Saxony and Philipp of Hesse, the Passau treaty recognized Lutheranism as a legal religion and called for a final settlement at an upcoming imperial diet. That diet took place in Augsburg in 1555, brokered by Charles's brother Ferdinand, who was King of the Germans. The resulting "Peace of Augsburg" established protection and rights of worship for all "adherents to the Augsburg Confession." It divided the Empire along confessional lines, according to a principle that was later known by the formula *cuius regio, eius religio* ("whose reign, his religion"): a prince's personal confession would become the official confession of his land. Inhabitants of the other confession were allowed to emigrate. Furthermore, Lutheran princes were given formal custody of the churches in their territories—recognizing a process that had begun with the 1526 Diet of Speyer.

With the Peace of Augsburg, the Lutheran Reformation in the Empire was secure. The fact that this was accomplished by an imperial diet rather than a church council is significant. The Council of Trent was still open in 1555 and could, at least theoretically, have served as a forum for religious peace. Protestants mostly did not attend the Council of Trent, however, and had by now given up hope that any papal instrument—including councils—would give them a fair and reasonable hearing. Resistance to the Interim had also shown how deeply entrenched Reformation convictions had become; this was a political fact that no theological judgment could overturn. Lutheran beliefs were there to stay. Even Germany's Catholic princes appeared to recognize this and, desiring peace and stability in the Empire, understood that it would have to come by political means. They were therefore willing to negotiate with their Lutheran counterparts. The losers in that process were the pope, who rejected the treaty but was powerless to change it; and the emperor, who saw his influence over the German princes diminish substantially. That was no accident; Catholic and Lutheran princes alike wanted to increase their territorial powers at Charles's expense. At the end of the day, the prospect of power united the princes where religion did not—and that, paradoxically, made peace possible.

The Peace of Augsburg established a certain kind of religious pluralism in Europe. Commentators have sometimes pointed to it as the beginning of religious tolerance, but that goes too far.

For one thing, the Peace did not extend to Calvinists[2] or to Anabaptists (much less to non-Christians). These groups continued to count as "illegal." Second, the Peace did not so much "create" a plurality as ratify one that was already present. If one looks beyond the theological differences between Catholics and Lutherans—most of which have since been found reconcilable—one sees a clash over polity and jurisdiction. When the princes took charge of their churches, they both revived and at the same time modernized the old medieval notion of royal church leadership. They created a religious jurisdiction apart from the pope—*churches* apart from papal authority. That was a clear rejection of the principles enunciated by documents such as *Dictatus papae* or *Unam sanctam*, which made subordination to the pope a requirement of true Christianity. At Augsburg in 1555, imperial law settled the medieval debate between royalism and papalism—not by declaring a victor, but by recognizing *both* in separate jurisdictions. Implicitly, of course, that was a serious setback for the papal model of church unity. Unlike that of the princes, it had universal ambitions, and these were now thwarted. This vision of unity had never been realized completely before the Reformation, and now, it seemed, it never would. The papal church that emerged after Augsburg and Trent would be one church among others, one ecclesial model among several.

Reformation Beyond the Empire

While the Reformation may have begun in the unique cauldron of the Empire's politics and religiosity, it spread beyond these bounds fairly quickly. Next to the special case of Switzerland, to

---

[2] The question of Reformed adherence to the Confession was somewhat controversial, complicated by Melanchthon's revisions to the original document. Calvin—and some of his German followers—signed a 1540 edition, known as the *Confessio Augustana variata*, which avoided specifying the mode of Christ's presence at the eucharist. Most Lutherans, however, rejected this document and insisted on using the original from 1530 (*C. A. invariata*).

which we shall return below, Scandinavia merits particular attention. Since 1397, the five countries of Denmark, Norway, Iceland, Sweden, and Finland were essentially ruled by a united monarch who in the early sixteenth century resided in Copenhagen. Here, too, lay the key that opened Scandinavia to Lutheranism.

The Reformation in Denmark provided so much human drama that even Shakespeare would have needed several *Hamlet*s to do it justice. Something, indeed, was "rotten in the state of Denmark" in 1520—but historians have long disagreed on what it was. King Christian II (1481–1559) is a likely candidate. His ruthlessness was remarkable even by that era's standards and made hard-bitten German princes seem wide-eyed by comparison. Many of his contemporaries thought him insane. On the other hand, he was also one of the most progressive social reformers in Europe and openly supported burghers and peasants at a time when that was not at all common. His endorsement of—and evident interest in—biblical humanism helped bring sweeping change to Denmark's cultural life. And while his radicality saw him exiled before those projects came to full fruition, his efforts helped set the stage for the Danish Reformation.

When Christian II was crowned in 1513, Denmark was effectively an empire, stretching from the German border in the south all the way north across the Arctic Circle, and reaching from Iceland in the west to Finland in the east. Geographically, it was much larger than the Holy Roman Empire ruled by Christian's brother-in-law, Charles V. To call all of this "Denmark," of course, requires something of a sleight-of-hand. The Danish king's authority over the other Nordic countries rested on the Treaty of Kalmar, signed in 1397, which agreed to unify the crowns of Norway, Denmark, and Sweden. The resulting union was not always happy, and Christian's ascendency came at a time when the Swedes, in particular, were eager to leave. Determined to prevent that, Christian marched into Sweden in 1520, defeated the anti-unionist forces, and had himself crowned and anointed by the pro-unionist Archbishop of Uppsala, Gustav Trolle. Inviting Sweden's church and secular leaders to celebrations in the palace afterwards, Christian used the opportunity to have his opponents arrested and tried by Trolle. The accused were sentenced to death.

Between 80 and 100 Swedish leaders, including the bishops of Skara and Strängnäs, were decapitated or hanged on November 9–10, 1520. The "Stockholm Bloodbath," as it came to be known, wiped out Sweden's elite, but did little to unify the realm. Reactions to Christian's brutality propelled Sweden to independence and lifted the Vasa dynasty to the Swedish throne in 1523.

Back in Denmark, Christian's opponents were aghast—but happy to use the massacre to their political advantage. Christian II was especially unpopular among the Danish nobility and higher clergy. They had good reason. Like other European rulers of his day, the king strove to undercut the powers of these elites wherever possible and to expand his own authority. In Christian's case, those efforts brought at least partial relief to the Danish peasants, most of whom lived on lands owned by the nobility or the church. Christian's new Code of Laws prohibited the selling of peasants, called for their education, and otherwise shifted the balance of social influence away from the higher nobility and clergy. Religiously, Christian also tended toward modernization. In terms of ecclesial polity, he desired to establish a national church under royal auspices. He also showed more than a passing interest in the Lutheran Reformation, inviting theologians from Wittenberg to come to Copenhagen in 1521 to teach. Even Karlstadt showed up for a few weeks. At the same time, a reform movement began to stir in parts of Denmark, drawing on progressive Catholic humanist foundations and including a popular preaching revival by Franciscans and Carmelites. Christian tentatively supported these efforts. All of this was controversial, and his opponents succeeded in overthrowing him in 1523, electing Frederick, Duke of Holstein, king in his place. Christian left Denmark and spent the rest of his life in exile—and plotting his return.

Frederick I promised to change his predecessor's progressive course and favored the previously harried counts and bishops—at the expense of the common people. That had less impact on the vision for a national church than one might expect, however. The bishops were no more fond of Rome than Christian had been, but their notion of a national church included independence from the king, as well. Rome had itself to blame for much of the Danish bishops' resentment; the papacy had rarely shown interest in the

Nordic churches and was often negligent about confirming episcopal appointments. In 1526, Frederick and the bishops took two steps toward founding a national church. They restricted eligibility for episcopal elections to the Danish aristocracy (which prevented the pope from sending them foreign candidates), and they ceased paying the pope to confirm those elections, diverting the fees to the king instead. This gave the bishops much of the influence they desired, but it did not make them independent of the king. In fact, Frederick surprised many by taking an unexpectedly avid interest in religious affairs—and that interest moved in a different direction from the reform-minded Catholicism of the bishops and leading humanists.

Beginning in 1526 and 1527, Frederick began offering protection to Lutheran congregations. He even exempted them from episcopal jurisdiction—effectively creating a parallel polity. Lutherans were still sparse; their churches grew around returning scholars who had spent time at Wittenberg and other German universities, and were encouraged by literature made available through Denmark's Hanseatic trade relations. Similarly to the Empire, Denmark's early Lutherans congregated in cities, especially Malmö and Copenhagen. The king's protection did not amount to an endorsement of the Reformation, but it allowed Lutheranism to gain a foothold in Denmark and it signaled Frederick's basic openness to this variety of reform over that of the more conservative Catholic humanism. That openness solidified into outright support a few years later, as Frederick invited a number of Lutheran theologians to Copenhagen in 1530 to draft a confession of faith, the *Confessio Hafniensis*, or "Copenhagen Confession."[3] Those assembled included the energetic Hans Tausen (1494–1561), a former monk who studied in Wittenberg and led a rapidly expanding Lutheran church in Viborg before the king called him to Copenhagen to continue his efforts in the capital. Tausen translated the Pentateuch as well as liturgical writings into Danish, helping lay a foundation for vernacular worship. He also played an important role in drafting the Copenhagen

---

[3]   An important document in its own right, the Copenhagen Confession was later superseded by the Augsburg Confession.

Confession. Frederick had intended to present the Confession to the National Assembly (*Herredag*) in July, 1530, coupled with a disputation, in order to ratify the Reformation with the assembly's support. The timing proved inopportune, however, as resistance from Catholic bishops and nobles remained strong, and the exiled Christian II threatened to invade. Formal adoption of the Reformation would have to wait.

Frederick's death in 1533 precipitated a civil war. Unnerved by his sympathy for Lutheranism, the Catholic bishops and noblemen refused to accept the subsequent election of Frederick's son, Christian III (1503–1559). The 30-year-old Christian was himself an outspoken supporter of Lutheranism and had already introduced the Reformation in his ducal territories in Schleswig and Holstein, creating a Lutheran seminary in the city of Haderslev. Opposition to Christian coalesced around Count Christopher of Oldenburg, whose military campaign sought to restore the deposed King Christian II. Known as the "Count's War" (*Grevens Fejde*), the conflict lasted several years until it was finally beaten back by Christian III, who took Copenhagen in July of 1536. Christian now moved quickly. He arrested all the Catholic bishops, accused them of having instigated the civil war, and then deposed them at a *Herredag* in October. Having thus cleared the table, the assembly then agreed to institute new Lutheran bishops (called superintendents) and to adopt a Lutheran church ordinance. Christian invited the Wittenberg reformer Johannes Bugenhagen to Copenhagen to draft the ordinance in 1537, and to ordain the new bishops. Upon his recommendation, Peder Palladius (1503–1560), who had studied in Wittenberg, took the most prominent spot as bishop of Zealand (*Sjælland*), the province that includes Copenhagen. Bugenhagen also presided over Christian's coronation on August 12. While Lutherans typically rejected the notion that monarchs derived their legitimacy by an act of the church, Christian insisted on a religious rite of coronation and anointment. Bugenhagen modified an existing Catholic liturgy, making it a "Lutheran coronation."

The Danish Reformation, which had begun as a grass-roots movement with intermittent royal support, had now become a king's Reformation along the patterns set by Germany's princes.

It was very much "top-down." While Christian III replaced the bishops, parish priests remained in office; they now simply had to "learn" the new faith and its practices. Remarkably, most seem to have done so without overt qualms of conscience; as a result, though, changes to traditional liturgical practice were often less radical than in the Empire. Parishioners by and large welcomed the reforms—though here, as in most of Europe, the perspective of the peasants, who had suffered significant setbacks over the previous decade, is not well-documented. Structurally, Christian's Reformation differed in one conspicuous respect from that of the German princes: it was episcopal. Where most of the church's authority in states such as Saxony was lodged in court consistories, in Denmark it lay with the bishops, or superintendents. It was men such as Peder Palladius who saw to the re-education of parish priests, implementation of new church ordinances, visitation of churches, and the introduction and administration of wide-ranging social programs.

Because of its broad and powerful aristocratic class, much of which saw itself as Catholic, Denmark's Reformation certainly profited from royal sponsorship and may even have required the kind of force that Christian applied on the counts and bishops to succeed. That situation was very different in Norway. Norway became a Danish province in 1537, losing its quasi-independent claim to the unified monarchy. In practice, Norway had been ruled by Danish kings for some time, but this streamlined that process and expedited the Lutheran Reformation's formal introduction into Norway. At the same time, it also hindered the Reformation. Norway's demographics were entirely different from Denmark's. The country was predominantly rural, with few aristocrats and a high percentage of free farmers (roughly 30 per cent compared to 10 per cent in Denmark [Oleson, 2003: 38]). Many of these people resented Danish rule on principle. And because Norway enjoyed a culture of humanistically trained and progressive clergy, the need for religious reform seemed less urgent. A greater danger lay in the confiscation of church properties by Danish aristocrats using the Reformation as a pretext. The fact that Lutheranism made use of the Danish language, with Danish Bibles and Danish hymnals, only deepened Norwegians' sense of alienation from the "foreign" religion that was being imposed upon them. For these and related reasons, Norway resisted the Reformation. Resistance was spearheaded by the last Catholic archbishop of Norway, Olav Engelbrektssøn (c. 1480–1538). Acting not only as the country's ecclesial leader, but also, as head of the Council of the Realm (*Riksrådet*), as its highest political official, Engelbrektssøn worked hard to achieve Norway's independence and to restore a purely Norwegian hereditary monarchy. To that end, he sought to impede the rise of Christian III, who stood for continued Danish rule as well as for the Lutheran Reformation, and supported the return of Christian II during the Danish Count's Feud. Denmark's royal representative in Norway, the Danish nobleman Vincens Lunge, was murdered by Engelbrektssøn's allies in January 1536, which further weakened the archbishop's position once Christian III emerged victorious. Engelbrektssøn fled Norway for the Netherlands, leaving the archbishop's chair vacant and Norway's Catholic church without a leader.

Engelbrektssøn's departure did not make introducing Lutheranism into Norway much easier for the Danish king, however. To begin with, he could find no suitable Norwegians to serve as bishops—the few who were qualified were unwilling. In some cases, deposed Catholic bishops were reinstated for lack of a better alternative. In others, Danes had to be brought in, which did little to win Norwegian hearts. Local priests showed such hostility to the new faith that Christian finally gave up and advised his administrators to soften their approach. Catholic practices remained largely in place and reform measures were suspended. In time, however, resistance gave way to a cautious acceptance of Lutheranism as memories of the tumultuous 1530s receded and the persistence of subsequent generations of Danish superintendents paid off. Jørgen Eriksøn (1535–1604), Bishop of Stavanger, who was born and educated in Haderslev, Denmark, threw himself into the work of bringing Lutheranism to the Norwegians. He used all the resources of his office to that effect, conducting countless visitations, stressing the education of priests, and even publishing his sermons. He also helped prepare Norway's own long-awaited church ordinance, adopted after his death, in 1607. This gave the Reformation firm institutional footing in Norway and eased its further implementation. As the seventeenth century unfolded, Norwegians began to claim Lutheranism for themselves—and typically on their own, often idiosyncratic terms.

Iceland showed no more enthusiasm for Danish domination than Norway did, but enjoyed certain natural advantages—one of which was an expanse of ice-cold ocean that separated it from the Danish king. Still, the Danes sent potent and often ruthless administrators to the island to impose their rule. After Christian III came to power, this included a forced introduction of Lutheranism.

The Reformation of Iceland illustrates very nicely the two modes of Christianization discussed earlier in this book. On the one hand, there was an institutional-political agenda, driven by the Danish overlords; it was resented by most Icelanders. On the other, there were the spiritual contents of Lutheranism, the new faith and values that the best of its proponents embodied and taught; these gradually took hold in Iceland. That makes the Icelandic Reformation a nuanced affair: though it contained the expected tensions between Icelandic nationalism and Danish subjugation, and between old and new faith, these did not always match. Some nationalists were Catholics, others were Lutherans. Consequently, additional factors drove Iceland's Reformation narrative, as well.

Demographically, Iceland was even more rural than Norway. Apart from the foreign lords, almost all of Iceland belonged to one of two social classes: peasants or clergy. Even these were not far apart: most clergy were nearly as poor as the farmers. The country's two bishops were exceptions to this, however. They were powerful figures who ruled from the two seats of Skálholt in the south, and Hólar in the north. At the time of the Reformation, each was occupied by a staunch and autocratic Catholic, Ögmundur Pálsson (c. 1475–1541) in Skálholt, and Jón Arason (1484–1550) in Hólar. Both fiercely opposed the new church ordinance commissioned by Christian III when it arrived in Iceland in 1538, with Ögmundur even sending out a pastoral letter to condemn it. Two Danish officials, Claus van Mervitz and Didrik van Minden, retaliated by attacking the ancient monastery of Viðey and confiscating its property. Now Icelandic national sentiments came alive, and the Althing, the country's ancient parliamentary assembly, promptly excommunicated the two Danes. At this moment, Lutheranism was identified with Danish oppression and theft of Icelandic property.

There were already Lutherans in Iceland, however, who, while practicing their faith in secret, were not agents of Denmark. One of these was Gissur Einarsson (c. 1512–1548), a protegé of Bishop Ögmundur who had studied in Germany. Shortly after the Viðey incident, the aging Ögmundur retired and nominated Gissur as his successor—apparently not fully aware of the latter's crypto-Lutheranism. Gissur now had to travel to Copenhagen to secure the king's approval, and, while he was away, Danish–Icelandic tensions again flared up around the Viðey issue. Didrik van Minden, on his way to further plunder, decided to stop in Skálholt to pay the bishop a visit. It was not cordial. Enraged, local farmers seized the Danish official and his nine aides and killed them. Word of this reached the king just as Gissur had his audience. Remarkably, the future bishop of Skálholt defused the situation, convinced the court of his Lutheran convictions, and promised to implement the new ordinance upon his return. Perhaps just as remarkably, he succeeded in introducing Lutheranism to southern Iceland after he arrived in Skálholt in 1540, becoming Iceland's first Lutheran bishop. Though practical changes were very modest, his patient and diplomatic approach allowed Icelanders to view a form of Lutheranism that was not synonymous with Danish oppression. He was aided by the efforts of a fellow Lutheran, Oddur Gottskálksson (?–1556), who translated the New Testament into Icelandic (published in Denmark in 1540 with a preface by the king), as well as a "postil" by the German Reformer Anton Corvinus, an annual cycle of sermons on the weekly lessons. Gissur encouraged his pastors to buy both, thus raising the level of their preaching and also ensuring that the new message was framed in the Icelandic language (avoiding the tensions caused by the lack of vernacular works in Norway).

Continued Danish intervention complicated Gissur's project, however. The Danish crown's relentless confiscation of secularized church properties was as unpopular as its forced imposition of the Lutheran ordinance. These were not helpful methods. Nor was the arrest of the frail former bishop, Ögmundur, who was carted off in 1541 to stand trial in Copenhagen for the murder of Didrik van Minden (Ögmundur died en route). Again, the new faith was linked with Danish autocracy, and resistance to Gissur remained strong, especially in the North. Bishop Jón still controlled the northern diocese and had managed to avoid Danish reprisals for retaining the Catholic faith there. After Gissur died unexpectedly in 1548, Jón saw an opportunity to reclaim the South, as well. Encouraged by Pope Paul III, who sent him a personal letter, Jón took his army to Skálholt in 1549 and dragged the new bishop away to a northern prison. The following summer, Jón went after the last of Gissur's allies in the South, but found himself surprised and captured instead. Rather than wait for royal officials to sail in from Copenhagen and put the bishop on trial, the local Danish magistrate had him executed right away. Jón and his two sons were beheaded in Skálholt on November 7, 1550. When the royal officials did arrive in 1551, they summoned leaders of Jón's territory to the northern town of Oddeyri in June and secured their allegiance to the Lutheran order. The last of the open resisters were now subdued.

While Lutheranism was herewith established institutionally in Iceland, it would take much more work to win over the Icelanders themselves. The most important early figure in that process was Guðbrandur Þorláksson (1542–1627), Bishop of Hórlar for an astonishing 57 years. A brilliant polymath, Guðbrundur published a complete Icelandic translation of the Bible (1584), an Icelandic hymnal (1589), a liturgical handbook that became the standard for two centuries (1594), and countless shorter works. Efforts like these ensured not only a higher level of clerical competence and liturgical accountability, they also impacted Iceland's literacy rate, which was nearly universal by the eighteenth century, and revived the island's venerable literary tradition. Iceland's appropriation of Lutheranism was enriched by such efforts. It was also made easier by the country's almost totally rural setting. Here, unlike the European continent, clergy lived in circumstances very similar to those of their peasant parishioners. The Reformation accentuated this by encouraging them to marry—which had the unintended side-effect of making pastors poorer. Since their incomes rarely sufficed to support a family, they often worked the land side-by-side with laypeople. That was not ideal—and Bishop Guðbrandur, for one, was concerned about raising clerical living standards to give pastors more time for study and preparation—but it did create a parish solidarity that was largely unique in Europe, and made Iceland's transition to Lutheranism comparatively smooth.

The Reformation of Sweden and Finland was a much longer and more complicated affair than that of western Scandinavia. Finland, though distinct from Sweden in culture and language, had been a Swedish province since the thirteenth century. The Reformation in both therefore followed the same institutional pattern directed by the Swedish crown. That made it heavily dependent on political considerations—and these, as it turned out, were enormous.

The Stockholm Bloodbath of November 1520 proved pivotal to the early-modern history of Sweden. Outraged at the brutal action of King Christian II and his Swedish helper, Archbishop Gustav Trolle, large parts of the population rose up in revolt. Many of these were peasants. Overwhelmingly rural, Sweden had only a tiny aristocracy; more than half the arable land was owned by free farmers, in Finland a staggering 95 per cent (Buchholz, 2003: 118). These peasants had no landlords, paid no rent, and were subject directly to the king. They were also accustomed to political freedoms and representation. In that respect, their situation was dramatically better than that of rural people anywhere else in Europe—even within Scandinavia. The only Swedish city of size was Stockholm, whose population of 6000 included a large number of merchants and craftsmen whose political interests overlapped with those of the region's peasants. Joining hands in rebellion against the Danish king, they laid the foundation for an independent Sweden and elevated Gustav Eriksson (1496–1560), later known as Gustav I Vasa, to the Swedish throne in 1523. His father Erik had been one of the victims in the Bloodbath. Gustav's ascent, which coincided with Christian II's forced departure from Denmark, marked the end of the Kalmar Union. Sweden was now in the hands of its own king.

One of Gustav's priorities lay in creating a national church. His incentive was likely economic rather than religious or particularly anti-Roman. Gustav badly needed money to repay the loans that financed the uprising. Secularizing church properties brought considerable wealth to the crown—and Rome's influence over Swedish dioceses had long been so negligible that it could hardly have inspired much animus. Gustav's agenda was helped by the simultaneous vacancy of nearly every episcopal see in his realm. Between the Stockholm Bloodbath, the subsequent backlash, and sheer fate, all but one of the Catholic bishops were gone. Irritated by the pope's desire to influence his choice of replacements (as well as by a disagreement over taxes), Gustav informed Rome that he would simply install bishops without papal confirmation. He solidified his plans in 1527 at a national diet (*riksdag*) in Västerås, which put the king in charge of all church properties and completed the break with Rome. Gustav had his national church.

The king showed little overt interest in religious content. And because much of the population remained religiously conservative (the peasants agreed to nationalizing the church primarily because they hoped to see their taxes lowered as a result), he saw little advantage in pressing forward with a reform program. On the other hand, Lutheran theology did have its uses. Gustav became acquainted with Lutheranism through two theologians associated with the cathedral of Strängnäs, near Stockholm: Olaus Petri (1493–1552) and Laurentius Andreae (c. 1470–1552). Petri, a student in Wittenberg when Luther posted his "Ninety-Five Theses," had been part of the Reformation from its first hour and returned to Sweden with an armful of Lutheran theology and a wealth of enthusiasm. Hired as a deacon in Strängnäs, he soon won over Andreae, who recommended him to Gustav. In 1524, the king appointed him city secretary of Stockholm. This not only gave him political clout, it also put him in charge of the city's printing press—which he put to good use. Laurentius moved to Gustav's court as a personal advisor and began teaching the king Lutheran theology. Above all, Gustav took an interest in ecclesiology, especially in the notion of a "people's church" as opposed to a clerical one—which he used to justify the church's nationalization at

Västerås. For Gustav, no one embodied "the people" as well as the king.

The Reformers had their own notions of what a "people's church" should mean, and this found expression in 1531, when representatives of the church elected Olaus's brother Laurentius Petri (1499–1573) Archbishop of Uppsala—bypassing the cathedral canons, who had traditionally elected the archbishop. They also defied the pope, who refused to acknowledge Petri's election and declared the archbishop schismatic. That failed to impress Gustav, however, and Laurentius Petri became the first Lutheran archbishop of Sweden, presiding at the king's wedding shortly thereafter.

Slowly but surely, Gustav appointed new bishops to vacant sees. One of these was the Finn Martin Skytte (?–1550), a Dominican friar who became bishop of Turku in 1528. This, too, took place without papal approval. Skytte, who did not adopt the Lutheran faith himself, nonetheless promoted Lutheranism in Finland, sending promising students to Wittenberg to study with the German Reformers. Michael Agricola (c. 1509–1557) was the most influential of these and traditionally takes credit for introducing Lutheranism into Finland. It was largely thanks to Agricola that the Reformation became more than a Swedish institutional act for Finnish-speaking people and gradually transformed their religious life. Aside from his skillful administration—as rector of Turku's Latin School, as assistant to the bishop, and later as bishop of Turku himself—it was his theological work that proved central to that effort. Importantly, those publications were in Finnish. In fact, his *ABC-Book*, a combination of primer and catechism, counts as the first book ever printed in the Finnish language. His 900-page prayer book, Finnish New Testament, and liturgical writings made Finnish a literary language—but also the language of this people's Reformation, making Finnish Lutheran culture distinctive even as it continued to labor under Swedish auspices on the one side and Russian expansionism on the other.

Sweden's royal Reformation was confused. Now that he had his national church, Gustav lost interest in reforming it, dithering for decades before dying in 1560. In 1541, the Petri brothers produced a Swedish Bible, called the "Gustav-Vasa-Bible." Olaus

Petri must have gritted his teeth at this, since Gustav had sentenced him and Laurentius Andreae to death only a year previously—for reasons unknown. Olaus's supporters managed to get the sentence suspended in time for him to present the Vasa-Bible. Clearly, Gustav was moving away from the Lutheran party—though the direction remained uncertain. Annoyed at having his overtures to the Schmalkaldic League rebuffed by the Germans, he began leaning toward Emperor Charles V. Any nascent revival of Catholic sympathy was quickly extinguished in 1542, however, by a peasant's revolt in southern Sweden that sought to defend traditional practices. Crushing the rebellion, Gustav now trumpeted his allegiance to the "new doctrine." Because there was no Swedish confession—nor an adoption of the *Augustana* or some other confession—the precise nature of that doctrine remained unclear. Institutionally, Gustav aimed at limiting the influence of the bishops, renaming them "ordinarii" and dividing dioceses to reduce their authority.

Because Gustav had concentrated so much ecclesial power in the throne and short-changed other structures, his death left the fate of the Swedish Reformation very much in the air. His son Erik XIV conquered Estonia, but appears to have lost his mind, and was deposed by his brother Johan III in 1568. Johan, who had fallen for a Polish princess, was enthusiastically Catholic and sought to restore the old faith to Sweden. Rome quickly sent a contingent of Jesuits to help. Even the Jesuits, however, expressed skepticism at the project's viability. As such, it is not surprising that a 1593 Swedish *riksdag* meeting in Uppsala upon Johan's death voted to reject his Catholic liturgy and to re-affirm the Lutheran ordinance it had approved in 1571. The clergy held to this even when subsequent monarchs vacillated. The Swedish church was beginning to find a *modus vivendi* with its fickle kings.

One of the most interesting sites of Reformation activity was Hungary. It was also the most ecumenical. Here, unlike virtually anywhere else in Europe, confessions learned to live peacefully side-by-side. The foundation for this remarkable state of affairs lay in Hungary's multi-ethnic cultural composition, which had brought together Magyars, Orthodox and Catholic Slavs,

Romanians, Greeks, Germans, and more for centuries. In addition, the Reformation coincided temporally with Hungary's occupation by Muslims.

Weak kings precipitated Hungary's decline during the fifteenth century, and a particularly intense peasants' rebellion in 1514 destabilized it further, setting the kingdom up for conquest by the Ottoman Turks in 1526. The Turks divided the kingdom into three parts: Habsburg Hungary, ruled by Austrians; Transylvania, governed by Hungarian princes under Ottoman suzerainty; and Ottoman Hungary, which was ruled directly by an Ottoman pasha. Prior to this, Hungary's Catholic population already had a strong taste for reform, cultivated by socially-critical Franciscans as well as by students returning from humanist universities and—by the 1520s—from Lutheran schools such as Wittenberg. While the Habsburgs brooked little dissent in other parts of Europe, their reach did not extend into Ottoman-occupied Hungary, and so the spirit of reform continued here. The Turks were perfectly happy to see Christians divided, and even seemed to enjoy the theological disputes themselves, often serving as judges at public disputations (Tóth, 2004: 216ff). Once Protestantism became better organized, they also recognized its value as a political buffer to a potential reconquest organized by Rome. As for the Hungarians themselves, they hoped for exactly that: for the pope to launch a crusade and liberate the kingdom. Therefore even the most fervent Protestants maintained an openness toward Rome. Ironically, few seemed to realize that they were better off under the religiously tolerant Ottomans than their counterparts in Catholic Spain or Italy. That was even more true for Anabaptists and for Antitrinitarians, who in fact fled those very countries to seek refuge in Ottoman Hungary and establish communities that could not have existed in either Catholic or Protestant-dominated Europe. It was an odd twist on the theme of a "magisterial Reformation." In Ottoman Hungary, the "magistrates" (the pashas and beys) could well have controlled religious affairs by imposing their own faith on the "infidels." Instead, they practiced an elaborate form of restraint, preferring instead to prevent one faith from dominating the others, and to maintain order by fostering religious pluralism.

Among the three Hungarian realms, Transylvania was the only one that actually institutionalized religious tolerance. While coexistence with confessional others may have taught the populations some measure of mutual respect, virtue was probably less instrumental than pragmatism. In Transylvania, there was no dominant confession. Ethnic Germans, known as *Siebenbürgen* Saxons, embraced Lutheranism early on, beginning in the 1520s and culminating by 1550. At that point, Reformed Calvinists started to establish vibrant communities in other parts of the country, most notably around Debrecen. Unitarian refugees joined them, winning converts among locals in Transylvania. Catholics and Orthodox had existed for ages, and now completed the religious tapestry. None of these faiths had enough numbers to dominate the other, and a balance of power ensued instead. Mutual tolerance was codified by a series of diets held in the city of Torda, the most famous of which took place in 1568. Here, lacking the resources to dominate or persecute each other, Christians of various confessions found a way to coexist peacefully, each "preaching the Gospel according to his own understanding" (Murdock, 2000: 110).

Calvin and Geneva

From its beginnings in Zurich, the Swiss Reformation spread outwards and quickly engulfed much of the German-speaking part of the Confederation, including the major city-states of Bern and Basel. Tensions between urban magistrates and their rural dependents remained part of that process. They were particularly sharp between the newly reformed territories and the five mountainous *Orte* of inner-Switzerland, which also happened to be the most rural. The *Fünf Orte*, as they were known, remained Catholic. They were not averse to reform; in fact, they were in many respects more progressive than the Protestant city-states. They had already negotiated special religious privileges with Rome, including an exemption from Lenten fasting (important for a society that had little grain and depended on meat and dairy products); they enjoyed considerable communal self-determination;

and they had even voted to end serfdom. In their eyes, the Reformation promised little additional gain, and even threatened to make their situation worse. The fact that it came from Zurich, whom the *Fünf Orte* suspected of using religion as a cover for political expansionism, made it distinctly threatening. Both sides formed military alliances and, in 1529, went to war: the First Kappel War. There was little fighting, and the peace was settled as soldiers from both sides joined together over an enormous bowl of fondue in the mountains. Two years later, hostilities erupted once again, yielding the Second Kappel War. The Catholic states had solicited support from Charles V, which precipitated a blockade by Zurich and Bern. On the verge of starvation, the *Fünf Orte* declared war on their Reformed neighbors in October 1531. Zurich mobilized, joined by Zwingli, who accompanied the troops as a field chaplain. When fighting ensued on October 11, Zwingli, too, drew his sword. He was killed. Catholic leaders recognized the corpse, held a posthumous trial for the "heretic," quartered him, burned the parts, and drowned the ashes.

Zurich's Reformation continued without Zwingli, though, as Zwingli was succeeded by the eminently capable Heinrich Bullinger (1504–1575). Bullinger's administrative talent continued where Zwingli's skill for agitation left off, and Zurich's Reformation took a firm and durable institutional course. Bullinger took charge of the churches and schools, passed a church ordinance in 1532, a new order of worship in 1535, and wrote two seminal confessional documents, the *Confessio Helvetica Prior* (1536) and the *Confessio Helvetica Posterior* (1566), which together with the Heidelberg Catechism became one of the most widely used confessions of the Reformed faith.

Meanwhile, reform began to spread to francophone Switzerland, as well. It came not from the German-speaking Swiss to the north, but from France. The most important site of those efforts was Geneva—thanks to its Reformer John Calvin (1509–1564).

The ancient trade center of Geneva did not belong to the Swiss Confederation as the Reformation began. It very much wanted closer relations to the Swiss, however, in order to rid itself of an unpopular ruler, the Duke of Savoy. On one level, the situation was fairly simple: Geneva had money but no army; the Swiss had superb armies and were happy to hire them out. In 1526, Geneva signed a pact of self-defense with the states of Bern and Fribourg. The following year it expelled Savoy's administrators—prompting the duke to attack Geneva. Unfortunately for him, the soldiers of Bern and Fribourg lay waiting, and his forces were crushed. By 1530, Geneva was free. Now, however, its affairs began to grow complicated.

Geneva's desire for independence seems to have been devoid of religious motives. Its primary interests were political (local self-determination), and economic (increased opportunities for trade). In fact, its allies were each of a different confession: Bern was Reformed and Fribourg Catholic. Here, too, motives for the alliance were primarily economic, and Geneva carefully declared itself religiously neutral. That tentative balance began to shift, however, as the French Reformer Guillaume Farel (1489–1565) came to the city.

Farel was a remarkable individual. His reforming career had begun in France, where he created the first French Protestant liturgy. A passionate evangelist, Farel won converts with compelling content and by sheer force of personality. Farel entered Geneva in 1532, but was driven out by ill-disposed residents. This, however, was not a man easily rebuffed. Sizing up the situation, Farel returned in 1533—and stayed. Previously agnostic Genevans were now surprised to find themselves Protestants. Farel's powerful preaching enflamed local passions against the mass, images and the clergy; the resident prince-bishop fled. By 1535, Farel had persuaded Geneva's council to ban Catholic mass and declare the city evangelical. The clergy were told to convert—or leave. Within a year, further measures were adopted, including a comprehensive code of morals. Having declared the city an independent republic in February 1536, the council met again in May to ratify Farel's reforms.

Later that summer, Farel came across a thin young traveler in Geneva. It was John Calvin (or Jean Cauvin), a French lawyer active in the reform movement centered at the University of Paris and now in exile, on his way to Strasbourg to escape religious persecution in France. Calvin had planned on spending only the night in Geneva, but Farel, who knew him by reputation, regarded this is a gift from heaven. Browbeating the sensitive Frenchman into staying, Farel tapped the most exceptional figure of the late Reformation.

Calvin hailed from the Picardie in northern France, where his father was an ecclesial administrator and comparatively well off. The young Jean was given church benefices from which he financed his education. Following his father's wishes, he studied law, finishing his degree in Orléans and Bourges before returning to Paris after his father's death in 1531 to take up theology. In Paris, Calvin joined a circle of reform-minded humanists around the biblical scholar Jacques Lefèvre d'Étaples (or J. Faber Stapulensis, c. 1455–1536), where he launched into intensive study of Scripture and began to read Luther. Sometime in 1533—he never provided a precise date—Calvin converted to the evangelical faith. The first public indication of his new convictions came in May 1534, when he returned to his hometown to rescind his benefices. In the meantime, however, others had already identified him as a "Lutheran" after he became involved in the so-called "Cop-Affair," a scandal surrounding his close friend Nicolas Cop, rector of the University of Paris, who had used his inaugural address on November 1, 1533 as a summons to evangelical reform. Conservative reactions were severe, and Cop and his allies had to flee. Calvin, whom many suspected of having written the address, eventually settled in Basel in 1535–1536. Here the recent convert—and quick study!—completed a textbook of theology, *Christianae religionis institutio* ("Institutes of the Christian Religion"), with a preface addressed to King Francis. He would revise the *Institutes* several times, culminating in a vastly expanded version of 1559. It is Calvin's most significant theological work. His letter to the king had little effect, however. After a brief reprieve allowed Calvin to return home in 1536, a new wave of anti-Protestant persecution put him on the road that, unbeknownst to him, would end in Geneva.

As a second-generation Reformer, Calvin may well have learned from observation that successful reforms required more than a change in faith, they also needed a new *order*. In Geneva, he and Farel embarked on the most ambitious program of societal transformation that the magisterial Reformation had so far seen.

In many ways, it had more in common with Anabaptist projects than with the reforms of Zurich or Germany—with the exception of attitudes toward money and property. Here, Calvin undertook little. On most other issues, however, *discipline* was the order of the day.

At the heart of Calvin's conception of church discipline lay the sacrament of communion. Unlike Zwingli, who was satisfied with four eucharistic celebrations per year, Calvin sought weekly communion. Whatever his appreciation for the sacrament itself, he especially saw it as a means for maintaining public discipline in the parish. As Calvin writes in his "Articles concerning the Organization of the Church and of Worship at Geneva" (Reid, 1954: 48–55), which he submitted to the Small Council[4] in November, 1536: "A church cannot be well ordered if the Lord's Supper is not celebrated often—and in such a good way that no one has the courage to participate unless he does so in holiness and with a special sense of respect" (Reid, 1954: 48; my translation).

Calvin and Farel thought of that "holiness" primarily in ethical terms, and they developed a plan to achieve it. Every neighborhood would have specially designated observers, who supervised the conduct of their neighbors and reported offenses to the pastor. If the pastor's admonishment did not resolve the issue, the offender would be excommunicated. When communion is held weekly, excommunication tends to be conspicuous to everyone, especially in the close quarters of Geneva's congregations. Calvin saw excommunication as a potent tool for moral improvement—assuming, of course, that the excommunicated desired reinstatement. Calvin and Farel submitted these proposals to the Small Council—along with a further provision: all Genevans should be required to swear an oath of allegiance to a "Confession of Faith" that Calvin wrote, and would be expelled if they refused.

[4] The Small Council had 25 members and ran the city's day-to-day affairs. For some decisions another 35 men were added to form the Council of Sixty. Weightier issues required a still larger body, the Council of Two Hundred. All registered Genevan citizens together comprised the General Council, which met once a year to elect the others.

These reforms proved too ambitious. The council initially adopted some of the measures, but they were unpopular and subsequent elections shifted the balance of power against Calvin and Farel. The conflict quickly crystallized around the issue of excommunication and its enforcement. The council decreed that it should have that right since the offenses in question were matters of civil discipline, while Calvin and the clergy countered that they should be the ones to excommunicate, since it is an ecclesial act. Neither side yielded. Shortly after Easter 1538, a joint session of the Small Council and the Council of Two Hundred fired Calvin and Farel and gave them three days to leave the city.

Calvin spent the next three years in Strasbourg—finally arriving in the city that had been his destination all along. Here he got to know Martin Bucer, observing first-hand how Bucer implemented the Reformation in Strasbourg, and discussing theology. Calvin was drawn to the moderate Lutheranism of Bucer's eucharistic teaching, affirming that Christ is present in the sacrament, but not specifying how. From Bucer, Calvin also adopted a doctrine of ministry and office that would figure prominently in his later work. Aside from serving a congregation of French refugees and teaching New Testament at the recently founded Strasbourg Academy, Calvin found time to get married—to Idelette van Buren, the widow of an Anabaptist.

Back in Geneva, the political climate changed once again and, in 1540, the city fathers invited Calvin to return. Calvin hesitated for nearly a year before going back, arriving in September, 1541. Now, however, he proceeded vigorously. Within two months, the council had adopted a new church ordinance (*Ordonnances ecclesiastiques de l'Eglise de Genève* ["Ecclesiastical Ordinances"], see Reid, 1954: 58–72) that implemented Calvin's vision for Reformed Geneva.

The church would have four offices (drawing on Bucer's model and using New Testament terminology): pastors, doctors (teachers), elders, and deacons. Prospective pastors were examined by the clergy—both in faith and morals—then approved by the city council, and finally accepted by the congregation. Replacing bishops, ecclesial oversight was carried out by the pastors collectively. Once a week, the city's clergy assembled as a Company of Pastors

(*Compagnie des Pasteurs*) to study the Bible and listen to Calvin, who served as moderator and closed the proceedings with reflections of his own. That was followed by an extended round of mutual assessment. Four times a year there would be an additional, formal *censura morum*, or examination of morals. Doctors taught in the schools—and later in the Genevan Academy, joining the *Compagnie*. Elders took over the task of the earlier "neighborhood monitors," watching over the moral conduct of the populace. There were 12 elders in Geneva, all of whom were "righteous and upstanding" members of the councils. Deacons were called to charity work, particularly in the hospitals and among the poor.

Once again, Calvin sought to make communion a centerpiece of church order. Chastened by the city's earlier refusal to adopt weekly celebration, he now asked for monthly communion. Again, the council refused and instead instituted the northern Swiss practice: communion would be held four times a year. That disagreement was fairly minor compared to the much weightier issue of excommunication. This was the point at which Calvin's earlier reforms had failed. Now, he suggested a compromise: excommunication would be the task of a mixed body containing the city's pastors and elders—and therefore representatives of both church and council; it would be called the Consistory. The council accepted this with a number of qualifications—insisting, for example, that civil offenses be tried by purely civil authorities. One point remained ambiguous, however: most council members understood the measure as allowing the Consistory to *recommend* excommunication and leaving its execution to the councils. Calvin, of course, favored a stronger reading that gave the Consistory full powers of excommunication. Herein lay seeds for further conflict.

Once these structural measures were passed, Calvin began a comprehensive ordering of Geneva's moral life. He banned activities such as gambling, card playing, dancing, fornication, and adultery; and all the usual crimes such as murder, theft, and acts of violence. Failure to attend church was punished, as was laughing during sermons, cursing, slander, and disobeying one's parents. Private homes were searched once a year to root out signs of Catholicism—one man was punished for owning a book on the saints. Parents were prohibited from giving their children "Catholic" names (for example, names of local saints) and encouraged to choose biblical names instead. Witchcraft and sorcery were punishable by death.

Not all these efforts were successful. Calvin ordered the taverns to be turned into devotional houses: in place of the tap he laid an open Bible, where visitors were now offered "spiritual refreshment." The barkeeper was told to lead devotions and encourage the patrons to pray at their tables. Remarkably, the project lasted nearly a month (Naphy, 1994: 99).

Offenses were reported to the Consistory. The effect was astonishing. After Calvin banned gambling, prostitution and other sources of pleasure, Genevans apparently turned with gusto to watching their neighbors. Sexual activity was monitored with particular care. In 1550, for example, the Consistory recorded 160 cases of sexual immorality (Naphy, 1994: 108ff); in other words, denunciations for fornication came in every other day. But transgressions of many kinds poured into the Consistory's records. Next to the expected descriptions of illicit sex, domestic disputes and slander ranked high on the list—as did skipping sermons. Less common, but still notable, were "Catholic practices," attacks on clergy, and magic. Since the councils listed actions defined as civil offenses separately, many items appear in those books instead—treason, slander against magistrates, theft, murder, duelling, and so on. Interestingly, financial corruption or greed was either extremely uncommon (which seems unlikely)—or Calvin's moral radar was simply tuned to a different frequency. People's selectivity in reporting vice probably reflected human frailty as much as the recorded vices themselves. Nonetheless, the Consistory's records offer a glimpse into the challenging process of disciplining an early-modern city of 15,000 inhabitants according to biblical values—a process that Calvin still found far too lax.

Calvin's vision for a Christian transformation of society was comprehensive. There were no exemptions from moral and credal accountability in Geneva. While it is easy to focus on the Genevans' fascination with sexual observation, it is important to remember that monitoring extended into the "soul," as well: beliefs were scrutinized wherever possible, often by seizing on external indicators such as possession of "Catholic" objects or the use of non-biblical names for children. Open disagreement with Calvin or his teachings brought punishment ranging from fines to banishment. As in most of Europe, cases of outright heresy met the death penalty. Michael Servetus, an anti-trinitarian scholar who made the mistake of seeking Calvin's protection in 1553, found himself put on trial by Calvin instead—and burned at the stake.

Social experiments of Geneva's intensity were fairly rare in Reformation Europe, but not entirely unprecedented. In 1534–1535, a group of apocalyptic Anabaptists took over the city of Münster, Germany. They too sought a complete transformation of societal behaviors, but they targeted wealth. Property and money were abolished, wealthy patricians stripped of their houses and belongings. Old Testament paradigms were applied much more forcefully than in Geneva: the Münsterites enforced polygamy (with the leaders enjoying the highest number of wives); they saw their leader as a Davidic "king." Executions, though certainly not uncommon in Calvin's Geneva, were swift and summary in Münster, often carried out by the leaders personally. Compared with Münster—which was soon crushed by outside forces—Geneva was not "revolutionary." Its existing social order was not turned upside down. Nor was it "theocratic," as is sometimes asserted. The intricate system of parliamentary councils and elections remained intact; it was simply supplemented by, and had to learn to live with, an assertive body of clergy. And as the events of 1538 had shown, Calvin could be "voted out" of the city at any time.

For more than a decade after his return, Calvin's hold on Geneva was insecure. For all his efforts at discipline, he could not overcome the city's ingrained factionalism. During Calvin's early years, Geneva's political life was dominated by two opposing groups, called "Articulants" and "Guillermins," who argued over how best to preserve Geneva's newly acquired liberties. The former had lobbied for a treaty with Bern (and were named after the treaty's "articles"), and feared that Calvin and Farel's aggressive reforms would not only deprive Genevans of liberties, but also threaten good relations with Bern and the Swiss Confederation. The Guillermins were named for their support of Guillaume Farel;

in their view, the greatest threat to Geneva's freedom came from the Articulants' kowtowing to Bern. As time went on, however, even some of the Guillermins began to sour on the Reformers' program. A new faction emerged during the 1540s to resist Calvin's incursions on what they felt were basic civil liberties; they were called "Libertines."

Connected with the Libertines' concerns about Calvin's discipline were anxieties over immigration. During this period, the influx of French Protestant refugees into Geneva was enormous. By some accounts there were up to 10,000 such refugees in the city at a time—and Geneva itself only had a population of 15,000. Because some of the foreigners came from the French upper classes and nobility, and were making efforts to settle permanently in Geneva, the established patricians grew nervous about the security of their own status. To make things worse, Calvin and nearly all the city's clergy were French. The threat of a creeping "revolution" seemed palpable.

Several high-profile cases heated Genevan political passions. One, in 1546, concerned an unfortunate councilman named Pierre Ameaux. Ameaux had many reasons to find Calvin irksome. First, he was a manufacturer of playing cards. That was no longer profitable in Calvin's Geneva. Second, Ameaux's wife appears to have been a nymphomaniac who, against all odds, managed to find a free-love society in Geneva and scandalized the poor councilman. Ameaux sought to divorce his wife, but that was derailed by Calvin and the council. Drowning his frustrations with friends, the drunken Ameaux let loose a barrage of insults against Calvin, the "awful Picard who just wants to be bishop." This tidbit made its way back to Calvin's ears, who responded with ice-cold fury: rather than let Ameaux apologize before the council—as many of his colleagues had suggested—Calvin ordered him to wear a hair-shirt and walk the streets of Geneva, begging everyone he met for personal forgiveness. Calvin interpreted the attack on his authority as an insult to God. Ameaux doubtless had other thoughts. Given the councilman's prominence in Genevan politics, the affair outraged many of the patricians and played into the hands of the Libertine opposition.

A few years later, a new crisis erupted. The issue itself was old; it concerned baptismal names. Patrician families, many of whom liked to pass on traditional names from generation to generation, were especially affected by Calvin's rejection of "secular" or "Catholic" names. More than once, such families had brought infants to church only to have the pastor refuse to perform the sacrament. A series of such incidents precipitated a clash between the clergy and the council, who ordered the pastors to go forth with the baptisms. But the conflict continued. One of those affected, a man named Philippe Berthelier, was excommunicated for his protests. He appealed to the Small Council in 1554, and the councilmen voted to overturn the excommunication. In Calvin's view, this was improper.

The old disagreement over excommunication rights had resurfaced with a vengeance—and now became a focal point for a wide spectrum of frustrations. Citizens were up in arms, council meetings broke down in fist-fights, slurs against the French flew in every direction, and the clergy themselves were irate. The entire Company of Pastors threatened to resign if the council did not back down. Finally, on January 24, 1555, the Council of Two Hundred overruled the Small Council and upheld Berthelier's excommunication. Calvin had won a major political victory. At last, his vision of church order as the linchpin of a godly society had been ratified. He spent the last nine years of his life in relative peace, founding the Genevan Academy, training a new generation of students who in a relatively short time would carry the Calvinist Reformation all over Europe and North America, and finishing the final version of his *Institutes*.

Catholic Reform and Counter-Reformation

Returning to the medieval trajectories of reform already described above (see Chapter 1), it should not surprise a reader to learn that some of these continued in the sixteenth century. Importantly, more than a few developed without involving an outright break with the Roman hierarchy. For some of the reform agendas, the pope was simply irrelevant. Others actively supported the papacy and made it a central feature in their own vision for a reformed Roman Catholic church. As the Protestant Reformation began to spread, a third agenda emerged as well and included persons whose primary motive was defensive: to defend the pope, the mass, and traditional rites and practices against Protestant attack. For a long time, historians have focused mainly on this third group, describing it as a "Counter-Reformation." More recently, reform movements whose origins predate the Reformation, or which developed in an independent context from it, have attracted attention and given rise to the notion of "Catholic Reform," or even a "Catholic Reformation."

The same yearning for a more authentic Christian life and witness that had driven the medieval monastic movement re-emerged as a powerful force in the fifteenth and sixteenth centuries. It is what gave the early Reformation so much of its promise. As time went on it was, among Protestants, perhaps most visible in parts of the Anabaptist movement, but it moved in other circles, too. There was a more prominent counterpart within Catholicism. It stayed closer to its medieval precedents, often working within existing orders for renewal and sometimes, when that seemed inadequate, launching new orders entirely.

The Franciscans were one of the most vilified groups within Catholicism. It did not take the Reformation to make the followers of Francis of Assisi so unpopular; indeed, the Reformers often simply borrowed tropes from pre-Reformation polemicists. Dishonest, overfed and hypocritical were among the milder epithets attached to the Franciscans. Much of this anti-fraternal hostility stemmed from the uncomfortable nature of the Franciscan witness itself—an example of radical poverty in a world dedicated to the accumulation of wealth. In many parts of Reformation-era Europe, the Franciscans remained a counter-cultural force— especially in places such as Hungary, where they helped organize a peasant revolution. In fact, Franciscans were often linked with the rural people to whom many of them ministered, and smeared with the same brush that disparaged the peasants. On top of that, they were accused of fomenting insurrection and of leading the innocent rustics to their destruction.

Despite all the charges of a softened, compromised mendicant ethos, the Franciscans could still bring forth a potent voice of social critique. On the other hand, there was more than a grain of truth to the charges, however much self-interest their subtext may have carried. The Franciscans did indeed have difficulty adjusting their ideals to the commercial, property-based society that grew around them. Internal divisions between Conventuals (those who lived in convents) and Observants (named for their more rigorous observance of the rule) undermined the integrity of their message and made them vulnerable to criticism. And if there had not been widespread corruption within the order, there would not have been so many internal calls for reform—such as those of the energetic Spanish archbishop and friar Francisco Ximenes de Cisneros. After repeated efforts to unite the various branches had failed, Pope Leo X formalized the division by declaring the two streams, Conventual and Observant, separate orders on May 31, 1517. That institutional clarity helped the Franciscans carry out internal reforms and, revitalized, regain some of the footing they lost through the Reformation.

Calls for greater rigor continued. The Italian Observantist Fra Matteo da Bascio (1495–1552), frustrated by the laxity of his Franciscan community, left his monastery to live a life closer to Francis's primitive ideals. In 1528, he obtained papal approval for the reform movement, named "Capuchins." By the end of the next century, and by now an independent order, it had 30,000 members. A corresponding order for women, the Capuchin Poor Clares, was founded in 1538. Committed to a life of poverty, the Capuchins were remarkable for their mission work, especially to the rural poor of Europe (but also overseas). Not known for their learning, the friars preached in a simple manner that drew its effectiveness as much from their nearness to the people as from their spirituality, cultivated by periodic retreats for contemplation. The Capuchins became a major arm, along with the Jesuits, in Rome's mission to the peasants during the later sixteenth and seventeenth centuries.

Angela Merici (1474–1540) was another Italian Franciscan (of the Third Order) who founded a movement of her own for women, in 1535, though they had been gathering informally for many years prior to that. Known as the Ursulines, her followers dedicated themselves to serving the poor and especially to the education of girls. Their remarkable schools in Italy and France played an analogous role for the formation of young women as schools for girls in Lutheran settings. Characteristically, the all-male Roman hierarchy was slow to recognize the potential posed by female groups such as the Ursulines. In Rome's view—underscored by the Council of Trent—religious women were better confined to the safety of enclosed convents, a notion very much at odds with the educational vision of the Ursulines. In fact, this was a tension faced by all female orders whose vocation made enclosure impractical; their effectiveness was hamstrung by the patronizing policies of their male peers. The Ursulines, however, prevailed long-term and became a particularly compelling example of Catholic reform and its promise for reshaping society through education.

The extraordinary Teresa of Ávila (1515–1582), perhaps the best-known religious woman of the sixteenth century, also undertook rigorous reforms of her Carmelite order in Spain, eventually founding her own branch, the mendicant Discalced Carmelites, with fellow Spaniard Juan de Yepes Alvarez (John of the Cross, 1542–1591). In Teresa's case, ecclesial recognition of her efforts was not only slow, it was initially hostile. She was even denounced to the Inquisition. Teresa was remarkable not only as a reformer, but also as a mystic and—unusually for a woman of her day—as an author. Her writings, which include her autobiography and the spiritual guide *The Interior Castle*, are still influential today. In fact, Teresa, who was canonized in 1622, was the first woman (along with Catherine of Siena) to be named a "Doctor of the Church," an honor she shares with Thomas Aquinas. That was in 1970.

As already mentioned (see Chapter 2), the fifteenth century saw the emergence of many groups that united laypeople and secular clergy in spirituality and works of charity, among them the Brethren of the Common Life and the Oratory of Divine Love. The latter confraternity provided the context for a new type of clerical order, as well. Several priests who belonged to the Oratory in Rome, including Gaetano di Thiene (St. Cajetan, 1480–1547) and the future Pope Paul IV, Giovanni Pietro Carafa (1476–1559), formed an order for clergy in 1524, called the Congregation of Clerks Regular of the Divine Providence, or "Theatines." It was dedicated to charity and preaching. The pattern soon caught on, and similar foundations such as the Barnabites of Milan and the Somaschi of Somasca followed. Northern Italy, ravaged by years of war, was particularly needy of such dedicated work. Unlike monks, whose spiritual life took place within a closed community and remained centered on an ordered regimen of prayer and contemplation, clerks regular were focused on ministry. They were priests who committed themselves in an exceptional way to serving the greater public by preaching, teaching, and charity. They are the most obvious Catholic counterpart to the Protestant emphasis on preaching and pastoral ministry. Though their theological language was very different, they were responding to many of the same needs.

The best-known and most successful of the new sixteenth-century orders combines aspects of both clerks regular and mendicants. Its origins lie in Spain, home to many of the most dynamic reform initiatives of the era. Its founder, Ignatius (Iñigo) of Loyola (c. 1491–1556), was a converted soldier. His religious vision emerged from a period of intense personal torment and spiritual struggle, guided by prayer and penance. Drawing on that experience, Ignatius created a guide for spiritual examination and discernment, the *Spiritual Exercises*, with which he sought to help other souls. Fleeing the Spanish Inquisition, Ignatius moved to Paris for further study in 1528, and within a few years had gathered a small group of companions. Initially pledging themselves to ministry in the Holy Land, they offered their services to the pope when that plan fell through. Pope Paul III recognized them as an order in 1540, thereby founding the Society of Jesus, known as the Jesuits.

The Jesuits could have been custom-tailored for the age. Like other clerks regular, their rule was structured to provide maximum flexibility and freedom of movement for the sake of effective pastoral ministry. There were no regular hours for prayer or communal devotion, as in Benedictine orders, that would have tied them down. Mendicant precedents encouraged the decision to forgo convents and depend on alms. Jesuits sought to find God in the people they served—and these structures, coupled with Ignatius's uniquely compelling spiritual vision, supported that. The recipe worked well. By Ignatius's death in 1556, the order had grown from less than a dozen members to over 1000; by the eighteenth century, there were over 20,000. Their focus on education, in particular, made the Jesuits a powerful agent of mission. Their colleges, smaller and more flexible than full-scale universities, responded to local needs and contexts, forming future leaders through Ignatius's spiritual guidelines. By the end of the century, their mission efforts spanned the globe—those in East Asia were especially noteworthy. Their educational emphasis applied to their own members, as well, and made them first-rate opponents of Protestant theologians. In Germany, their college at the University of Ingolstadt became something of an anti-Wittenberg in the late-sixteenth and seventeenth centuries. Robert Bellarmine (1542–1621) set the tone of Catholic–Protestant debate with his monumental *Disputations on the Controversies of the Christian Faith* (published between 1581–1593), a comprehensive engagement with Protestant theology. Responses from Lutheran and Reformed scholars (whose positions Bellarmine tended to lump together) followed quickly. Though often polemical, these exchanges raised the standards of theological discourse and even contributed, however indirectly, to ecumenical understanding.

The sixteenth century saw many more new orders, and many more reforms to older orders than can be described in this brief survey. Taken as a whole—and particularly when combined with the similarly impressive initiatives of laypeople—they offer a glimpse into a uniquely Roman Catholic world of reform. For all its diversity, Protestantism developed nothing comparable. Many Protestants, whether justly or not, held a deep theological skepticism toward what they saw as a mentality of "works righteousness" (that is, earning one's salvation by works rather than relying on God's grace) attached to monastic vows. Cultural and economic factors also motivated the closure of convents and monasteries in Protestant lands. And the disappearance of celibacy reduced the number of people who would have been available for such single-minded vocations. Vows of poverty are not compatible with raising a family. The Catholic orders profited, therefore, from a continuity in traditions, values, and spiritual practices with which most Protestants had broken. The success of the orders in turn strengthened the institutions that sought to preserve those specific values. One of those institutions was the papacy. While the pope may have had only tangential relevance for many orders—and sometimes his influence was destructive—other orders, such as the Jesuits, stressed obedience to the pope as a core value. The Jesuits dedicated themselves "to the greater glory of God," but they were happy to see some glory, at least, go to the pope.

Given the state of the Renaissance papacy, serious institutional reform of the Catholic church had to come from a council. The Fifth Lateran Council of 1512–1517 had seen a few stirrings of reform, but these were both tepid and, due to the nature of its attendees, focused one-sidedly on questions of episcopal authority. The results were inadequate. Furthermore, they were quickly eclipsed by the events of the Protestant Reformation. While the Reformation certainly sent shock waves through parts of the curia, there were also some church leaders who, far from surprised, saw merit in many of the Reformers' concerns. Pope Paul III, elected in 1534, moved to convoke a council in the Italian city of Mantua after only two years in office, but was unable to summon sufficient political support—conflicting interests of the French, the emperor, and the German princes, who insisted on a council on German soil, worked against him. Paul III was hardly an obvious champion of reform. Unashamedly nepotistic, he furthered the careers of his children (!) and even made cardinals of two teenaged grandsons. Yet Paul applied genuine interest to the matter and commissioned a group of nine cardinals that included the reform-minded Gasparo Contarini and the uncompromising Gian Pietro Carafa to prepare a report on the state of the church. Their *Consilium de emendanda ecclesia* ("Advice on Reforming the Church," 1537) was scathing in its criticism of the curia, the system of benefices, episcopal absenteeism and pluralism, and the generally poor quality of clergy. Though confidential, a copy of the text was leaked and made its way to Luther, who published a German translation adorned with his own scornful comments.

It was a remarkable document, "a compilation of those diseases and remedies" (Olin, 1969: 187) that plagued the church. It set the stage for the next council.

After much delay and negotiation, Pope Paul III succeeded in convoking a council that opened on December 13, 1545, in the northern Italian city of Trent. The location was a compromise; Trent was part of the Empire (and technically "on German soil"), but it was south of the Alps and near to the pope's sphere of influence. As it happened, the Protestants still refused to attend since they had also insisted on a "free" council—that is, a council over which the pope did not preside. Charles's attack on the Schmalkaldic League a few months later put an end to that discussion in any case. The council met in three phases. The first lasted until March 1547; the second from May 1551 to April 1552; and the third from January 1562 to December 1563. The council was attended by a variety of hierarchs and theological consultants, of which cardinals, bishops, and other high-ranking clergy had voting rights. Their theological positions also varied. Despite the pope's formal control of the council, its outcome was in many ways unpredictable—especially since three popes were involved by the time it was over. The council had two principal agendas: addressing the Protestant "heresies," and reforming the institutional church. The sessions alternated between these two agendas.

Theologically, Trent established several important positions. Countering the Protestant principle of scriptural authority (*sola Scriptura*), the council insisted on two sources of authority: Scripture and tradition. In addition, it decreed that it is the church, represented by the pope's teaching office, who interprets Scripture authoritatively. The Latin Vulgate edition was defined as the church's standard; the number of sacraments fixed at seven; the doctrine of transubstantiation made binding; and communion under one species (that is, laypeople were to receive only bread) defended, though final decision on this matter was now deferred to the pope. The most significant doctrinal discussions took place at the Sixth Session and dealt with justification. The council members brought a number of different positions to the table, some close to Luther. In the end, though, the council chose a narrowly scholastic definition of justification as an infusion of grace, and rejected the more Augustinian understanding of justification centered on forgiveness and "imputed" righteousness. Many at the council thought that this condemned the Lutheran doctrine. Subsequent studies have challenged that notion. It appears far more likely that Trent, by narrowing the concepts used to describe justification, "talked past" the Lutheran position.

Measures for reforming the church institutionally focused heavily on the bishops. Acting on the kinds of concerns raised by the 1537 *Consilium*, the council emphasized the bishop's role as pastor, restricting absenteeism and pluralism, and calling for the bishop to preach regularly in his diocese. This went hand in hand with increasing the bishop's authority—so far, in fact, that some saw a threat to papal superiority. While skillful maneuvering by papal legates avoided that outcome, the topic remained sensitive. The council closed in 1563 without ever addressing the office of the pope.

While enormously significant as a catalyst for Catholic reform—and for launching a vigorous Counter-Reformation against Protestantism—the Council of Trent also fell short in several respects. Institutional reforms of the church, while partly successful, were too narrowly focused on the episcopacy, and left undefined the relationship of bishops to the pope, the nature of the papacy itself, and the role of princes and other secular leaders in the church. These issues had provided some of the central dynamics of the Protestant Reformation, and the council failed to address them—probably because it lacked the necessary unanimity to address them adequately, or at least to achieve results compatible with curial expectations. As a result, Trent consolidated a particular kind of Roman Catholic polity—without finding a way to engage the ecclesial "others" that had emerged through the Reformation. The post-tridentine Roman Catholic church was surely an improved church, but it was now one church among several. Unable to envision a path to reconciliation, it had entered an age of open competition with the Protestants.

In some circles, that recognition fueled a redoubled effort to eradicate, rather than integrate Protestantism. Those efforts would last well into the seventeenth and even eighteenth century, and chronicling them goes beyond the scope of this book. The pontificate of

Gian Pietro Carafa, as Paul IV, gives a foretaste of those developments, however. Paul IV was 79 when he took office in 1555—between sessions of Trent. He was a fierce opponent of the Peace of Augsburg, which was signed that same year. One of his primary interests lay in supporting the Roman Inquisition, a more local Italian variant of its Spanish cousin and described by at least one historian as a "regime of terror." Former colleagues in the reform commission of the 1530s suddenly found themselves in Carafa's sights—hauled before the Inquisition and imprisoned. He was also responsible for introducing another method of controlling thought and speech: the papal Index of Forbidden Books. The lists included works not only by the Protestant Reformers, but also by Catholic humanists such as the venerable Erasmus. This was papal power in its most naked form—and the spectacle shocked even loyal Catholics such as Ignatius of Loyola.

Though at times unedifying, the Counter-Reformation did little to change the balance of confessional power in Europe. Countries and territories that were Protestant in 1555 mostly remained so. Some efforts at clamping down on Protestant populations within Catholic-led territories simply backfired. In the Netherlands, for example, they sparked a national independence movement, as Reformed constituencies identified Catholicism with Spanish-Habsburg oppression. After several decades of violence, the Dutch prevailed; their independence was recognized formally in 1648. Efforts to suppress Protestantism were more successful in other regions under Catholic control. In France a series of bloody religious wars led to the consolidation of a Gallican national church under the Catholic king. Protestants, known as Huguenots, were recognized as a tolerated minority by the Edict of Nantes (1598), but expelled from France after Louis XIV revoked the measure in 1685. Nearly half a million Huguenots were uprooted and fled. In Austria, heartland of the Habsburg dynasty, Protestants constituted a majority of the population in some regions. Here the principle of *cuius regio, eius religio* worked to their disadvantage—those who did not leave were forced back to the Catholic faith of their ruler. Similar fates befell Protestants in much of Eastern Europe, including Croatia, Slovenia, Bohemia, and Poland.

If the devil had offered the pope a deal in 1517: "Germany and Scandinavia for the New World," it is hard to imagine any of the shrewder pontiffs turning him down. Whatever conspired to cause it—that, more or less, is what they got. The Reformation limited Rome's jurisdiction within early modern Europe, but it came at a time when Catholicism's horizons were expanding dramatically. The early explorers of the Americas, as well as those who pursued trade and fortune in Africa and Asia, were almost all Catholics and sailed for the Catholic crowns of Spain and Portugal. Those explorers were accompanied by missionaries—often Franciscans, Dominicans, or Jesuits—whose Christian convictions were frequently at odds with the financially-driven agendas of the soldiers. The Spanish Dominican Bartolomeo de las Casas (c. 1484–1566), who came to the "New World" in 1502 and later became Bishop of Chiapas, proved a forceful advocate for extending human rights to the native peoples. Though his efforts halted the enslavement of "Indians," they opened the door to another tragedy of the burgeoning colonial age: the importation of slaves from Africa. Undeterred by mendicant apprehensions, Europe's feudal values and commercial avarice reached new intensity in the mayhem of the Americas.

References

The following is a list of works cited and consulted in this chapter. Though it is only a small selection of relevant literature, it is a good place to start for further reading.

Buchholz, Werner. 2003. "Schweden mit Finnland" [Sweden with Finland]. In *Dänemark, Norwegen und Schweden im Zeitalter der Reformation und Konfessionalisierung: Nordische Königreiche und Konfession 1500 bis 1660* [Denmark, Norway and Sweden in the Age of Reformation and Confessionalization: Nordic Kingdoms and Confession, 1500–1660], ed. Matthias Asche and Anton Schindling, pp. 107–243. Münster: Aschendorff.

Luther's Works. 1955–. (LW). *American Edition*, vols. 1–55. Philadelphia: Fortress Press.

Murdock, Graeme. 2000. *Calvinism on the Frontier 1600–1660: International Calvinism and the Reformed Church in Hungary and Transylvania*. Oxford: Clarendon.

Naphy, William G. 1994. *Calvin and the Consolidation of the Genevan Reformation*. Manchester: Manchester University Press.

Oleson, Jens E. 2003. "Dänemark, Norwegen und Island" [Denmark, Norway and Iceland]. In *Dänemark, Norwegen und Schweden im Zeitalter der Reformation und Konfessionalisierung: Nordische Königreiche und Konfession 1500 bis 1660* [Denmark, Norway and Sweden in the Age of Reformation and Confessionalization: Nordic Kingdoms and Confession, 1500–1660], ed. Matthias Asche and Anton Schindling, pp. 27–106. Münster: Aschendorff.

Olin, John C. 1969. *The Catholic Reformation: Savonarola to Ignatius Loyola*. New York: Fordham.

Reid, J. K. S., ed. 1954. *Calvin: Theological Treatises*. Library of Christian Classics vol. 22. Louisville: Westminster John Knox Press.

Tóth, István György. 2004. "Old and New Faith in Hungary, Turkish Hungary, and Transylvania." In *A Companion to the Reformation World*, ed. R. Po-chia Hsia, pp. 205–20. Oxford: Blackwell.

Further Reading

Appold, Kenneth G. 2006. "Early Lutheran Attitudes toward Jews." *Lutheran Quarterly* XX(2): 170–89.

Appold, Kenneth G. 2006. "Frauen im frühneuzeitlichen Luthertum: Kirchliche Ämter und die Frage der Ordination" [Women in Early Modern Lutheranism: Church Offices and the Question of Ordination]. *Zeitschrift für Theologie und Kirche* 103(2): 253–79.

Bireley, Robert. 1999. *The Refashioning of Catholicism, 1450–1700: A Reassessment of the Counter-Reformation*. Washington, DC: Catholic University of America Press.

Brady, Thomas A., Jr. 1978. *Ruling Class, Regime and Reformation at Strasbourg 1520–1555*. Leiden: Brill.

Cameron, Euan. 1991. *The European Reformation*. Oxford: Clarendon.

Chatellier, Louis. 1997. *The Religion of the Poor: Rural Missions in Europe and the Formation of Modern Catholicism, ca. 1500–1800*, transl. Brian Pearce. Cambridge: Cambridge University Press.

A Companion to the Reformation World. 2004. Ed. R. Po-chia Hsia. Oxford: Blackwell.

Dänemark, Norwegen und Schweden im Zeitalter der Reformation und Konfessionalisierung: Nordische Königreiche und Konfession 1500 bis 1660 [Denmark, Norway and Sweden in the Age of Reformation and Confessionalization: Nordic Kingdoms and Confession, 1500–1660] (2003). Ed. Matthias Asche and Anton Schindling. Münster: Aschendorff.

Eire, Carlos M. N. 1986. *War Against the Idols: The Reformation of Worship from Erasmus to Calvin.* Cambridge: Cambridge University Press.

Fell, Michael. 1999. *And Some Fell into Good Soil: A History of Christianity in Iceland.* New York et al: Peter Lang.

Forster, Marc. 1992. *The Counter-Reformation in the Villages: Religion and Reform in the Bishopric of Speyer, 1560–1720.* Ithaca/London: Cornell University Press.

Heininen, Simo and Heikkilä, Markku. 2002. *Kirchengeschichte Finnlands* [Church History of Finland]. Göttingen: Vandenhoeck & Ruprecht.

Hendrix, Scott. 2004. *Recultivating the Vineyard: The Reformation Agendas of Christianization.* Louisville: Westminster John Knox Press.

Hillerbrand, Hans J. 2007. *The Division of Christendom: Christianity in the Sixteenth Century.* Louisville/London: Westminster John Knox Press.

Hsia, R. Po-chia. 1998. *The World of Catholic Renewal, 1540–1770.* Cambridge: Cambridge University Press.

Jedin, Hubert. 1957. *A History of the Council of Trent*, 2 vols. St. Louis: Herder.

Kaufmann, Thomas. 2009. *Geschichte der Reformation* [History of the Reformation]. Frankfurt/Leipzig: Verlag der Weltreligionen.

Kingdon, Robert M. 1967. *Geneva and the Consolidation of the French Protestant Movement, 1564–1572.* Geneva: Droz.

Kohnle, Armin. 2001. *Reichstag und Reformation* [Imperial Diet and Reformation]. Heidelberg: Gütersloher Verlagshaus.

Lausten, Martin Schwarz. 2008. *Die Reformation in Dänemark* [The Reformation in Denmark], transl. Lise Miller Tönnies. Heidelberg: Gütersloher Verlagshaus.

Lindberg, Carter. 1993. *Beyond Charity. Reformation Initiatives for the Poor.* Minneapolis: Fortress Press.

Lindberg, Carter. 2010. *The European Reformations.* Second Edition. Oxford: Wiley-Blackwell.

Lindhart, Poul Georg. 1983. *Kirchengeschichte Skandinaviens* [Church History of Scandinavia]. Göttingen: Vandenhoeck & Ruprecht.

MacCulloch, Diarmaid. 2003. *The Reformation.* London: Penguin.

McGrath, Alister E. 2007. *Christianity's Dangerous Idea. The Protestant Revolution—A History from the Sixteenth Century to the Twenty-First.* New York: Harper One.

McKee, Elsie Anne. 1984. *John Calvin on the Diaconate and Liturgical Almsgiving*. Geneva: Droz.

McKee, Elsie Anne. 1999. *Katharina Schütz Zell*. Vol. I: *The Life and Thought of a Sixteenth-Century Reformer*; Vol. II: *The Writings, A Critical Edition*. Leiden: Brill.

Minnich, Nelson H. 2008. *Councils of the Catholic Reformation: Pisa I (1409) to Trent (1545–63)*. Aldershot, England; Burlington, VT: Ashgate.

Mullett, Michael A. 1999. *The Catholic Reformation*. London: Routledge.

Oberman, Heiko A. 2003. *The Two Reformations: The Journey from the Last Days to the New World*. New Haven/London: Yale University Press.

O'Malley, John. 2000. *Trent and All That: Renaming Catholicism in the Early Modern Era*. Cambridge: Harvard University Press.

Ozment, Steven. 1980. *The Age of Reform, 1250–1550: An Intellectual and Religious History of Late Medieval and Reformation Europe*. New Haven/London: Yale University Press.

Pettegree, Andrew. 2000. *The Reformation World*. London: Routledge.

Pettegree, Andrew. 2002. *Europe in the Sixteenth Century*. Oxford: Blackwell.

The Scandinavian Reformation. From Evangelical Movement to Institutionalization of Reform. 1995. Ed. Ole Peter Grell. Cambridge: Cambridge University Press.

Schilling, Heinz. 1988. *Aufbruch und Krise: Deutschland 1517–1648* [New Beginnings and Crisis: Germany 1517–1648]. Berlin: Siedler.

Spijker, Willem van't. 2009. *Calvin: A Brief Guide to His Life and Thought*. Louisville: Westminster John Knox Press.

Stjerna, Kirsi. 2009. *Women and the Reformation*. Oxford: Blackwell.

Wengert, Timothy J. 2008. *In Public Service: Priesthood, Ministry and Bishops in Early Lutheranism*. Minneapolis: Fortress Press.

Wicks, Jared. 1978. *Cajetan Responds: A Reader in Reformation Controversy*. Washington, DC: Catholic University Press.

Wiesner-Hanks, Merry. 2006. *Early Modern Europe, 1450–1789*. Cambridge: Cambridge University Press.

Epilogue:
The Reformation's Legacy

Scholars often argue over when, exactly, the Reformation "ended." That question is as difficult to answer as the related issue of when the Reformation started. As the preceding pages have shown, efforts to reform the church are as old as the church itself, and provided a driving force in the Christianization of Europe. In a similar vein, a yearning for reform and renewal extended far beyond the Reformation's traditionally ascribed "endpoints"—and continues to the present day. The rise of new movements, such as Pietism in the seventeenth and eighteenth centuries, or Pentecostalism in the twentieth century, and even modern-day ecumenism, testifies to the energy and timelessness of Christian reform.

What made the events of the sixteenth century distinctive was not the desire for reform itself, but the unique constellation of political, economic, religious, cultural, and personal ingredients that allowed those desires to find durable institutional forms. That combination of factors launched a re-formation of Europe's ecclesial communities. While many of these ingredients pre-date the Reformation considerably—and it is therefore important to identify continuities within the overarching narrative—it is also clear that Luther's "Ninety-Five Theses," however unintentionally, turned into something like a firing pin for a far more condensed and explosive process. Within just a few decades, centuries-old tensions and ideological divisions within Western Christendom were exposed and—in a way—settled. An internally

The Reformation: A Brief History, First Edition. Kenneth G. Appold.
© 2011 Kenneth G. Appold. Published 2011 by Blackwell Publishing Ltd.

divided church had yielded an institutional plurality of churches. For the Holy Roman Empire, that meant the creation of Protestant state churches that would now exist next to a reduced but strengthened papal church of Rome. A suitable end-point for that development is the Peace of Augsburg of 1555. Momentous as that treaty was, however, it did not settle the issues as durably as many would have liked. Tensions continued—fueled both by political opportunism and by Rome's refusal to acknowledge the treaty—and erupted once again in military conflict: the Thirty Years' War of 1618–1648. That war settled matters politically, giving the rising nations and states far more sovereignty—but came at a devastating cost to the general population.

Assessing the legacy of the Reformation is complex. Much depends on one's perspective. Even before the Peace of Augsburg was signed, distinct confessional cultures had begun to form. That process was especially interesting in Germany, where two or more confessions lived side by side. In Scandinavia and in much of Switzerland, where Protestant majorities dominated, cultural shifts took place as well—though lack of direct competition may have made confessional identity less impassioned. The Catholic reform process brought equally remarkable changes to lands that did not adopt Protestantism. Both "sides" had a great deal in common as well. Particularly significant was the rise in overall levels of education. Education had been a linchpin of Luther's reform efforts—and all Protestants prided themselves on their schools. But Catholics recognized their value, as well, even if implementation tended to be less systematic. Here, the orders—such as the Jesuits or the Ursulines—took the initiative and frequently surpassed the efforts of Catholic bishops or princes. The impact on European culture was profound. Because it coincided with the emergence of printing, attention to education raised literacy rates and, over time, transformed much of Europe into a literate society. People not only learned to read and write, they thought differently, as well. Religion acquired a verbal and intellectual character, often at the expense of ritual, that owed as much to this underlying transformation as it did to Protestant commitments to "the Word" (which would have been impracticable without a rise in literacy).

With the focus on education came a heightened role for its elites: the universities and their scholars. Universities and university-trained intellectuals formed the core of a new societal order as the princes made use of educated public servants to increase their administrative control and lifted such people to positions of prominence. For the churches—more so for Protestants, but more than before for Catholics—the interest in higher education produced better-educated clergy. Socially, the fact that Protestant clergy could marry led to dynastic families of theologians, who, generation for generation, produced leaders for church and society. Academic culture also had an enormous impact on the articulation of theology. The post-Reformation period saw the emergence of the first theological "systems," thematically-organized treatments of the important topics of faith, designed to prepare pastors for an intellectually grounded ministry. Such attention to thought also affected dialogue between the confessions, as nuanced and detailed "controversial theology"—also known as "polemics"—came into its own.

The Reformation's impact on worship would be hard to overstate. Even the interiors of churches gave powerful first impressions of these confessionally-based differences, ranging from the stark simplicity of Anabaptist meeting houses, and the slightly more "solid" feel of similarly spare Reformed churches, to ornate interiors and altar paintings of the Lutherans, all the way to the triumphant splendor of the Catholic baroque. Almost all Protestants insisted on vernacular worship, with Catholics retaining Latin. Anabaptists and Reformed frowned on music in church, especially liturgical chanting, which continued to form the core of a Catholic mass. Lutherans, on the other hand, thrived on music. In addition to new (vernacular) liturgies and an extraordinarily rich hymnody, Lutherans cultivated choral and instrumental church music to an unprecedented degree. The most brilliant—but by no means only—example of Lutheranism's impact on musical culture comes with Johann Sebastian Bach (1685–1750). Bach revolutionized Western music—and he did so while working as a cantor in a Lutheran church.

From the vantage point of social history, the undisputed "victors" of the Reformation were Europe's princes. Almost all saw their powers increase. That change was not caused by the Reformation as such (the trends had begun earlier), but the Reformation gave it an enormous boost. Protestant rulers—and even, if more subtly, Catholic ones—rid themselves almost entirely of an independent ecclesial authority. Having repelled the pope's jurisdictional authority, they established themselves as the highest religious authorities in their lands, subsuming oversight and custody of the church into their ever-expanding court administrations. Princes within the Empire got the additional benefit of seeing the emperor's wings clipped at their expense. Internally, princely custody of religion allowed the ruler to take charge of his people's moral and spiritual life, giving rise to the modern notions of "police" and "social discipline." Even the free imperial cities, whose magistrates initially played a role analogous to that of the princes, saw their status come to an end by the late sixteenth century, as most were swallowed up by the states that surrounded them.

It is perhaps too easy to view the post-Reformation rise of princely absolutism as a negative development—particularly if one does so from the comforts of an affluent modern democracy. But the development brought benefits as well as restrictions. In the hands of competent rulers, these increased powers led to the construction of school systems, universities, hospitals, and an unprecedented social welfare system. It was here that Lutheranism as a social model probably worked best. The educational and cultural support, and the nearly unique social systems of contemporary Scandinavia and Germany trace their roots to the schools, the church music, and the common chest of Luther and his peers.

Rural peasants, on the other hand, profited far less from the Reformation's promise. After the defeat of 1525, peasants mostly returned to their prior lives—sobered, sullen, and quietly resistant. In Germany, serfdom would continue for another three centuries, with many peasants not tasting freedom until the 1800s. Whether Catholics had more to offer the rural people than Protestants remains an open question. In countries such as France, there were at least missions aimed at further evangelizing the peasants, led by energetic Capuchins and Jesuits. In Switzerland, the rural cantons remained resolutely Catholic—and fiercely anti-Protestant—and saw advantages to this. In Scandinavia, most rural populations gradually warmed to Lutheranism—but often on their own terms, expressed forcefully in laypeople's Pietism, for example. Some rural communities embraced Anabaptism. Though persecuted terribly in Europe, they held out in its remote corners. Many Anabaptists saw hope—and found religious freedom—in America, where their experience helped inspire the rigorous separation of church and state, and the ethos of religious tolerance enshrined by the Constitution of the United States.

Non-Christian minorities had a fate analogous to that of the Anabaptists—with the exception that Jews and Muslims often found even America less welcoming. Informal, culturally engrained hostility to these religious "others" was deep, and its European currents ran in ways that were mostly independent of the Reformation's particular dynamics. Institutionally, the Fourth Lateran Council (1215) already placed severe restrictions on both Jews and Muslims living in the Empire, forbidding them from holding public office, mandating "distinctive clothing," and prohibiting their appearance in public on Christian holy days. Many of Western Europe's Jews were driven out during the fourteenth century as a reaction to the Black Death, for which they were frequently blamed. Of course, the plague was unimpressed by the Jews' departure—and some were allowed to return once that became apparent. Segregation was often the social recipe for "allowing" their presence. Pope Paul IV, for example, found time from his work for the Inquisition to force Rome's Jews into a special neighborhood—the first European "ghetto." A number of Protestant princes and magistrates expelled them from their territories during the sixteenth century. Luther, whose initial support of and interest in Jews was remarkable for his day, turned to an equally remarkable hostility late in life, arguing that their synagogues should be burned to the ground. Fortunately, these late writings had virtually no impact on early Lutheranism (they were mostly ignored until they were resurrected by twentieth-century fascists). Lutherans in Germany navigated between the social alternatives of segregation and cautious integration, often aiming at the latter in hopes of converting Jews to Christianity.

Their successes were modest. On the other hand, any adoption of a long-term perspective for coexistence was an improvement over the dominant alternatives.

Women accounted for half the European population. Scholars debate whether their lives were improved by the Reformation. For women of the elites—who are typically the most interesting to scholars—the results are mixed. Closing convents reduced vocational opportunities for religious women in Protestant territories. There would be no direct equivalent to compensate them. On the other hand, the greater emphasis on domestic religiosity, coupled with schooling for girls in most Protestant settings created important, if less conspicuous roles for women—arguably no less significant for taking place "in the home" rather than the public eye. Some of the exceptional women who took leadership roles during the early years of the Reformation—for example, Katharina Schütz-Zell in Strasbourg, Argula von Grumbach in Bavaria, Katharina von Bora (Luther) in Wittenberg, or Marie Dentière in Geneva—not only made an immediate impact through their writings and their public support of the Reformation, their resonant examples helped shape a culture. While Protestants did not take the additional step of ordaining women to pastoral offices, they actively encouraged women to involve themselves in ministry. By 1575, for example, Wittenberg had a female schoolteacher—who received the same salary as her male predecessor, an ordained pastor.

Most of Europe's women did not have the luxury of worrying about the size of their salaries. They were peasant women, and they had no salaries. They worked long, hard days, slept short nights, raised families, and committed their full resourcefulness to the difficult art of survival. They enjoyed few rights. Of course, neither did their husbands. The Reformation did little to change that.

To what extent the Reformation brought rural people a deeper spiritual relationship to the Christian faith remains an open question. For many peasants, Lutheranism, Calvinism, and Catholicism were all "religions of the authorities." Denied the right to elect their own pastors, the women and men of the countryside simply had to accept—and feed—the clergyman who was sent to them. Sometimes those relations were tense and fraught with resentment. But one also hears stories that are much more edifying—of priests and pastors who dedicated themselves to this oft-neglected ministry, welcomed the personal and material sacrifices it demanded, and shone a local light in forgotten country chapels.

Index

The Reformation: A Brief History, First Edition. Kenneth G. Appold.
© 2011 Kenneth G. Appold. Published 2011 by Blackwell Publishing Ltd.

Las Casas, Bartolomeo de, 182
laypeople/laity, 6, 14, 22, 25, 32,
        34, 36, 40, 54–6, 58–9, 75,
        77, 84, 86, 101, 112, 115,
        157, 175, 177, 179, 189
League of Torgau, 138, 141
Lefèvre d'Étaples, Jacques, 165
Leipzig Disputation (1519), 64–5,
        100
Leipzig Interim, 145
Leo I, pope, 17
Leo III, pope, 18
Leo IX, pope, 21–3, 29, 31, 66
Leo X, pope, 46, 49, 174
Libertines, 171
literacy, 1, 41, 59, 69–70, 143,
        156, 187
Lotzer, Sebastian, 108
Louis XII of France, 51–2
love, see charity
Lucius III, pope, 36
Lunge, Vincens, 153
Luther, Martin, 11, 43, 45–50,
        54–5, 57–79, 81–7, 91–2,
        96, 98, 100–1, 103, 108,
        111–12, 114–19, 123, 126,
        128, 135–6, 138–41, 143–4,
        158, 178–9, 186–7, 189–90
    Admonition to Peace, 115–18
    *Babylonian Captivity of the
        Church*, 75–6
    death of, 144
    early life, 60–2
    excommunication of, 64, 66
    "Invocavit Sermons", 84–5
    Luther and
        Jews, 190
        Karlstadt, 84, 86–7
        Müntzer, 111–12
        peasants, 108, 114–19, 126
        Zwingli on eucharist, 138–40

Luther's theology, 65, 71–9
    "Ninety-Five Theses", 43,
        46–50, 57, 59, 62, 158, 186
    On the Freedom of a Christian, 73
    Small Catechism, 143
    *To the Christian Nobility of the
        German Nation*, 77–9, 81

Magdeburg, 60, 138, 145
magistrates (see also: individual
        city councils), 53, 67, 81,
        85, 88, 90, 95, 97–100,
        102, 122, 124, 135, 143,
        156, 161–2, 169, 189–90
Mantz, Felix, 119–23
Marburg Colloquy (1529), 139–41
Marburg, university, 143
Marpeck, Pilgram, 128
marriage, 2, 7, 14, 23, 70, 78, 83,
        93, 95–7, 100–1, 103–4,
        140, 157, 188
Marsilius of Padua, 51
Martin V, pope, 105
martyrdom, 12–13, 53, 122–3, 128
Martyrs' Synod, 127
Maximilian I, emperor, 64, 89
Melanchthon, Philipp, 71, 75,
        82–4, 86n, 108, 114, 137,
        139–41, 143, 145, 147n
    as *praeceptor Germaniae*, 71
    at Augsburg, 140–1
    Examen ordinandorum, 143
    Loci communes, 71
Memmingen, 108, 114, 137, 142
mendicant ethos, 38–9, 41, 55–6,
        78, 93, 118, 174, 182
mendicants (see also: individual
        orders), 38–9, 41, 43, 47,
        55, 60, 78, 84, 90, 93, 95,
        118, 175–6
Mennonites, 118n, 129

Waldburg, Truchsess Jörg von, 109
Waldensians, 36–7, 66
Waldes of Lyons, 36–7
Waldshut, 107, 113, 123–4
Walpot, Peter, 131
Wartburg, 69, 81, 85
wealth, 9–11, 16, 32, 34, 36–8, 41, 45, 53, 78, 87, 98, 100, 112, 115–17, 119, 158, 170, 173
Weingarten, Treaty of (1525), 109
Weinsberg, 110
wergeld (blood money), 15, 44
William of Ockham, 38
Wittenberg, 46, 66–8, 70, 75, 82–7, 93, 111, 139, 144, 149, 191
  Castle Church (All Saints), 49, 82–3, 144
  City Church, 62, 101
  City Council, 83–5
  Ordinance, 84
  university, 43, 54, 61–3, 71, 82, 86, 150–1, 158–9, 161
Wittenberg Concord, 140
women (and girls), 14, 23, 36, 55, 70, 93, 128, 143, 174–5, 191
Wyclif, John, 65

yieldedness, see *Gelassenheit*

Zurich, 88–91, 93–102, 107, 112, 118–24, 126–7, 162–3, 166
  City Council, 89–90, 93–9, 119–22
Zurich Disputation
  First (1523), 95–8, 140
  Second (1523), 98–9, 119, 123
Zwickau Prophets, 83
Zwilling, Gabriel, 82–4
Zwingli, Huldrych, 76, 91–102, 108, 114, 118–20, 122–3, 126–7, 138–40, 142, 163, 166
  conflict with Anabaptists, 99, 118–20, 122–3, 126–7
  death of, 163
  Divine and Human Righteousness, 119
  early life, 91–3
  on fasting, 94
  "Sixty-Seven Articles", 95–7
  Von Erkiesen und Freiheit der Speisen, 94
  (see also: Luther and Zwingli on eucharist)

Printed in the USA
CPSIA information can be obtained
at www.ICGtesting.com
LVHW050425060224
770915LV00018B/190